Personal Injury Claims in the County Court

Tolley Publishing Company Limited

Personal Injury Claims in the County Court

Second edition

by Janet Bettle LL B (Lond), Barrister
and John A Hamey MA (Cantab), Barrister

Tolley Publishing Company Limited
A UNITED NEWSPAPERS PUBLICATION

ISBN 0 85459 921–5

First published 1992
Second edition November 1994

Published by
Tolley Publishing Company Limited
Tolley House
2 Addiscombe Road
Croydon
Surrey
CR9 5AF
0181-686 9141

A catalogue record for this book is available
from the British Library

Typeset in Great Britain by Action Typesetting Limited,
Northgate Street, Gloucester

Printed and Bound by
BPC Wheatons Ltd, Exeter

Contents

Contents

Contents

Contents

Contents

Table of Statutes

Table of Statutory Instruments

Table of Cases

Foreword

In the last 150 years there have been over 50 reports on procedure in the civil and criminal jurisdictions. Whether despite or because of this, the subject of civil procedure has remained complicated and indeed become increasingly technical.

It is against this background that, under the provisions of the Courts and Legal Services Act 1990, the High Court and County Courts Jurisdiction Order 1991 took effect. As from 1 July 1991, procedure in the county courts has been governed by the terms of this Order. This is of particular significance to those in the legal profession involved with personal injury litigation since all such cases, save those with a value of £50,000 or more, must now commence life in the county court.

Since that time there has been obvious and urgent need for guidance in the form of the publication of a book which deals with the procedure for PI cases in the county court in a logical and detailed yet concise and easily readable manner. This is that book.

This need has been occasioned not only by the changes in the Rules which are in themselves complex, but also by reason of the fact that there is now for example, as a result, a much greater necessity to heed the timetables laid down in the Rules and also the fact that not all personal injury litigation in the county court is conducted by specialist solicitors or counsel, automatically familiar with the new structure in place.

John Hamey and Janet Bettle have been successful in adopting a very careful approach to each topic and the thoroughness of their very considerable research is impressive. In addition to the obvious areas which require to be dealt with in a book of this kind, attention is also given to less colourful but important matters including costs and appeals. There is even a short chapter giving practical tips on negotiating.

The authors take the reader through the whole process from arrangements for funding the action, including the handling of legal aid, and the obtaining of instructions, statements and other evidence, through to trial. Where necessary ample and appropriate precedents are provided. Particularly appealing to the busy practitioner, to whom an *aide-mémoire* is invaluable, will be the 'shorthand' checklist to be found at the end of most chapters.

Considerable assistance is given as the reader is taken through the potential minefield of e.g. limitation, tactics, discovery, planning the claim and pensions. Many practitioners from both branches of the profession will find the chapters on damages (including the assessment of past and future pecuniary loss and the recoupment of State benefits) of particular value.

The former follows a step-by-step approach through the variety of contingencies which have to be considered and for which calculations have to allow. The latter contains a clear exposition of the recoupment provisions and their effect for example upon payments into court, an area with which not all practitioners are familiar.

The authors have correctly captured and explained the attitude of the Court of Appeal regarding the 'Fifteen-month rule' under CCR, O.17, r.11(9) and the need for a plaintiff's solicitor to concentate his mind on the necessity to request the court to fix a date for hearing within the timescale provided by the Rule.

I commend this book to all practitioners, both barristers and solicitors, who deal with personal injury cases in the county court whether for plaintiff or defendant.

The authors have considerable knowledge of their subject and have been able to call upon their significant professional experience in order to provide a book which is completely up to date, deals with the procedural problems in a practical and understandable way and results in a work which will constitute an invaluable guide and reference book and an essential addition to the practitioner's library.

John Cherry QC

Preface

The need for a second edition of Janet Bettle's book presented the ideal opportunity to add a section on the assessment of damages. Like the procedural section, this is aimed not at the established personal injury specialist, but at those who need a short, easily digested statement of the bare bones of the law coupled with the detailed practical guidance which can convert an admissible head of loss into an entry in the Schedule of Special Damage. The specialist practitioner will always need the specialist textbooks, but we have tried to write for a person very familiar to us both, the overworked general practitioner who asks for advice on the telephone. 'Look,' he or she says, 'I've got an rta ... Can I claim this? How do I calculate that? Do I have to give credit for the other? What sort of evidence should I be getting? Have you got something I can quote to the other side?' This book aims to give such people the quick, simple answer they need.

We have tried to keep constantly in mind the needs of a solicitor in a medium-sized practice. We have assumed he or she has ready access to the statutes, to *The County Court Practice*, to *Current Law* and to basic reports. For that reason we have set out in full the relevant parts of statutory instruments, have cited few unreported cases and have cited the mainstream reports wherever possible.

The principles which govern the assessment of damages are clear enough. Speaking as county court practitioners, however, we are only too well aware of the mismatch between everyday practice and strict legal theory — *Smith* v *Manchester* awards must be the most striking example. Since the divergence between practice and law often foreshadows developments in the law, we would be delighted to hear from practitioners whose experience fails to meet the expectations created by our book.

Each of us owes a great debt to those who have helped in the preparation of this book. Our colleagues in Chambers have put up with 'the Janet and John book' for many months — usually without complaint! The Bettle family — Vernon, Rosie and Will — have been similarly supportive and deserve tribute.

We are extremely grateful to Caroline Pinfold of Field Fisher Waterhouse for her help in providing the tables that are set out in the Appendix.

We gratefully acknowledge the co-operation of Butterworth & Co (Publishers) Ltd for permission to quote from *The All England Law Reports* and from *Butterworths Personal Injury Litigation Service* (price £245). Readers who go on to develop a specialist practice in personal injury litigation will find it an excellent guide, particularly strong on practice, procedure and tactics; it is also a good place for finding authority, since it cites a vast number of decisions.

The co-operation of Sweet & Maxwell Ltd for permission to quote from Kemp & Kemp's *The Quantum of Damages* is gratefully acknowledged. We owe an incalculable debt to the authors and editors, past and present, of Kemp & Kemp — it has helped to shape the modern law of damages, and is an indispensable handbook which the specialist practitioner consults almost every working day (the main work currently costs £290). Permission from Sweet & Maxwell Ltd to quote from their *Personal Injuries and Quantum Reports* (annual subscription, including bound volume service, currently costs £187) is also acknowledged gratefully.

Full acknowledgment is given to the Judicial Studies Board, as the authors, and to Blackstone Press Ltd, as the publishers, for permission to quote extracts from the Judicial Studies Board's *Guidelines for the Assessment of General Damages in Personal Injury Cases* (currently priced at £15.95).

Extracts from the Law Reports (Queen's Bench, Chancery and Family Divisions; Appeal Cases) and from the Weekly Law Reports are reproduced with the kind permission of the Incorporated Council of Law Reporting for England and Wales.

Finally, we would like to thank Her Majesty's Stationery Office for allowing us to quote from statutory material which is Crown copyright, and Paul Coppin of Eversheds for his assistance with points of practice.

The law is stated to 4 August 1994.

Janet Bettle
John A Hamey

PART I:

PRACTICE, PROCEDURE AND TACTICS

Chapter 1

The county court jurisdiction

1. Introduction

Before 1 July 1991, there were good reasons to commence most personal injury actions in the High Court. The upper limit of the county court jurisdiction was £5,000, although this could be exceeded with the consent of all parties to the case. The jurisdiction of the High Court, however, was unlimited and there were no penalties for starting proceedings there provided that the plaintiff obtained at least £3,500. There was a general feeling amongst solicitors that the absence of a jurisdictional limit provided a more favourable background to negotiations.

Relatively few of these cases, however, found their way to trial in the High Court. Considerable use was made of the provisions for transfer between the High Court and the county courts under s 40 of the County Courts Act 1984. Under s 40, any of the parties could apply to transfer the litigation. In addition, the court could order transfer of its own volition.

This power was used extensively by the High Court, and in recent years there has been a thorough screening of all cases at the setting down stage. All but the most serious or difficult claims were sent to an appropriate county court. This had the effect of considerably reducing the pressure on the list at the Royal Courts of Justice — to the extent that the wait between setting down and trial was shortened to a period of months rather than years.

2. The county court jurisdiction since 1991

Since 1 July 1991, the situation has been governed by the High Court and County Courts Jurisdiction Order (SI 1991/724). This Order was made under the provisions of the Courts and Legal Services Act 1990 and was aimed at channelling the majority of personal injury actions through the county court system. The Order has brought about a re-drafting of s 15 of the County Courts Act 1984; see the notes on s 15 in *The County Court Practice* (the 'Green Book'). The most important change is that all personal injury actions must now start in the county court unless the value of the claim is £50,000 or more.

(a) Transferring from the High Court to the county court

Under the amended s 40 of the County Courts Act 1984, if the High Court is satisfied that proceedings before it fit within the criteria for hearing in the county court, it can order a transfer. However, there is a sting in the tail of this provision in that if the High Court is satisfied that the person bringing the proceedings knew or ought to have known that the case should have been brought in the lower court, it shall order that the claim be struck out.

This was enforced strictly in *Groom* v *Norman Motors* [1993] PIQR 215, but this draconian ruling has been disapproved in *Restick* v *Crichmore* (The Times, 3 December 1993) in which the court's discretion to transfer rather than strike out was confirmed.

3. How the claim is valued

Article 9 of the Order provides that the value of an action will be 'the amount which the plaintiff reasonably expects to recover'. In determining this, no account will be taken of the following:

- contributory negligence, unless this is admitted by the plaintiff;
- where a claim for provisional damages is made, the possibility of a future application for the additional monies;
- payments to be made to the Compensation Recovery Unit under the Social Security Act 1989 (now the Social Security Administration Act 1992);
- interest;
- costs.

4. The trial venue

Under Article 7 of the Order, a claim valued at less than £25,000 will normally be heard in the county court. In some cases, however, it will be possible to transfer a case for hearing in the High Court. The criteria for transfer are set out in Article 7(5) of the Order:

- the financial substance of the claim, including the value of any counterclaim;
- whether the action is otherwise important, and, in particular, whether it raises questions of importance to persons who are not parties or questions of general public interest;
- the complexity of the facts, legal issues, remedies or procedures involved;
- whether transfer is likely to result in a speedier trial of the action (although transfer cannot be made on this ground alone).

If the case is valued at £50,000 or more, it will be heard in the High Court unless:
- it was started in the county court and the court does not feel it needs to be transferred to the High Court using the criteria set out in Article 7(5);

- the High Court, using the same criteria, considers that it ought to transfer the case to the county court for trial.

Further assistance in considering whether a case should be transferred is given in the Practice Direction reported at [1991] 3 All ER 349. Paragraph 9 of the Practice Direction, gives guidance on the type of case which 'whether by claim or counterclaim may be considered important and therefore suitable for trial in the High Court'. These include cases involving professional negligence, and fatal accidents.

It is made quite clear in the Practice Direction that the court still has the power to transfer a case of its own volition. Under paragraph 3, a Judge, Master or District Judge who considers that the case should be transferred should give notice to the parties in form PF 202 (unless the parties are already before the court). Objection to transfer must be made within 14 days of receipt of the notice, when an appointment will be set for the hearing of the objection.

No guidance is given on the venue for claims valued at between £25,000 and £50,000, other than confirmation in the Order of 1991 that proceedings in which both the High Court and county court have jurisdiction may be tried in either court. However, as the case in question will have been commenced in the county court it will presumably stay there for trial unless transfer is felt appropriate on the basis of the Article 7(5) criteria.

5. Statements of value

Under SI 1991/1329, a statement of value must be served on all parties and lodged with the court if the case is one to which Article 7(1) of the 1991 Order applies — in other words, if it is a case which could be tried in either the High Court or the county court (valued between £25,000 and £49,999 inclusive). It seems, however, that in practice a statement need only be served if the case is proceeding in the High Court, as the sanction for failure to lodge is that the case will be transferred to the county court.

6. Trial before the District Judge

Before 1991, the District Judge was empowered to sit in open court to hear claims for up to £1,000. This limit has now been increased to £5,000 by the County Court (Amendment No 2) Rules 1991 (SI 1991 No 1126).

Under the 1991 Rules, if the Particulars of Claim do not contain a statement that the amount involved is likely to exceed £5,000, the court will assume that the value of the claim falls within the District Judge's jurisdiction (Rule 3). The Particulars of Claim should therefore indicate, if appropriate, that damages in excess of £5,000 are claimed. If for any reason the value of a claim falls to below £5,000 after proceedings have been commenced, the plaintiff must notify the court accordingly by filing an amendment.

7. Quantifying the claim

One of the effects of the new rules will be that plaintiffs' solicitors will be forced to consider at an early stage and in some detail the question of the likely level of damages. This will create difficulties, especially where the prognosis is uncertain. What follows is a short examination of the basic approach to assessing quantum — for a more detailed account, see the later chapters of this book.

In an action for personal injuries, the starting point is that the plaintiff should be compensated for the suffering and losses sustained by reason of the defendant's negligence or breach of statutory duty. These losses are likely to be wide-ranging. In addition to suffering considerable pain for a long period of time, the plaintiff may well have sustained a substantial loss of earnings. He may be at risk of losing earnings in the future and be forced to pay for nursing care, equipment and so on.

Over the years, the heads of damage for which claim may be made have been categorised. These categories, however, should never be regarded as closed.

(a) General and special damages

The most basic distinction is that between general damages and special damages. It is an important distinction because different rates of interest apply to the amounts recovered under each category. Despite this, there is some debate as to the precise nature of the difference.

The starting point is the case of *Prehn* v *City of Liverpool* (1870) LR Ex 92 where Martin J pointed out that:

'General damages ... are such as the jury may give when the judge cannot point out any measure by which they are to be assessed, except the opinion and judgment of a reasonable man ... special damages are given in respect of any consequences reasonably and probably arising from the breach complained of.'

This distinction has given rise to the traditional view that general damages are those which cannot be expressed in terms of pecuniary loss. However, the judgment of Ormrod LJ in *Daly* v *General Steam Navigation Co Ltd* [1980] 3 All ER 696, [1981] 1 WLR 120, included a different distinction between the two heads of damage:

'So far as the special damage is concerned, that ... represents "actual" as opposed to "estimated" loss. So far as general damage is concerned, that loss necessarily has to be estimated.'

Thus we do not look to the nature of the damage, but whether it can be accurately assessed or only estimated. On this basis, a claim for future loss of earnings would be categorised as general damages. Whatever the merits of such an argument, it seems that this latter approach is rather at odds with current practice. Certainly, a statement of special damages would be regarded as incomplete without a section on future losses.

(b) Quantifying general damages

The only guidance to be had in compensating the plaintiff for his pain, suffering and loss of amenity is by consulting the Judicial Studies Board's *Guidelines for the Assessment of General Damages in Personal Injury Claims* and by examining previous cases concerning similar injury. Traditionally, the reference point for these is Kemp and Kemp's *Quantum of Damages in Personal Injury and Fatal Accident Claims*. In fact, the wider the search for comparable cases the better, and Goldrein and de Haas include a useful section on awards in volume 2 of their *Personal Injury Litigation Service* ('*PILS*'). (See Chapter 17.)

For up-to-date quantums, use should be made of the monthly editions of *Current Law*. These reports are well indexed on a cumulative basis and are a considerable help to practitioners in the personal injury field. Those practitioners who have access to *Lawtel* will also be able to avail themselves of the injury awards details available under the *Decisions* heading. These are both numerous and useful, although they tend to be somewhat brief.

In any event, any award to be used should be updated to take account of inflation. There is a useful table for this purpose at the beginning of *Kemp*.

One of the problems posed by the new rules is that early quantification of a claim may well be difficult or even impossible. A serious prognosis, for example, may often not be made until some years after the accident. All that practitioners can reasonably be expected to do is make a rough guess at quantum. If this turns out to be grossly inaccurate, an amended Statement of Value can always be made, coupled, if necessary, with an application for transfer under Article 7.

Compensating for future disadvantage on the labour market: An injured employee may find that he is able, after a suitable period, to return to work. Even if he has sustained a permanent injury, he may be able to continue working, especially with a helpful employer who is prepared to tailor his duties if required.

There is, however, a risk to a plaintiff in this situation. If he were to lose his job in the future, he would find himself competing for a new job with able-bodied workers. As a result, it may take him longer to obtain suitable replacement employment — or he may never find another job.

This is obviously a real risk in many cases, and a practice has grown up by which the plaintiff's general damages may be increased to include a sum to compensate him for his disadvantage on the labour market — commonly called a *Smith* v *Manchester* claim.

Such a claim (which should always be expressly pleaded) will probably be difficult to quantify. It is essentially a question of compensating the plaintiff for a risk which might never materialise. In addition, the losses which might arise should unemployment occur cannot be calculated as no one is in a position to predict how long it would take the plaintiff to obtain alternative employment.

Essentially, the court in considering this question will look at the general circumstances of the case and try to evaluate the degree of risk and the seriousness of the handicap on the job market. The award should take into account the plaintiff's salary at the date of trial, the type of work, security of the employment and the plaintiff's age.

Damages for loss of congenial employment: Practitioners should also be aware that it has recently become clear that if the plaintiff loses employment which he found particularly congenial, he will be allowed to claim damages to represent this loss. The leading case is that of *Champion* v *London Fire and Civil Defence Authority* — The Times 5 July 1990, where a fireman had lost job satisfaction as a result of his discharge from the fire service. It was held that such an award would normally form part of the claim for general damages, although in the *Champion* case, a suitable figure had been agreed between the parties and was therefore awarded separately.

(c) Quantifying special damages — earnings loss

In practice, the largest item of special damage in a serious case will be the claim for loss of earnings, both past and possibly future.

If the plaintiff has returned to work, his loss (apart from a possible *Smith* v *Manchester* claim) can be calculated in the following way:

(i) Obtain from his employers a schedule of his gross earnings, together with a separately itemised list of deductions each week for tax and national insurance.

(ii) Check that the tax and national insurance deductions have been properly calculated, using the tables in the Appendix. It is surprising how often the tax deductions shown for a particular week are unrepresentative of the annual situation.

(iii) Arrive at an average weekly wage, net of tax and national insurance.

(iv) Multiply the average net weekly wage by the number of weeks that the plaintiff was away from work. This figure will be the potential loss.

(v) Subtract from this figure any wages received by the plaintiff whilst he was away from work.

This calculation ignores the receipt of State benefits. Since the introduction of the changes wrought by the Social Security Act 1989, benefits are ignored for the purpose of calculating special damages, although the plaintiff will find that his damages cheque will be reduced by an amount equal to the relevant benefits which he has received.

In more serious cases, where the plaintiff has been away from work for several years, it will be necessary to increase the average net wage used to calculate his potential loss so that wage increases may be brought into the picture. The employers should firstly be asked to provide details of comparable earners for the years in question. It must be said, however, that these figures are often unforthcoming, especially where the employer is the defendant. In this situation, the plaintiff may be able to produce pay slips and P60s from colleagues on the same grade. This, of course, requires the co-operation of fellow employees. As an alternative, the Department of Employment *New Earnings Survey* researches and publishes average gross earnings received by workers in a wide range of jobs each year. The service is both cheap and quick, taking on average about two weeks. It can be obtained simply by writing to The New Earnings Survey, Department of Employment, Exchange House, 60 Exchange Road, Watford WD1 7HH, indicating the years for which figures are sought and the occupation of the plaintiff. If nothing else, the use of figures from the *New Earnings Survey* often stimulates the production of figures from the plaintiff's employers.

If the plaintiff has been unable to return to work by the time that proceedings are issued, the question of claiming his future loss of earnings will arise. The extent to which this can be calculated will depend upon the firmness of the prognosis given by the medical experts. If the prognosis is that the plaintiff is unlikely to work again, the future loss of earnings can be arrived at by taking his average net earnings at the time of calculation, and projecting this figure forward by an appropriate multiplier.

This multiplier cannot be arrived at by simply deducting the plaintiff's actual age from his likely date of retirement had the accident not occurred. As he will obtain his damages as a lump sum, the multiplier is reduced to avoid the plaintiff being over compensated. In addition, the multiplier will include a provision for the risk that the plaintiff might in any event have failed to work to the normal retirement age.

Selecting the multiplier is not an easy task and is likely to remain an issue between the parties. *Kemp* carries a list of multipliers which have been applied in previous cases, arranged to show the age of the plaintiff. It should not, however, be regarded as the final word on the subject. In particular, careful regard should be had to the nature of the plaintiff's work. If he had been employed as a manual worker, the multiplier will seem low as account will be taken of the fact that he may well have given up work before the normal retirement age.

Other items of special damage are usually easier to calculate. The plaintiff should be asked to keep all relevant receipts to make dealing with this aspect of the claim as straightforward as possible.

If the plaintiff needs a considerable amount of equipment, consider the use of a rehabilitation costs consultant. This expert should visit the plaintiff in his home and carry out a detailed survey of his equipment needs. The expert will be able to identify just about every item available which might assist the plaintiff and will produce a fully costed list of these. The list should also explain for how long each item will last so that the cost of replacement can be included in the claim. These reports are, however, expensive and only appropriate in cases of serious injury.

Checklist

1. Valuing the claim:

   General damages — use *Kemp*, *PILS* and *Current Law*
   — Inflate using *Kemp's* table
   — Consider claim for disadvantage on the labour market

   Special damages — loss of earnings
   — cost of care
   — cost of equipment
   — any other item

2. If claim is worth £50,000 or more issue a writ in the High Court. The writ should be endorsed with a statement that the value of the action exceeds £50,000. The case will be heard there unless it is deemed to be appropriate for transfer.

3. If claim is worth less than £50,000, proceedings should be issued in the county court nearest to the defendant — whilst it is possible to issue in another court, the case will probably be transferred to the defendant's court.

4. If there is no Statement of Value in the Particulars of Claim, the case will be assumed to be worth £5,000 or less and will be listed for trial before the District Judge. This can be done by simply indicating that damages in excess of £5,000 are claimed.

Chapter 2

Funding the action

1. Legal aid

(a) The Green Form scheme

The legal aid system can help the potential plaintiff in two ways. First, it is possible for him or her to give instructions and receive advice under the Green Form scheme. Under the scheme, the solicitor is able, with the aid of a regularly updated key-card, to assess the client's eligibility on the spot. If the client qualifies (a contribution may be required), the solicitor can carry out a cash limited amount of initial work. It is possible to extend the Green Form to allow for additional work to be carried out if circumstances demand.

(b) Application for legal aid certificate

If the prospects for a successful claim look good, an application for a legal aid certificate should be made. This is done by filling out a CLA 1 application form together with a CLA 4 financial circumstances form. In addition, if the client is working, his employers should fill out an L 17 form confirming his wages. If the client is in receipt of State benefits, a specially expedited legal aid form is available.

Filling out the application forms is reasonably straightforward. There is a page set aside for a resumé of the case, and it is quite acceptable for the solicitor to fill this in subject to the client's approval. Obviously, the case should not be overstated, but if the solicitor thinks that the chances of success are very good, he should say so and give his reasons. This may lead to an unlimited certificate being granted, which will save time and costs in the long run.

Once the application forms are received and checked, the Area office will make further enquiries of the applicant's circumstances. If a contribution is required from the applicant, he and his solicitor will be sent a form headed 'Offer of Legal Aid'. This will explain how much is required by way of contribution, expressed as a total and as a set of monthly payments. It is important to note that this offer must be accepted and a certificate issued before the solicitor is covered by the fund for work carried out.

(c) Limited certificates

The Area Office will often issue a certificate limited to taking various preliminary steps. If the issue of liability is uncertain, for instance, the certificate may be limited to taking counsel's advice only. It is all too easy to forget the limitation, but it should be borne in mind that it will be interpreted strictly by the Area Office and that unauthorised work will not normally be paid for.

If the case looks reasonably sound, the certificate may well be limited to 'all steps up to and including close of pleadings, discovery and counsel's opinion thereafter'. This will cover the solicitor up to, but not including, setting down. Counsel's opinion will be needed before the limitation can be removed and the case allowed to progress further.

(d) Notice of issue

The fact that a plaintiff is legally aided carries important ramifications for the other parties to the litigation. Firstly, they will know that the legally aided litigant is, to some extent at least, in funds to continue to prosecute or defend the claim.

More importantly, crucial rules exist on the subject of recovering costs against a legally aided opponent. The normal approach to costs in litigation is, of course, that the loser pays his own and the winner's costs. However, under s 17(1) of the Legal Aid Act 1988, a legally aided party's liability for costs will not exceed the amount which it is reasonable for him to pay. In deciding what is reasonable, account can be taken of his resources and his conduct during the litigation. This liability will frequently be limited by the court to a sum equal to the contribution (if any) which he has made towards his legal aid. This can leave his successful, but privately funded, opponent very much out of pocket.

Section 18 of the Legal Aid Act helps an unassisted winner to some extent in that it allows him to claim his costs from the legal aid fund in certain circumstances. Such a claim can only be made where the action was commenced by the legally aided party. In determining whether a claim can be made in this way, the court will have regard to the following:

- whether it would be just and equitable for the unassisted defendant to recover his costs in this way;
- whether consideration has been given to making an order for costs against the legally aided plaintiff;
- proceedings must have been resolved in favour of the unassisted party;
- whether an order for costs would have been made against the plaintiff had he not been legally aided;
- whether the unassisted party would suffer severe financial hardship without such an order.

Many parties will not be able to avail themselves of the provisions of s 18 and in any event, even those who qualify will not know whether they can claim their costs in this way until the proceedings have been disposed of. It is therefore only fair that privately funded parties are made aware that they face a legally aided opponent. To this end, a Notice of Issue of Legal Aid Certificate must be served on all parties and filed at the court. Note, however, that it is not necessary to disclose on the Notice any limitations which appear on the certificate.

(e) The legal aid charge

One of the most frequent complaints levelled by clients at their solicitors relates to the failure to advise them about the effects of the legal aid charge. It is vitally important that this is discussed with the client at the earliest opportunity and that the advice be followed up by letter. It may well be helpful to have a standard form letter on the word processor — a suggested draft is provided at the end of this chapter.

The Law Society's *Guide to the Professional Conduct of Solicitors* indicates that where a client is legally aided in civil proceedings, he should be informed of the effect of the charge at the outset of the case 'and at appropriate stages thereafter'. In addition, the client should be given the following information:

- that if he loses the case, he may still be ordered by the court to contribute towards his opponent's costs even though his own costs are covered by legal aid;
- that even if he wins, his opponent may not be ordered to pay the full amount of his costs and may not be capable of paying what he has been ordered to pay;
- that he has an obligation to pay any contribution assessed, together with the consequences of any failure to do so.

Under s 16(6) of the Legal Aid Act 1988, a charge is created on 'any property which is recovered or preserved in . . . the proceedings'. It can be used by the Legal Aid Board to pay any sums unpaid by the applicant's contribution, or any deficiency which has arisen because the applicant's total contribution was less than the Legal Aid Board's liability.

The charge will normally arise where there is a shortfall between the costs paid to the applicant's solicitor by the Legal Aid Board and the costs actually recovered against the opponent.

The solicitor acting on behalf of a legally aided client should not release the damages cheque to him until the question of the charge has been dealt with.

(f) Disbursements

It is impossible to avoid disbursements in dealing with a personal injury claim. There will certainly be a medical report to pay for. There may be further bills for engineer's reports, police reports and the like.

Legal aid certificates will often specifically give authority to obtain a medical report. If the case demands a relatively expensive report, or a report which has not been expressly authorised on the certificate, it is worth applying to the Area Office for specific authorisation to obtain it. Application is made by way of letter, which should explain the circumstances and the cost of the planned disbursement.

If authorisation is given by the Area Office, payment of the disbursement is guaranteed. If it is not given, the solicitor will recover the full cost of the disbursement only if he can justify it on taxation. If it is not allowed, he will bear the cost of it himself as the client cannot be approached to pay for it.

If authority is given for the disbursement, the solicitor can improve his cash flow by applying to the Area Office for payment promptly. This is made by filling out the Board's form. Application can be made for disbursements already incurred, and those 'likely to be incurred'.

(g) The effect of a payment in on a legally aided plaintiff

If a payment in is made (see page 92), the plaintiff's solicitor should first consult the legal aid certificate to remind himself whether a limitation has been imposed requiring the notification of any payment in to the Area Office.

Second, the legally aided plaintiff is vulnerable following the payment in. If he fails to beat it, the statutory charge will descend upon the damages which he is awarded, to pay his own legal expenses (assuming that, because of the failure to beat the payment in, he is not awarded all of his costs). In addition, he runs the risk of being ordered to pay all or some of his opponent's costs as the court can take into account the damages which he has received in deciding whether to make a costs order against the plaintiff.

(h) Sample letter to client explaining legal aid

Dear . . . .

Re: Legal Aid
I have already spoken to you about the legal aid system and how it works. I realise, however, that this is a rather complicated area and I am therefore sending you this written reminder of the important points you should bear in mind if you are successful in your application for legal aid.

1. *Change of address and Change in Financial Circumstances*
    Once you have been granted legal aid, you are under a duty to the Legal Aid Board to inform them of any change in your address or any alteration to the financial information you have provided them with. This is an obligation upon you and simply informing me will not be sufficient.

2. *The statutory charge*
    In an ideal world, if you are successful in your claim, you would not only come away from your case with the compensation you sought, but also with all of your costs met by the Defendants. However, in reality, it is possible that there will be a shortfall between the costs

that the Defendants are ordered to pay and those which I am entitled to charge. In these circumstances, the Legal Aid Board will meet this shortfall in my costs, first, from any contribution which you have had to pay to the Legal Aid Board and then out of your damages. Although this sounds very worrying, I should add that it is a situation that does not usually come about in practice. However, it is a possibility that you should be aware of.

3.   *Discharge/Revocation of Certificate*
Discharge: If your legal aid certificate is discharged, which may happen if you have become financially ineligible or have required the case to be conducted reasonably, or have fallen behind with your contributions, then you will cease to be an assisted person under the scheme. However, you will retain all the benefits of assistance in respect of matters which arose in the life of the legal aid certificate. Most importantly, this includes costs incurred under the certificate up to the point of discharge. The statutory charge may apply to the costs under the certificate in the same way as I have outlined above.

Revocation: Your legal aid certificate may be revoked if you have lied to the Legal Aid Board in respect of your finances or the facts of your case. Revocation is far more serious than discharge, in that the Legal Aid Board will treat you as if you were never, in fact, assisted. This means that they will not meet any of the costs incurred during the validity of the certificate and you will have none of the protection from an Order for costs that a legal aid certificate would normally give you. The Legal Aid Board may also seek to recover from you all costs paid to me.

I hope that the above clarifies the obligations which you enter into upon accepting legal aid. If you are not clear about anything, or wish to discuss any other aspect of your claim with me, please feel free to contact me at any time.

Yours sincerely,

2. Other forms of funding

Many prospective plaintiffs do not qualify for legal aid. However, those who are members of Trade Unions may well be able to take advantage of a legal assistance scheme provided by the Union.

Alternatively, legal expenses insurance policies are becoming increasingly common, and it is always worth suggesting that a prospective litigant checks his household and/or car insurance policies to check whether legal expenses cover has been included.

Thirdly, anyone, regardless of means, is entitled to take advantage of The Law Society's ALAS scheme. This is a scheme run by participating firms which agree to provide half an hour's free legal advice to prospective plaintiffs. The main contact points for the scheme are the Citizens' Advice Bureaux, which refer enquirers on to the scheme administrator. It is often the case that a prospective plaintiff will be prepared to proceed on a privately funded basis if his case is strong.

3. Contingency and conditional fees

Opinion was canvassed, in the Green Paper on Contingency Fees (Cm 571), on the subject of the funding of litigation. A full contingency system operates where the plaintiff's solicitor acts on the basis that he obtains a stated percentage of the plaintiff's damages. If his client loses, he collects no fee. The response to the Green Paper was against the introduction of a full contingency system. However, a more favourable response was received to the idea of a conditional fee system, which operates in Scotland. Under this system, the arrangement is for payment of normal fees, rather than a percentage of the damages, to the plaintiff's solicitor only if the plaintiff wins.

Such an arrangement in itself would be unlikely to appeal to a prospective plaintiff's solicitor as there would be no additional fee to compensate him for the risk involved in taking on a case for which he might receive no fee at all. With this in mind, provision can be made for the payment of a stated uplift to the solicitor's fees on the successful outcome of the case.

Arrangements allowing conditional fee agreements were introduced by s 58 of the Courts and Legal Services Act 1990. This provides that conditional fee arrangements must be in writing and must comply with such regulations as may be prescribed by the Lord Chancellor. A percentage uplift can be charged, but this must be set out in the agreement and cannot be above a maximum set by the Lord Chancellor.

It is also worth bearing in mind that under s 15(4A) of the Legal Aid Act 1988 a person may not be refused legal aid on the ground that it would be more appropriate for him to enter into a conditional fee arrangement.

Checklist

1. Obtaining legal aid — forms CLA 1, CLA 4, L 17.
2. On receipt of certificate — check for limitations.
3. When issuing proceedings, file Notice of Issue. If proceedings are not issued at the time that the certificate is issued, tell your opponents that you are legally aided, as this may persuade them to settle your claim earlier.
4. Always advise your client about the charge.
5. Seek specific authorisation for disbursements and claim them promptly from the Board.
6. If you are keen to take on plaintiff work, contact your local ALAS scheme administrator and the head offices of trade unions covering your local workforce.

Chapter 3

Limitation

1. The limitation period

Personal injury actions are subject to special rules so far as the issue of limitation is concerned. The relevant provisions are found in s 11 of the Limitation Act 1980 which provides that the appropriate limitation period is three years from either the date on which the cause of action accrued; or the date of knowledge (if later) of the person injured.

If the potential plaintiff dies before the expiration of the limitation period, s 11 further provides that the appropriate period will be three years from whichever is the later of the date of death or the personal representative's knowledge.

2. Defining knowledge

It can be seen from the above that defining the date of a person's knowledge that he has a claim is of crucial significance. Section 14 of the Limitation Act helps in this respect. It provides that a potential plaintiff first had knowledge of the cause of action, when he was aware of all the following facts:

(a) That the injury in question was significant. A helpful case on this point is *McCafferty* v *Metropolitan Police Receiver* [1977] 2 All ER 756, [1977] 1 WLR 1073. This was an industrial deafness case in which the plaintiff first became aware that he was having problems with his hearing in 1968. The plaintiff however regarded these problems as being only 'an irritating nuisance'. He did not tell his employers of the results of the test carried out in 1968, and in 1973 an audiogram showed signs that he had suffered severe acoustic trauma. Geoffrey Lane LJ stated that one should look at the nature of the injury as known to the plaintiff at that time — 'taking that plaintiff, with that plaintiff's intelligence, would he have been reasonable in considering the injury not sufficiently serious to justify instituting proceedings for damages?'

(b) That the injury was attributable in whole or in part to the actual omission which is alleged to constitute negligence, nuisance or breach of duty. What is required is knowledge, rather than suspicion or belief. In some cases it may even be that such

17

knowledge cannot be obtained until expert evidence is obtained; see, for example *Davis* v *Ministry of Defence* The Times 7 August 1985.

(c) The identity of the defendant. It can sometimes take time to discover a defendant. Company structures, for example, can be notoriously complex and plaintiffs will not be prejudiced by any problems which are experienced in this respect.

(d) If it is alleged that the act or omission was that of a person other than the defendant, the identity of that person and the additional facts supporting the bringing of an action against the defendant. This problem arises most commonly where the plaintiff is suing an employer on the basis of vicarious liability.

3. Knowledge — subjective or objective?

Whilst the tests set out in s 14 appear to be largely subjective, practitioners should be aware of s 14(3). This provides that a person's knowledge will include knowledge which he might reasonably have been expected to acquire either from facts observable by him or from facts ascertainable by him with the help of expert advice which it is reasonable for him to seek. Potential plaintiffs thus cannot hide behind any delay on their part in finding out the appropriate facts, or any delay by advisers or experts.

As might be expected, these provisions have attracted a considerable amount of litigation. So far as the plaintiff's own conduct is concerned, it is assumed that provided that he has worked for a reasonable period in a particular industry he will be aware of the type of injury likely to be suffered whilst he is at work. He will also be assumed to know that injuries of the type in question attract compensation from his employer — *Davies* v *British Insulated Callenders Cables Ltd* (1977) 121 SJ 203. Thus, so far as expert advice is concerned, s 14(3) of the Act provides some help to the plaintiff in that he will not be fixed with knowledge of a fact ascertainable only with the help of expert advice, so long as he has taken all reasonable steps to obtain and act upon that advice. There is an apparent anomaly in the reported decisions concerning incorrect legal advice given to a potential plaintiff. In *Central Asbestos Co Ltd* v *Dodd* [1973] AC 518, [1972] 2 All ER 1135, [1972] 3 WLR 333, it was held that if a potential plaintiff is wrongly advised that the facts which he has discovered would not give rise to a cause of action, the limitation period would run notwithstanding the fact that the advice was wrong and was indeed relied upon by the plaintiff. (See also *Farmer* v *NCB* The Times 27 April 1985.) However, after *Hendy* v *Milton Keynes Health Authority* [1992] PIQR 281 a Judge can take into account the nature of the plaintiff, with reference where relevant to his limited education.

If, however, the plaintiff is wrongly advised by his solicitors that there are no further facts to be discovered and as a result he remains in ignorance of facts which may assist his claim, the limitation will not run against him — see *Fowell* v *NCB* The Times 28 May 1986.

The above distinction appears to be difficult to support and stems from a decision made several decades ago, but it has been upheld by the Court of Appeal in the decisions referred to above.

4. When does suspicion become knowledge?

In many cases, the plaintiff may not be sure that he has suffered injury as a result of anyone's negligence. This issue arises frequently in medical negligence actions where it is often argued that the plaintiff cannot be fixed with the knowledge required by the Limitation Act until he receives an expert's report on the treatment which he has undergone. In *Hendy* v *Milton Keynes Health Authority* The Times 8 March 1991, it was held that such an argument might well be appropriate in a complicated case. In easier situations, the date of knowledge would be when the plaintiff appreciated in general terms that her problems were attributable to the operation, even if the precise terms of what had gone wrong were not known. In this particular case, the plaintiff had been given sufficient information to set the limitation period running against her (although the court used its discretion under s 33 to disapply the limitation period).

In *Bentley* v *Bristol and Western Health Authority* The Times 6 December 1990, it was held that the plaintiff's state of knowledge that the injury he had suffered was attributable to an operation would not arise until he became aware of some act or omission which could have affected the safety of the operation. It was not enough simply to show broad knowledge on the part of the plaintiff that the injury had been caused by the operation.

5. Proceeding after the expiry of the limitation period

An action commenced after the limitation period has expired will not automatically fail. Section 33 of the Limitation Act 1980 allows the court, in effect, to ignore the expiration of a limitation period if it feels that it would be equitable to do so in the circumstances. In particular, it will have regard to any prejudice to the plaintiff and the defendant. So far as the defendant is concerned, this means something more than simply being deprived of a defence based on limitation arguments. Generally, the longer the delay, the greater the defendant's chance of showing that he is prejudiced, in that he will have more problems in tracing witnesses and keeping their memories refreshed. The court will look at all the circumstances of the case and, under s 33, must pay particular attention to the following six factors:

   (a) the length of and the reasons for the delay on the part of the plaintiff;
   (b) whether the plaintiff's or defendant's evidence is likely to be less cogent because of the delay;
   (c) the conduct of the defendant after the cause of action arose;
   (d) the duration of any disability of the plaintiff arising after the date of the accrual of the cause of action;

(e) the extent to which the plaintiff acted promptly and reasonably once he was aware that he might have an action for damages;
(f) the steps taken by the plaintiff to obtain medical, legal or other expert advice and the nature of any such advice.

Interestingly, after *Jones* v *G D Searle & Co Ltd* [1978] 3 All ER 654, a plaintiff can be ordered to disclose the nature of any legal advice which he has received.

The operation of s 33 was discussed in *Halford* v *Brookes and Another* The Times 18 November 1990, where the plaintiff was the administratrix of her deceased daughter's estate. The daughter had been strangled in 1978. The person initially charged with murder was acquitted in 1978, and his defence involved allegations that his stepfather had carried out the murder. The question of civil proceedings was not however contemplated until 1987, when a writ was quickly issued. The plaintiff argued firstly that the limitation period had not expired in that she did not receive legal advice in respect of a civil claim until 1985. This argument was rejected on the basis that expert advice was not needed to become aware of the matters outlined in s 14. Moving on to the question of the court's discretion under s 33, the court of first instance had felt that the passage of time would have made a fair resolution of the conflict between the two defendants unlikely. This argument was rejected on appeal. It was further held that the court was entitled to take into account a plaintiff's ignorance of her legal rights. For these reasons the appeal was allowed, and Mrs Halford was able to bring a claim against the defendant.

The factors set out in s 33 are not exhaustive. Every application will be dealt with on its own particular facts. Some other elements of relevance were discussed in the case of *Mills* v *Dyer-Fare* March 1987 (unreported). Steyn J was prepared to take into account the size of the claim and its prospects of success in deciding whether to exercise his discretion under s 33. There was a further discussion of whether the fact that a solicitor may have been negligent in handling the claim is a matter which the court can properly take into account. To some extent, such an argument is a double edged sword. Whilst a fairly made allegation of this type will naturally elicit the sympathy of the court, it is quite common for judges to opine that in such a situation, the potential plaintiff is left with a perfectly adequate remedy against his solicitor. Steyn J felt that this was highly relevant, although not a decisive factor. In the *Mills* case, he found nothing to indicate negligence on the part of the plaintiff's solicitors and his comments were thus necessarily *obiter*.

Further consideration of this issue was given in *Hartley* v *Birmingham City DC* [1992] 2 All ER 213, [1992] 1 WLR 968 where a writ was issued one day out of time. The defendants argued that this had given them a cast iron, windfall defence, and that to allow a s 33 application would be to deprive them of this. It was held by Parker LJ that, in nearly all cases, the relative prejudice suffered by the plaintiff in the application of the limitation period and the defendant in a s 33 order would be equal and opposite, but that the strength of the case would be relevant in that, in a strong case, the plaintiff's degree of prejudice would be greater. So far as the question of a claim against the plaintiff's solicitors was concerned, whilst this could be taken into account, so too could the fact that the defendant was insured against the claim. Further, it was relevant that the plaintiff might have a more difficult time suing his solicitor, who would know any weak points of his case, which might not have been so apparent to the defendant. The courts are therefore keen to look at all the circumstances of the case, and show a marked reluctance, demonstrated in *Ramsden* v *Lee* [1992] 2 All ER 204, to commit themselves to specific guidelines.

6. Lapsed proceedings

One situation in which it will be difficult to persuade a court to use its discretion under s 33 is where the plaintiff has already begun an action for the same damage against the same defendant but has failed to proceed with it — *Walkley* v *Precision Forgings Limited* [1979] 2 All ER 548, [1979] 1 WLR 606. This gives rise to particularly harsh results where a plaintiff's solicitors have issued proceedings but have neglected to serve them in time. Subject to the points raised in Chapter 7 the original proceedings will fail, and the plaintiff will be most unlikely to obtain the indulgence of the court under s 33. To all effects and purposes, he is in a worse position than had his solicitors forgotten to issue proceedings at all. The only remedy is likely to be against his legal advisers.

7. Dealing with limitation arguments

If a defence of limitation is raised, it can be dealt with either at an interlocutory hearing before the District Judge or before the Judge in open court. If it is dealt with by the Judge, it can arise either as a preliminary issue or as part of the trial itself.

It is generally felt that referral to a District Judge should only be made if there is a very clear distinction between the facts relating to the limitation action and those relating to the action itself. If the limitation issues can be singled out in this way, an interlocutory hearing before the District Judge has the advantage of keeping the plaintiff's costs to a minimum.

If it is possible to refer the case to the District Judge in this way, it is normally the defendant who takes the initiative by issuing a notice of application. In most cases, this would take the form of an application to stay the action, although where the defendants are particularly confident of success, their application may be to strike out the claim on the basis that it is frivolous, vexatious and an abuse of the process.

A form of application for an order under s 33, and an application for striking out a time-barred claim, are set out on page 23.

Checklist

1. Missing the expiry of a limitation period could well give rise to a cause of action against the solicitor. There are a variety of techniques available to minimise the risk of a date being missed. These include:

- diarising the date by which proceedings should have been issued;
- having different colour files for each year — this should direct one's attention to which files are getting old;
- keeping a cardex list of all cases in which proceedings have not been issued, kept by reference to dates.

2. If expiry of a limitation period is drawing nigh but you do not have enough information, it may well be advisable to issue without serving the proceedings on the defendant. The County Court Rules allow the plaintiff's solicitors to wait up to four months after issue for service. It may also be possible to apply to extend the validity of the summons (see page 50).

3. As an alternative, after *Lubovsky* v *Snelling* [1944] KB 44 it is possible to enter into an express agreement with the defendant to waive the limitation period. This is relatively uncommon, but such a practice was upheld by Griffin J in *Doran* v *Thomas Thompson & Sons* [1978] IR 223.

4. It will be noted that the fact that negotiations are in train is not a ground for the exercise of a discretion under s 33. Being involved in negotiations is one of the easiest ways of missing the expiry of the limitation period. In this situation, insurance companies are quite accustomed to agreements whereby proceedings are served but no further steps are taken for a given period of time to allow negotiations to be concluded. Beware, however, of leaving matters for too long on this footing. The county court has the power to strike out a claim which is not set down for action by 18 months after the close of pleadings.

Notice of application for Order under s 33 Limitation Act 1980

IN THE BARCHESTER COUNTY COURT

(Case heading)

NOTICE OF APPLICATION

TAKE NOTICE that the Plaintiff intends to apply to the District Judge at Barchester County Court, 9, High Street, Barchester on . . . . day the . . . . day of . . . . 19 . . . at . . . am/pm for an Order that pursuant to Section 33 of the Limitation Act 1980 the provisions of Section 11 of the said Act shall not apply to this action.

AND that the costs of and occasioned by this application be costs in the cause.

DATED the . . . . day of . . . . 19 . . .

> . . . .
> Davies & Co
> 10 High Street
> Barchester

Notice of application for order that the plaintiff's claim be struck out

IN THE BARCHESTER COUNTY COURT

(Case heading)

NOTICE OF APPLICATION

TAKE NOTICE that the Defendant intends to apply to the District Judge at Barchester County Court, 9, High Street, Barchester on . . . . day the . . . . day of . . . . 19 . . . at . . . am/pm for an order that the Plaintiff's claim be struck out on the ground that it sets up a cause of action which is barred by the provisions of the Limitation Act 1980 at the time of service of the Statement of Claim.

AND that the costs of and occasioned by this application be paid by the Plaintiff in any event.

DATED the . . . . day of . . . . 19 . . .

> . . . .
> Smith & Co
> Barchester Tavern
> Barchester
> Solicitors for the Defendant

Chapter 4

The role of the Motor Insurers' Bureau and the insurance companies

In most personal injury cases, the identity of the defendant will be clear and he will be sued as the original tortfeasor. However, in certain situations, the position will be less clear. Difficulties will obviously arise, for example, where the injury arose out of a 'hit and run' accident and it has been impossible to trace the driver concerned. In this chapter, we look at the role of the Motor Insurers' Bureau ('MIB') in hit and run cases and in cases where the defendant driver proves to be uninsured. We also look at the role of insurance companies in dealing with personal injury claims.

1. The Motor Insurers' Bureau

The MIB will become involved in a claim concerning a road traffic accident in two circumstances — where the driver tortfeasor is uninsured, and where he cannot be traced. In such circumstances, it is clearly unjust for the innocent party to go uncompensated and the MIB has entered into two agreements to make appropriate compensation in suitable cases.

(a) Where the defendant is uninsured (the 'First Agreement')

Under this agreement, if judgment is obtained in respect of any 'relevant liability' and such judgment is not satisfied within seven days, the MIB will pay any sum payable under the judgment to the plaintiff.

'Relevant liability' under the agreement is defined as 'a liability in respect of which a policy of insurance must insure a person in order to comply with the Road Traffic Act 1988'.

It is important to note that before the MIB will satisfy a judgment in this way notice must have been given to it within seven days of the commencement of proceedings. This notice should be accompanied by a copy of the summons, and the plaintiff's solicitor should provide the MIB with such information as it may reasonably require. The importance of this provision was underlined in *Stinton* v *Stinton and the MIB* [1993] PIQR 135 in which it was held that letters written at an early stage in the preparation of the plaintiff's case could not constitute sufficient notice.

The scheme does not apply, however, to the following:

(i) accidents involving Crown vehicles;

(ii) accidents involving local authority or police vehicles, unless the vehicle is being driven without the local authority's or police's control;

(iii) accidents which occurred where the claimant knew or had reasonable cause to believe that the vehicle had been taken without the consent of the owner, unless:

- he believed or had reason to believe that he would have had the owner's consent if the owner had been aware of the situation; or
- he had learned of the circumstances of the taking of his vehicle since the journey began and it would be unreasonable to expect him to have alighted from the vehicle;

(iv) the claimant owned or was using the vehicle knowing that there was no policy of insurance.

With regard to (iv) above, however, see *Limbrick v French and Another* [1993] PIQR 121 (although the case itself was heard in June 1989) where it was held that 'relevant liability' would extend to the boyfriend of the plaintiff who was driving the plaintiff's car with her consent when he was not a named driver on her insurance policy and was thus uninsured. It was held that the onus is on the MIB to show facts from which it could be concluded that the plaintiff knew the defendant to be uninsured. Compare this with the result in *Stinton v Stinton and the MIB* [1993] PIQR 135 where it was found that the plaintiff, a passenger in his brother's vehicle, knew that his brother was uninsured. A useful discussion was held in the latter case on the idea of what constitutes a 'user' of a vehicle, and recourse had to the idea of a joint enterprise. No reference was made in the *Stinton* case to the *Limbrick* decision.

In addition, it should be remembered that the maximum amount payable under the agreement will not exceed £250,000. In practice, bringing a claim against the MIB is normally quite straightforward. On receiving the appropriate notice, the MIB will nominate an insurance company to deal with the claim on its behalf. The claim can of course be settled before trial. The MIB will pay costs in the usual way.

(b) The untraced motorist (the 'Second Agreement')

Under the MIB's untraced driver's agreement, the MIB will deal with a claim by anyone involved in an accident who can show that:

(i) he cannot find the person responsible for the accident;

(ii) he was injured in the accident and that, on the balance of probabilities, the injury was caused by the untraced person in such circumstances that he would be otherwise liable to pay damages; or

(iii) the liability of the untraced driver is one required to be covered by the Road Traffic Act 1988 (in practice, this means liability for personal injuries, but not damage to goods).

The agreement will not apply in the following circumstances:

(i)   where the accident was caused by a vehicle owned or in the possession of the Crown;

(ii) where the claimant was being carried in the vehicle and knew that it had been taken without the consent of its owner.

The usual rules with regard to notice apply, and the claim must be made within three years of the date of the accident. Once the MIB has been notified, it will investigate the claim and the applicant must give the MIB all the help which it reasonably needs.

(c) The award

The MIB will then consider whether to make an award. Damages are to be assessed in the same way that a court would assess them, although the award will not include:

(i)   damages for loss of expectation of life or pain and suffering which the claimant could otherwise have claimed under the Law Reform (Miscellaneous Provisions) Act 1934;

(ii) where the application is made in respect of death, any amount with regard to solatium for grief of any relative under Scottish law;

(iii) if the applicant was paid wages whilst sick he is deemed not to have suffered any loss of earnings even if he is under a duty to reimburse his employer for his sick pay.

(d) Several drivers

Clause 5 of the agreement deals with situations where only one of several drivers is untraced. It applies in the following cases:

(i)   where the applicant has obtained a judgment in respect of death or injury against one or more of the identified persons, or any person liable for such as the master or principal of any such persons, and that judgment has not been satisfied within three months;

(ii) where the applicant has not obtained, and has not been required by the MIB to obtain, a judgment against an identified person and has not received any payment by way of compensation from such a person.

In these two situations, the MIB will, in effect, top up any compensation received to equal the untraced person's contribution to a full award if the judgment is fully satisfied; or, if the judgment is only partially satisfied, an amount equal to the untraced person's contribution to the shortfall.

(e) The MIB's decision

If the MIB rejects an application, reasons must be given. If an offer is made, an appeal can be made within six months of the decision. The case is then sent to an arbitrator, and each party must bear its own costs.

(f) Streamlined applications

A less formal procedure was introduced by a 'supplemental agreement'. This covers the situation where the claim is for less than £20,000 and is straightforward. In addition, the claimant must be legally represented and the claim should not involve an unidentified driver.

(g) Bringing an action where the MIB is involved

Under the First Agreement, proceedings must always be issued where the MIB is involved, as an unsatisfied judgment is a precondition of payment. The MIB is often added as the second defendant, so that it can exercise some control over the proceedings (or make a payment in).

Under the Second Agreement, there cannot be proceedings, as there is no identified defendant to sue. Even if proceedings are brought against an identified defendant who is only partially responsible for the accident, the MIB cannot be joined − *White* v *London Transport Executive* [1971] 2 QB 721, [1971] 3 All ER 1, [1971] 3 WLR 169.

Normally, the MIB cannot accept service, but under O 7 r 8 CCR, an order for substituted service can be made if it is impracticable for the summons to be served in the normal way. If the defendant has given a false address, it may be possible to obtain an order for service on the MIB. The application should be made to the District Judge and an affidavit supplied, showing that reasonable efforts have been made to find the defendant's address.

2. Insurers

In the vast majority of personal injury claims, the initial discussion of the case will be between the plaintiff's solicitors and the defendant's insurers. Most insurance companies will form an initial view of the case through their inspectors and, if liability is indefensible, will conduct negotiations themselves.

In less clear cases, the insurers may well invite the plaintiff's solicitors to issue proceedings and may nominate solicitors to accept service. The summons should not be served upon the insurer as, unless an appropriate order has been made, it will not be good service — *Foster* v *Turnbull & Others* The Times 22 May 1990.

(a) The Third Party (Rights Against Insurers) Act 1930

It is also worth bearing in mind the provisions of the Third Party (Rights Against Insurers) Act 1930 if the defendant becomes insolvent. This Act was introduced to by-pass a practical problem which had arisen from the strict application of insolvency principles. Before the Act, if a tortfeasor driver became bankrupt, the insurance monies which he received to meet the claim against him would form part of his estate, with all creditors taking a bite. The 1930 Act changed this and allows the innocent third party to take the place of the tortfeasor driver, so that the insurance monies are paid directly to him. The other creditors are, in effect, by-passed and the third party obtains his compensation.

However, as the innocent third party stands in the shoes of the bankrupt driver, he stands or falls by the negligent driver's relationship with his insurers, but the insurance company cannot allow any of the following factors to defeat a claim (RTA 1988 s 148):

- the age or physical/mental condition of the driver;
- the condition of the vehicle;
- the number of persons in the vehicle;
- the weight or characteristics of the goods carried in the vehicle;
- the times when or areas where the vehicle is used;
- the cylinder capacity of the vehicle;
- the carrying of apparatus on the vehicle;
- the carrying of identification required under the Vehicles (Excise) Act 1971.

If the Third Party (Rights Against Insurers) Act 1930 applies, proceedings can be brought against the insurance company direct. It should be pleaded that the rights of the third party were vested in the plaintiff who can therefore enforce them against the defendant.

(b) The Road Traffic Act 1988

Section 151 of the Road Traffic Act 1988 provides help for the plaintiff who discovers that the insurance policy of the negligent driver has been cancelled. The following conditions must be satisfied:

(i) the innocent third party must have given formal notice of proceedings to the insurers;

(ii) there must be a certificate of insurance or security;

(iii) there must be a judgment against either any person insured by the policy, or any other person provided that the judgment is in respect of a liability which would be covered if the policy covered any driver;

(iv) the judgment must have been obtained in respect of a liability which must be covered by insurance under s 145 of the 1988 Act;

(v) such liability must be covered by the terms of the policy (apart from the right to cancel).

In certain situations, however, s 151 will not help the third party — for instance, if the use to which the vehicle was being put was outside the cover provided, or if the policy is avoided on the grounds of non-disclosure of a material fact. In the latter case, it is for the insurance company to commence proceedings to obtain a declaration that the policy may be avoided.

Checklist

The MIB — First Agreement (uninsured drivers)

1.   Always notify the MIB within seven days of issuing proceedings.
2.   MIB will cover liability for which compulsory insurance is required under the RTA.
3.   MIB may well apply to be made party to the proceedings.

— Second Agreement (untraced drivers)

1.   Apply to the MIB within three years of the date of the accident.
2.   Consider the supplemental agreement if the claim is for less than £20,000.

Insurance companies

1.   Never serve the summons on the insurer.
2.   Use the Third Party (Rights Against Insurers) Act 1930 if the tortfeasor becomes bankrupt.
3.   If the tortfeasor's insurance policy is cancelled, consider s 151 of the Road Traffic Act 1988.

Chapter 5

From taking instructions to issuing proceedings

1. Statements

It is good practice to obtain a statement from the client at the earliest possible opportunity, ideally at the initial interview. The nearer this is to the date of the accident, the more difficult it will be for it to be attacked on the basis of a lapse of memory.

In addition, the discipline of taking a statement can often help the conduct of a case. It forces the conducting solicitor's mind to the elements of the case that must be proved. It will indicate where further evidence from witnesses will be relevant, and the efficient solicitor will obtain this at the earliest possible opportunity.

2. Photographs

In many cases, photographs will be helpful. They are particularly useful in tripper cases, where the height of the protruding flagstone is likely to be crucial. It goes without saying that in such cases, a ruler should be placed beside the offending object in order that the scale can be determined.

Providing that the camera is of reasonably good quality, there will normally be no need for a professional photographer to be engaged. A camera with a zoom facility is especially useful, and several shots, from varying angles and distances, should be taken. At the time of taking the photographs, a log should be kept indicating from where each was taken. The appropriate details should then be recorded on the back of each developed print. The person who took the photograph should also sign it and date it.

3. Taking a statement

The mechanics of taking a statement depend largely on the relationship between the solicitor and the client. There is an increasing tendency towards creating an atmosphere of informality, and putting the client at ease. Against this must be balanced the need to impress upon the client the absolute importance of accuracy. He or she must tell the solicitor everything which is relevant to the case — both helpful and unhelpful. At the end of the day, it is all a question of balance and the good solicitor tends to vary his or her approach to the different types of client that come into the office.

Most solicitors will start the interview by inviting the client to tell them, in a fairly straightforward way, exactly what happened. In many cases, this will create no difficulties. In others, such as factory accidents, the facts giving rise to the accident will be less easy to understand.

The importance of understanding exactly how the accident occurred cannot be overstated. Too many lawyers are embarrassed to press the plaintiff too far for fear of revealing their own ignorance. Remember that the plaintiff may have to make a Judge understand how the accident occurred. If he can't make his solicitor understand, the chances are that he will not be able to explain the accident to the Judge either.

When the way in which the accident occurred has been described, the questions to be asked will depend upon the likely causes of action. Often the potential claim will be in negligence after a road traffic accident, or under the Factories Act and negligence in an industrial accident. The golden rule is to remember what needs to be proved and question the client accordingly.

One useful trick is to try to imagine that you are drafting the Particulars of Claim then and there. Thus, in a straightforward case, you will need to show:

- the duty of care;
- the breach;
- the damage arising from the breach.

The duty of care will be straightforward. The breach? Perhaps driving on the wrong side of the road, failing to stop in time or failing to keep a proper look out in a running down case. Alternatively, in a factory accident situation, failing to fence dangerous machinery or, more generally, failing to provide a safe system of work.

It is often easy to concentrate too much on alleging negligence or breach of statutory duty. What must be remembered is that damages now need to be quantified at the earliest possible stage and this must be covered with the client. Make enquiries of his employer as to his loss of earnings as soon as possible. Encourage the client to keep receipts for everything which he needs to purchase because of his injuries.

4. The form of the statement

The statement must be signed and dated by the person on whose behalf it has been drafted. The reason for this is that, should the person concerned die or become otherwise unavailable before trial, the statement will be admissible under the Civil Evidence Act if signed and dated.

Apart from this, the plaintiff's solicitor has always had a free hand in determining the form of the statement. It is usual to head it with the name, address and occupation of the witness – eg 'I, John Smith, joiner, of 1 Acacia Avenue, Surbiton, will say as follows ...'. The rest of the statement should be expressed in the first person and should deal with the circumstances of the claim in chronological order.

31

As we will see at a later stage, the court now has power to order the exchange of witness statements between the parties. Under the new rules, the parties will, in effect, be confined to giving evidence within the parameters of their statements.

Order 20 r 12A of the County Court Rules and the Rules of the Supreme Court O 38 r 2A give guidelines on the desired form of the statement. These are really no different from the traditional approach outlined above and provide, in particular, that the statement should be expressed in the first person and should state:

- the full name of the witness;
- his place of residence or, if he is making the statement in his professional capacity, his work address, the position which he holds and the name of his firm or employer;
- his occupation, or if he has none, his description;
- the fact that he is a party to the proceedings or is the employee of such a party (if appropriate).

The notes to the RSC indicate that the statement should be treated as if the witness was giving evidence. It should be clear and straightforward and chronologically set out. Dates, sums and numbers should be expressed in figures.

In addition, the statement should comply with O 66 RSC. In other words, it should:

- be on A4 ISO paper of durable quality;
- have a margin of not less than 1½" wide on the left of the side facing the reader;
- be in the form of printing, or clear and legible writing, or typewritten (but not a carbon copy).

The notes further recommend that the statement should be signed and, if possible, witnessed. As it will be filed with the court's papers, it should not be bound with thick plastic strips. If it makes reference to other documents in the trial, their references should be put in the margin.

5. The initial letter

One of the advantages of formulating the claim in this way will be that when the plaintiff's solicitor writes to the tortfeasor, he or she will have a detailed account of the circumstances of the accident. The decision which now needs to be taken is whether the statements already obtained are enough, or whether further information is needed.

In many factory accident cases, the statements of the witnesses will not be enough and it will be necessary to instruct an expert to deal with the possible breaches of statute and/or duty of care. The next section below deals with pre-action access to the factory for this purpose.

At around this time, the solicitor will also be writing the initial letter of claim to the tortfeasor. This will normally invite him to refer the matter to his insurer. Traditionally, the advice has always been to make this letter as vague as possible. This is good advice when it is expected to instruct an engineer or other expert to advise on practices at the factory, as it will probably not be possible fully to formulate the claim at this stage.

If, however, there is enough evidence at this stage, the letter may as well give a fairly detailed account of the claim. This will have to be done in any event when proceedings start and if done at this early stage, will by-pass the usual insurance company's inquiries for further details of the case and the allegations of negligence.

6. Pre-action access to the scene of the accident

It is normally quite acceptable to obtain engineering evidence after proceedings have commenced. However, in a complicated case, or in a situation where the plaintiff himself is unsure how the accident occurred, it is advisable to obtain an expert's report before the Particulars of Claim are settled.

Application for such facilities should first be made to the prospective defendant's insurers. If permission is refused, application can be made under O 29 r 7A RSC (which applies in the county court by reason of O 13 r 7 CCR). Application is made by way of originating application and a precedent, together with supporting affidavit, is supplied at the end of this chapter.

7. Preservation of property

It may become apparent that there is a risk the prospective defendant may dispose of property which is relevant to the proceedings. In such a case, application can be made under s 52 of the County Courts Act 1984 for an order for:

- the inspection, photographing, preservation, custody or detention of the property;
- the taking of samples of any such property and the carrying out of any experiments on or with any such property.

Again, application is by way of originating application supported by an affidavit which must specify the property and show that it is relevant to the proceedings. The affidavit must be served with the summons. A sample application is set out at page 37.

8. Videotaping of industrial processes

Under s 38 of the County Courts Act 1984, the county court is entitled to make any order within the powers of the High Court. This provision is useful in that it allows an application to be made for an order providing for the videotaping of an industrial process; see *Ash v Buxted Poultry Ltd* The Times 29 November 1989.

9. Disclosure of documents

A full discussion of the rules relating to discovery will be found in Chapter 12. However, an application can be made for disclosure of relevant documents before proceedings are issued. This application is made under s 52(2) and s 53(2) of the County Courts Act 1984, and O 24 r 7A RSC.

These rules apply only in personal injury actions, and allow a potential plaintiff to obtain documents from a likely party to the proposed litigation.

Four conditions must be satisfied before an order can be made:

- the person making the application is likely to be a party to proposed proceedings;
- a claim for personal injury or death is likely to be made;
- the person against whom the order is sought is likely to be a party to such proceedings;
- such person appears likely to have had in his possession custody or power documents relevant to the proposed action.

The application, once again, is made by originating application with supporting affidavit which should be served with the summons. The affidavit must:

- specify the documents;
- show their relevance to the action;
- show why the person against whom the order is served is likely to have the documents; and
- show why that person is likely to be a party to the subsequent proceedings.

In *Dunning* v *Board of Government of Liverpool Hospitals* [1973] 2 All ER 454, [1973] 1 WLR 586, it was held that 'likely to be a party' could depend upon the result of the discovery.

A sample application for pre-trial discovery is set out on page 38.

10. Obtaining the first medical report

Under O 6 r 5(a) CCR a medical report must be served with the Particulars of Claim. Note that reference is made to 'a' report — it need not be the final report. All that is required is that it substantiate all the injuries alleged in the Particulars of Claim which the plaintiff proposes to adduce in evidence as part of his case at the trial.

If the prognosis cannot yet be given, the report should say so. Indeed, there is nothing in the rules to prevent a first report being short and even rather vague.

Normally, the appropriate expert to instruct will be a consultant specialising in the area of medicine covering the plaintiff's injuries. GPs will normally only provide a report if they know the patient. They are most unlikely to deal with the amount of medico-legal work that a consultant will, and their reports are normally shorter and less helpful to the court.

The most commonly used medical experts in personal injury cases are orthopaedic consultants. They deal with bone injuries and tend to be the first port of call for most road traffic injuries. Other useful specialities are listed below:

children — paediatrician
head — neurologist/neurosurgeon
internal injuries — general surgeon
eyes — ophthalmologist
personality disorders — psychiatrist

There is a growing tendency amongst some consultants to take on so much medico-legal work that they have developed reputations as almost professional witnesses. Such consultants can often not see a client for many months. However, local consultants are often received extremely well in the county court. They can usually see patients much more quickly than consultants of national renown and will probably be considerably more flexible when it comes to being available for court. If local consultants are reasonably good at giving evidence, it is a good idea to use them.

Most consultants know how a report should be set out. However, it may be worth indicating that the report required at this early stage is a preliminary one and need not be as detailed as the report(s) to follow.

11. The statement of special damages

Order 6 r 5(b) CCR provides that the plaintiff should file with his Particulars of Claim a statement of the special damages claimed. This is defined further in r 3(7) as 'a statement giving full particulars of the special damages claimed for expenses and losses already incurred and an estimate of any future expenses and losses (including loss of earnings and of pension rights)'. There is no set form for the statement — as long as it is reasonably clear, it will suffice. An example of a straightforward statement is given at the end of this chapter.

If the injury is more serious, the drafting of the statement may be difficult in that some estimate of future losses should be provided. Whilst there have been no guidelines, it is suggested that solicitors should take their cue from the prognosis given by the medical expert. If this is uncertain, and there is a risk that the plaintiff will not be able to return to work, a suitable paragraph should be inserted in the statement, indicating that more information will be provided as and when the prognosis becomes clearer.

12. Report or statement not provided

If the medical report or statement of special damages is not filed, the court can specify the time in which these should be provided, or 'make such other order as it thinks fit' (including an order dispensing with the requirements or staying the proceedings).

Checklist

1. Obtain statement. Include: Name
   Address
   Occupation
   Date
   Signature
2. Consider whether statements will be required from other witnesses.
3. Consider whether other evidence is needed before the decision to issue proceedings can be taken. If answer is yes, apply under CCA 1984 ss 52(2) and 53(2).
4. Is there a risk that relevant property will be destroyed?— s 52(1) CCA 1984.
5. Obtain medical report.
6. Draft statement of special damages.

Application for pre-trial access to the scene of the accident

(Case heading)

I, ... of (address and occupation) apply to the Court for an Order pursuant to Order 29 Rule 7A of the Rules of the Supreme Court in the following terms:

(1) That the Respondent do upon seven days notice give inspection to the Applicant, the Applicant's solicitor and the Applicant's engineering expert of the Respondent's premises situate at . . . . and do allow the making of any drawing and the taking of photographs at the property by such persons.

(2) That the Respondent do pay the costs of this application.

The grounds upon which I claim to be entitled to this Order are:

(1) That the Applicant and Respondent are likely to be parties to subsequent proceedings in this Court in which a Claim is likely to be made by the Applicant against the respondent in respect of personal injuries sustained by the applicant on 9th October 1994.

(2) That the safety of equipment situate at the Respondent's premises will be likely to be relevant to the issue of liability in the said proceedings.

(3) That the Applicant is unable properly to formulate his claim in such proceedings until the said inspection has been carried out.

The name and address of the person upon whom it is intended to serve this application is (insert Respondent's name and address).

My address for service is . . . .

Dated this   day of

Affidavit in support of application for pre-action inspection

(Case heading)

I, John Smith of Smith and Co, 20 Museum St, Barchester, MAKE OATH and say as follows:

1. I am a solicitor of the Supreme Court and have the conduct of this personal injury claim on behalf of the prospective Plaintiff, Mr Kevin Jones. I am duly authorised to make this affidavit on behalf of Mr Jones and do so on the basis of instructions received from my client.

2. Mr Jones was injured on the 9th October 1994. He was employed as a radiator repairer at the Defendant's premises in Gorse Road, Barchester. My instructions are that as Mr Jones used an air hose to check whether a radiator was leaking, a small explosion occurred, causing injury to his left eye and hand.

3. I am of the opinion that the equipment being used by the Defendant was faulty and have written to the Defendants and their insurers accordingly. A bundle of the correspondence that has passed between us is now shown to me and produced marked JJ1.

4. On 21st December I wrote to the Defendant's insurers requesting that our engineering expert might be allowed to visit the factory and examine the equipment. This will obviously assist the proper conduct of the claim as it will allow us to identify the faults which we believe were present in the equipment at the time of the accident.

5. The Barchester insurance society, who insure the Defendant, are not prepared to allow such inspection.

6. I am informed by my client and verily believe that the air hose and radiator may well be the subject matter of proceedings arising out of the accident. I therefore respectfully ask that the Plaintiff, his solicitor and his engineering expert be permitted to inspect and photograph the scene of the accident and the equipment being used at the time it occurred.

SWORN etc.

Application for preservation of property pending trial

I . . . of (address and occupation) apply to the court for an Order pursuant to s 52 of the County Courts Act 1984 in the following terms:

1. The air hose and radiator situate at bench 6 and being the equipment used by the Plaintiff at the time of his accident on 19th October 1994 be preserved without alteration or removal pending trial of this action

(finish as before).

Application for pre-trial discovery

. . . in Order that

1. The Defendant do make and serve on the Plaintiff's solicitors a list stating whether the following documents are in his possession custody or power AND if such documents were once but are not now in the possession custody or power of the Defendant then to list such documents and state when they were last in the possession of the Defendant and where the Defendant believes them now to be:

   (i) Maintenance records from 1988 to date concerning Acme Air Pressure System used by the Defendant

   (ii) Operating instructions for said system

   (iii) Maintenance instructions for said system

   (iv) Installation records for such system

(finish as before).

Initial statement of special damages

(case heading)

STATEMENT OF SPECIAL DAMAGES TO 30.9.94

1. Loss of earnings
   Plaintiff absent from work for 10 weeks @ £90 net per week
   . . . . £900

   Less sick pay advanced £500

   Loss £400

2. Painkilling tablets £20

   Physiotherapy £100

   TOTAL £520

DATED this   day of

Chapter 6

The Particulars of Claim

Once the basis of the client's claim is understood, the medical report has been prepared and a preliminary quantification of special damages has been made, the next stage will be the preparation of the Particulars of Claim. By this stage, the plaintiff's solicitor will have been in touch with the defendant and his insurers and should have some idea of the stance which they are adopting. The insurers may well be fairly non-committal at this stage. If this is so, and liability looks good, proceedings should always be issued to force the pace.

1. Using counsel to draft pleadings

Opinion can vary as to the merits of this. It certainly is infuriating to have to wait months for a perfectly straightforward pleading to come back from counsel. On the other hand, if a pleading is urgent, many barristers will generally do their best to meet a time limit.

The following are some of the advantages in using counsel:

- A second head will consider the claim. It is surprising how easy it is to miss something important.
- If counsel is to present the case in court, it is only right that he or she should have had the opportunity to plead it.
- Barristers draft more pleadings. Of course, many solicitors are equally competent, but the two most important specialities of the Bar are advocacy and pleadings. A reasonably experienced barrister should be able to draft pleadings relatively quickly and, therefore, cheaply.
- There should not be any problem in justifying the use of counsel to settle proceedings on taxation (whether a particular fee can be justified is, of course, another question).
- Occasionally, pleadings can get difficult and there are pitfalls for the unwary in certain causes of action. For an example, see *Johnston* v *Caddies Wainwright Ltd* [1983] ICR 407.

2. Formulating the claim

Personal injury actions are characterised by the nature of the harm suffered by the plaintiff, rather than the cause of action itself. However, when it comes to the causes of action available, two distinct groups emerge — negligence and breach of statutory duty.

The boundaries of negligence are forever shifting, but the traditional view is that the plaintiff must show three things — the existence of a duty of care, a breach of the duty, and damage resulting from the breach. So far as breach of statutory duty is concerned, there is below a table showing some of the commonly used statutory provisions. Recourse should be had to Redgrave & Machin, *Health and Safety*, and Munkman *Damages for Personal Injury and Death*, for their nuances.

Workplaces — Factories Act 1961

Definition of factory	s 175
Adequate ventilation	s 4
Floors, steps, stairs, passages and gangways	s 28(1)
Place of work over 2 metres high	s 29(2)
Lifting tackle/machines	ss 22 – 27
Fencing vats and dangerous liquids	s 18
Explosive/inflammable substances	s 31
Steam boilers	ss 32 – 38
Fencing of machinery	ss 12 – 16
Training and support of young persons on dangerous machines	s 21(1)
Self acting machines	s 19
Dust/fumes	s 63(1)
Washing facilities	s 58
Protection of eyes	s 65

Other regulations

The Construction (General Provisions) Regulations 1961
The Construction (Lifting Operations) Regulations 1961
The Construction (Working Places) Regulations 1966
The Woodworking Machines Regulations 1974
The Power Presses Regulations 1965
The Abrasive Wheels Regulations 1970
The Iron and Steel Foundries Regulations 1953
The Docks Regulations 1934
The Mines and Quarries Act 1954
The Electricity Regulations 1944
The Offshore Installations (Operational Safety, Health and Welfare) Regulations 1976
The Diving Operations at Work Regulations 1981
The Agriculture (Safeguarding of Workplaces) Regulations 1959

3. The Consumer Protection Act 1987

Special mention should be made of the new cause of action provided by this Act, which applies to items supplied after 1 March 1988. If injury is caused by a defect in a product supplied after this date, an action under the Act should be considered. To succeed, the plaintiff must show the following:

(a) the product was not as safe as persons are generally entitled to expect (s 3);

(b) the supply was made in the course of a business (s 4(1)(c));

(c) the defect existed at the time of supply (s 4(1)(d));

(d) the damage suffered falls within the meaning of the Act.

Under s 45(1) 'goods' can include crops and agricultural products which have undergone an industrial process. The term also includes products which are component parts of another item, such as industrial machinery or cars.

Evidence showing that the product is defective should be gathered from experts, trade and consumer journals, British Standards and EC Directives. Enquiries of local Trading Standards departments may well prove fruitful.

Under the Act, proceedings are commenced against the producer, or, if the product was made outside the EC, the importer. If the plaintiff does not know the identity of the producer, he can ask the supplier to identify the importer or producer. If no help is given, the plaintiff can sue the supplier instead.

Defences are set out in s 4:

- the defect is attributable to compliance with any requirement made by an enactment or with any EC obligation;
- the product was not supplied by the defendant;
- the supplier was not a business;
- the item was not defective when supplied;
- the state of scientific and technical knowledge at the relevant time was not such that the producer could be expected to have discovered the defect.
- the defect was in the subsequent product, rather than the component part supplied by the defendant.

4. Pleading the claim

In drafting the Particulars of Claim, it should be remembered always that the purpose of the pleading is to summarise, as succinctly and elegantly as possible, how and why the cause of action arose and what is claimed. Order 6 of the CCR indicates that 'a plaintiff shall, at the time of commencing an action, file particulars of his cause of action and the relief or remedy which he seeks and stating briefly the material facts on which he relies'. There is no magic in standard precedents. Indeed, there are far too many examples of cases in which standard precedents have been used and which give no clue how the accident arose.

Guidelines on the subject of pleadings can be found in O 18 RSC. It provides that each pleading should state the year in which proceedings were issued, the letter and number of the action, the description of the pleading and the date on which it was served. The pleading should be divided into paragraphs, if possible with each allegation in a separate paragraph. Dates should be expressed in figures and the pleading should be endorsed with the name and firm of the solicitors conducting the case.

The rules provide that facts, not evidence, should be pleaded. This sometimes causes difficulties as the line between facts and evidence is not always easy to draw. An admission by the defendant, for example, should not be pleaded, although it will of course be highly relevant at trial. However, a conviction arising out of the same facts should be pleaded.

Further, only the material facts of the case should be pleaded. It is important to consider carefully which facts are material to the case. Every element of the case must be included, but the temptation to include material which has no bearing on the outcome is to be avoided, as this will simply make the pleading appear imprecise.

There is generally no need to use antiquated language. Colloquialisms are to be avoided, but the case should be expressed as simply and precisely as possible. Remember that the Judge who deals with the case is likely to read the pleadings before the hearing starts. The first document he will read will be the Particulars of Claim — a golden opportunity to gain the advantage over the defendant. A well drafted, comprehensive yet concise pleading should assist and impress the Judge.

A full guide to the pleading of personal injury claims is outside the ambit of this book, but an example, using a simple claim, may be helpful. Let us assume that we are dealing with a straightforward claim for a whiplash injury resulting from a motor accident. The client is Jenny Smith, a 30-year old married woman. She was driving her Volvo to work on 19 April 1994. She stopped at traffic lights and was hit from behind by a Ford Orion driven by one Sidney Street. She suffered a whiplash injury in the accident and made a full recovery after six months.

The first question to deal with is 'what are the material facts?'. They are listed below:

- the names of the parties;
- the date of the accident;
- the place of the accident;
- the fact that the plaintiff was hit from behind by the defendant;
- the fact that the plaintiff was injured because of the accident.

Having decided what the material facts are, the next question will be how to present them in the most effective way for your client. It would be possible to plead the case on this basis perfectly competently thus:

The Particulars of Claim

IN THE BARCHESTER COUNTY COURT   **Case No 941234**

BETWEEN: JENNIFER SMITH   <u>Plaintiff</u>
                                       and
                                  SIDNEY STREET   <u>Defendant</u>

PARTICULARS OF CLAIM

1. The Plaintiff is the owner of a Volvo motor car, registration number A610 LFJ.
2. On 19th April 1994, whilst the Plaintiff was driving her said motor car at Saxon Place, Barchester, she was in collision with a Ford Orion motor vehicle, registration no G631 VJD driven by the Defendant.
3. The said accident was caused by the negligence of the Defendant.

PARTICULARS OF NEGLIGENCE

i.   Driving too fast.
ii. Colliding with the plaintiff's vehicle.
iii. Failing to keep a proper look out.
iv. Failing to stop, steer or turn aside so as to avoid the plaintiff's vehicle.

4. By reason of the matters aforesaid the plaintiff has suffered personal injury, loss and damage.

PARTICULARS OF PERSONAL INJURY

The Plaintiff, who was thirty years of age at the time of the accident suffered a whiplash injury of the neck. She was seen by her GP and subsequently at the Barchester Hospital and recovered from her injury after six months.

PARTICULARS OF SPECIAL DAMAGE

i.   Painkillers £5.00
ii. Travel to doctor/hospital £20.00

5. The Plaintiff further claims, pursuant to the provisions of s 69 of the County Courts Act 1984 to be entitled to interest at such rate and for such period as the court shall think fit.

AND the Plaintiff claims:

1) Damages
2) Interest as pleaded

                                              . . . .
                                              Messrs Slope & Co
                                              Barchester Chambers
                                              Barchester

Served this . . . . day of September 1994.

A little more thought, however, would make this pleading considerably more effective.

In the first paragraph of the Particulars of Claim, the identity of the plaintiff is set out. In this case, as the identity of the defendant is unlikely to cause any difficulty, space can be saved by introducing him at this stage.

Secondly, the real strength of the case lies in the fact that the client was stationary at traffic lights when hit from behind. She cannot therefore be expected to shoulder any of the blame for the accident. Revealing the strength of our case on this point will not cause any problems as the defendant can have no answer to it. On the other hand, it will underline the strength of our claim to our opponents, and, should the case get that far, to the Judge. Paragraph two of the pleading should thus be strengthened.

So far as the allegations of negligence are concerned, a properly drafted second paragraph will take you halfway there. When setting out the allegations, we should put the most specific first.

In a case such as this, where liability is extremely strong, the likelihood is that the case will only be contested on the subject of quantum. It is easy to concentrate too hard on the subject of liability and forget to give a proper account of the injuries. Although the medical report will be served with the pleading, this is only to verify the allegations of injury made. It does not therefore remove from the plaintiff the need to plead her injuries properly. As these may be in dispute, it is worth summarising them as carefully and effectively as possible.

Interest should be pleaded specifically, and the appropriate rate inserted into the Particulars of Claim.

Thus the corrected pleading may well look something like this:

IN THE BARCHESTER COUNTY COURT **Case No 941234**

BETWEEN: JENNIFER SMITH <u>Plaintiff</u>
and
SIDNEY STREET <u>Defendant</u>

<u>PARTICULARS OF CLAIM</u>

1. At all material times the Plaintiff was the owner and driver of a Volvo motor vehicle, registration no A610 LFJ. The Defendant was the driver of a Ford Orion motor vehicle, registration no G631 VJD.

2. On the 19th April 1994 when the Plaintiff was stationary in her vehicle at traffic lights situated at Saxon Place, Barchester the Defendant drove his Ford Orion motor car into the rear of the Plaintiff's vehicle.

3. The said accident was caused by the negligence of the Defendant.

PARTICULARS OF NEGLIGENCE

The Defendant was negligent in that he:

    i. Drove into the back of the Plaintiff's stationary vehicle
    ii. Failed to keep a proper lookout
    iii. Drove too fast
    iv. Drove too close to the vehicle in front of him
    v. Failed to brake in time or at all
    vi. Failed to stop, slow down, turn aside or so manage or control his vehicle as to avoid the said collision.

4. By reason of the matters aforesaid, the Plaintiff, who was thirty years of age at the time of the accident, suffered personal injury, loss and damage.

PARTICULARS OF PERSONAL INJURY

The plaintiff suffered a whiplash injury to the neck together with shock. Severe pain in the neck caused the plaintiff to visit her GP on the day after the accident and she was referred for physiotherapy to the Barchester Hospital. The plaintiff attended the hospital on eight occasions and followed a physiotherapy programme which was demanding and painful.

The plaintiff continued to suffer from pains in her upper back and neck for a period of around six months. During this period she experienced difficulties in dealing with household tasks and in playing with her two children. She was required to wear a neck brace for two weeks which she found uncomfortable. She was unable to pursue her hobbies of gardening and walking and her sex life was adversely affected.

A full account of the injuries sustained by the plaintiff is set out in the medical report of Mr. Denis Smith FRCS served herewith.

PARTICULARS OF SPECIAL DAMAGE

    i. Painkillers £5.00
    ii. Travel to doctor/hospital £20.00

5. Further, pursuant to the provisions of s 69 of the County Courts Act 1984 the plaintiff is entitled to and claims interest of 2% on General Damages from the date of commencement of proceedings and interest at the full court short term investment rate on the special damages from the date when each item of loss accrued.

AND the Plaintiff claims:
1. Damages
2. Interest as pleaded.

        . . . .
        Slope & Co
        Barchester Chambers
        Barchester
        Solicitors for the
        Plaintiff

Served this   day of   1994.

5. Instructing counsel

If counsel is used to settle pleadings, instructions should be drawn up. The instructions should give a brief indication of what the case is all about, and any potential areas of difficulty. The instructions should be accompanied by the medical report, the details of special damages and, most importantly, the client's statement.

The barrister selected should have some experience of personal injury law. Further, ensure that the Chambers concerned has at least three or four trusted civil practitioners. If, at the trial stage, the brief has to be returned because the person originally chosen is no longer available, it is preferable for it to go to someone practising in the same Chambers.

Using counsel who practises in the geographical area in which the case will be heard is often a canny move. Obviously, local sets of Chambers will fall into this category. In addition, many London sets tend to seek work in particular areas of the country. A barrister who is known and respected by the local judiciary can often be a distinct asset. In addition, he or she will be aware of any foibles of the local Bench and will be able to present the case accordingly.

Checklist

1. Consider whether to instruct counsel.
2. Consider appropriate factory legislation in industrial accidents.
3. Plead facts, not evidence.
4. If using counsel, include statement and medical report with the instructions, together with photographs, maps, etc.

Chapter 7

Issuing proceedings

If negotiations with the insurers are proving fruitless, the only way to progress the case will be by issuing proceedings. This may well be the stage at which the insurers will appoint solicitors to deal with the case on their behalf and the client should be told how this affects the question of costs. His authority must be sought before proceedings are issued.

1. Which court?

Under r 40 of the County Court (Amendment No 2) Rules 1991, the plaintiff can commence proceedings in any county court of his choice.

2. The summons

The plaintiff's solicitor now has a choice. He can fill in a request for issue of a default summons. This is delivered to the local county court which will, if required, serve the defendant with the summons which it draws up.

Alternatively, under the County Court (Amendment No 2) Rules 1991, the plaintiff's solicitor can prepare and serve the summons himself in a personal injury action. This change has found its way into the County Court Rules as O 3 r 3(1A) and is likely to be helpful where the plaintiff is running into limitation problems. See pages 53 to 56 for forms.

The summons, if served by the solicitor, should be sent by first class post to the defendant at the address stated in the summons. If it is not served in accordance with the rules, but the defendant delivers a defence, admission or counterclaim, the summons will be deemed to have been properly served unless the contrary is shown.

If the defendant is out of the jurisdiction, special rules about service apply. These are set out in O 8 CCR, which was redrafted in the light of the Civil Jurisdiction and Judgments Act 1982 and the Hague Convention 1965. Order 8 r 2(2) allows for service of an originating process out of England and Wales without the leave of the court in two cases:

  (a) Where:
- the court has power to hear and determine the claim under the Civil Jurisdiction and Judgments Act 1982;
- no proceedings between the parties concerning the same

cause of action are pending in the courts of any part of the UK or any other Convention territory (in effect, most EC countries). *and*

- either the defendant is domiciled in the UK or any other Convention territory, or the proceedings are covered by Article 16 of Sch 1 or Sch 4 to the 1982 Act. These Schedules set out certain situations in which a particular court will have exclusive jurisdiction, for example, where the claim concerns immovable property, the courts of the country where the property is situated have jurisdiction. Full reference should be made to these Schedules as their repetition is outside the scope of this book. They can be found in volume 11 of *Halsbury's Statutes*;
  or
- the defendant is a party to an agreement conferring jurisdiction to which Article 19 of Sch 1 or Sch 4 applies.

(b) Where the claim is one which by virtue of any other enactment the court has power to hear and determine notwithstanding that the person against whom the claim is made is not within England and Wales, or that the wrongful act did not take place within England and Wales.

Where the summons can be served without leave, the time for service of a defence is extended to 21 days where the defendant is in Scotland, Northern Ireland or the European territory of another contracting state, or 31 days where certain other states are concerned.

In other cases, leave will be needed to serve process out of the jurisdiction. The precise situations in which leave will be required are set out in O 8 r 2(1).

3. What documents are required?

The following documents are required:

- the request for a default summons, or the summons;
- Particulars of Claim — under O 6 r 1, the plaintiff must supply, at the time of commencing his action, 'particulars of his claim, specifying his cause of action and the relief or remedy which he seeks and stating briefly the material facts on which he relies';
- a medical report (O 6 r 5(a));
- a statement of the special damages claimed (O 6 r 5(b)).

4. Judgment in default

The first step in seeking judgment by default will be to calculate the date of service. This will normally be seven days after the date of posting as shown by the postmark, although if the plaintiff can prove that service was affected before that date, the earlier date will stand. If the defendant is a limited company, and the summons has been sent to its registered office, service will be deemed to be effected in the ordinary course of the post, rather than on the seventh day after posting.

If the defendant has not responded by filling in the appropriate part of the summons and returning it to the court within 14 days of service, the plaintiff can make an application for judgment in default. If the plaintiff's solicitors served the summons, the application should be accompanied by an affidavit of service. The application is made under O 9 r 6 CCR; note also that by dint of r 5 of the County Court (Amendment No 4) Rules 1991, it is no longer necessary to file the plaint note when applying for judgment in default.

5. Setting judgment aside

Often, a judgment in default is obtained because of the defendant's administrative problems. Perhaps he forgot to send the summons to his insurers, or the insurers lost it. For these reasons, a judgment obtained in default will often be the subject of an application to set aside. Application is made under O 37 r 4. For a form, see page 59. The rules do not require the defendant to explain why he allowed judgment to be entered, but in practice it is wise to do so. The defendant should also show that he has a defence on the merits.

This type of application can cause practical problems for the plaintiff's solicitor. On the face of it, one should not agree to such an application as it is clearly not in the interests of the plaintiff. However, it should be remembered that, provided the defendant agrees to pay the costs thrown away, most applications of this type are successful. Waiting for an appointment to set aside can take months — months which will be lost if the case is held in limbo pending the application.

Possibly the most sensible course of action is to let the defendant's insurers know at the end of the 14-day period that judgment is about to be entered. They should be allowed a week to put their house in order before applying for judgment. This should stand the plaintiff in good stead in dealing with any later application to set judgment aside.

6. Time for service

The summons must be served within four months of its issue (County Court (Amendment No 4) Rules 1989, r 7 and O 7 r 20 CCR).

(a) Extension of time

Under O 7 r 20, the court can extend the period of validity of the summons if it is satisfied that 'despite the making of all reasonable efforts, it may not be possible to serve the summons within four months'. This period can be extended for up to a total of 12 months. A form of application, and affidavit in support, appear on pages 59 to 60.

There must be good reasons for such an extension (*The Mouna* The Times 7 May 1991) and each case will be examined on its own facts. Application should normally be made before the summons has expired. The normal situations in which leave will be granted will occur when, for example, there are problems in finding the defendant or where there is a clear agreement that service be deferred.

The following are not good reasons for obtaining an extension:

- the fact that negotiations are continuing (*The Mouna*, above);
- the fact that a grant of legal aid is awaited;
- the fact that the solicitors are experiencing difficulty in tracing witnesses;
- carelessness on the part of the solicitor.

(b) Effect on limitation period

It may be that the three-year limitation period is set to expire during the proposed period of extension. Generally, a summons will not normally be renewed to deprive the defendant of a limitation argument (*Heaven* v *Road and Rail Wagons Ltd* [1965] 2 QB 355, [1965] 2 All ER 409, [1965] 2 WLR 1249), although this rule is not absolute.

The provisions for extension remain unaffected by s 33 of the Limitation Act (see page 19). Further, the plaintiff cannot show that if the extension were granted, he would be more likely to persuade the court to exercise its discretion in its favour under s 33. The reason for this is that the cause of prejudice in such cases will be the solicitor's omission rather than the existence of a limitation period (*Walkley* v *Precision Forgings Ltd* [1979] 2 All ER 548, [1979] 1 WLR 606).

The application for extension is made *ex parte* and is supported by an affidavit showing the circumstances relied upon. The High Court Rules provide that the affidavit should be accompanied by the original writ, so it seems wise to incorporate the copy of the summons in this way. Whilst application is made under O 7 r 20, the guiding principles are those set out in the O 6 r 8 RSC.

The defendant has a particularly alarming tactic available to him, best used in cases where leave has been granted to serve the summons out of time and the expiry of the limitation period is fast approaching. The defendant then waits for the summons to be served and makes an application to the District Judge to discharge the order for renewal and set aside service.

This puts the plaintiff's solicitor in an invidious position if the order granting the extension is set aside. The original action is now likely to be time-barred, although the plaintiff may be able to avail himself of the provisions of s 33 (the *Walkley* v *Precision Forgings* decision may cause severe problems in this respect).

7. Minor plaintiffs and plaintiffs under a disability

If the plaintiff is under the age of 18 or has a mental disorder within the meaning of the Mental Health Act 1983 which makes him incapable of managing his property and affairs, he will be regarded as being under a disability. In such a situation, there are important procedural steps which the plaintiff's solicitor must take.

The plaintiff who is under a disability cannot sue in his own name. An adult must be appointed as his next friend. Often, this will be a parent, but there should be no conflict of interest between the next friend and the plaintiff. A potential problem might arise in this respect if, say, the infant plaintiff was a passenger in a car driven by a parent who was partly to blame for the accident.

The next friend must undertake to take responsibility for the costs of the case. He or she is named on the summons and, when proceedings are issued, must file a form indicating his or her consent to being the next friend.

In many cases, especially those involving young children, instructions during negotiations will be, in effect, taken from the parents. A plaintiff under a disability will be deemed incapable of giving a valid consent to the settlement of his or her case. The plaintiff could therefore reopen the case when he attains his majority or recovers, on the basis that it was undersettled. In addition, he may pursue a claim against his parents and/or his solicitor for undersettling the case.

To minimise the risks of this happening, O 10 r 10 CCR provides that in such cases, no settlement shall be made without the approval of the court. This allows, in effect, an independent third party, in the person of the District Judge, to examine the terms agreed upon, and to give the court's approval if appropriate. If proceedings have not already been commenced by the time that settlement terms are agreed, O 10 r 10 provides that the particulars of claim can be brief, setting out the cause of action, together with a request for the approval of the court to the terms arrived at.

Application is made on notice to the District Judge. He will want to see the medical report, and, often, counsel's advice on quantum. He may also want to see the child to gauge the extent of the injuries.

Both sides should attend the hearing. If the District Judge approves the settlement, he will give directions as to the investment of the monies under O 10 r 11. This will normally be in the court's own account.

Forms of application are set out on pages 60 to 61.

Checklist

1. Issue in the county court most convenient to the plaintiff.
2. Remember that the plaintiff's solicitor can now serve the summons. This must be served within four months of issue, unless time is extended.
3. If no response within seven days of deemed service, consider entering judgment in default. It is probably wiser to warn the defendant of this, although this is not required under the rules.
4. Minor plaintiffs/plaintiffs under a disability — remember to obtain the court's approval to settlement terms. Do not accede to insurance company requests to deal with the matter by way of a parental discharge form as the status of such a document is doubtful in the light of O 10 r 10 CCR.

Request for issue of default summons

Request for Issue of Default Summons

- Please read the notes over the page before filling in this form

For court use only

Case Number	

Summons in form   N1 ☐

    N2 ☐

Service by: Post ☐

Plaintiff('s solr) ☐

1 Plaintiff's full name address

2 Name and address for service and payment *(if different from above)* **Ref/Tel No.**

3 Defendant's name address

- Please be careful when filling in the request form. Do not write outside the boxes.
- Type or write in BLOCK CAPITALS using black ink.
- If the details of the claim are on a separate sheet you must also give the court a copy for each defendant.
- You can get help to complete this form and information about court procedures at any county court office or citizens' advice bureau.

4 What the claim is for

Give brief description of the type of claim

5 Particulars of the plaintiff's claim

6

Plaintiff's claim	
Court fee	
Solicitor's costs	
Total Amount	
for court use Issued on	

How the claim will be dealt with if defended

If the claim is worth £1,000 or less it will be dealt with by arbitration (small claims procedure) unless the court decides the case is too difficult to be dealt with in this informal way. Costs and the grounds for setting aside an arbitration award are strictly limited. If the claim is for £1,000 or less and is not dealt with by arbitration, costs, including the costs of help from a legal representative, may be allowed.

If the claim is worth over £1,000 it can still be dealt with by arbitration if either you or the defendant asks for it and the court approves. If your claim is dealt with by arbitration in these circumstances, costs may be allowed.

Please tick this box if your claim is worth over £1,000 and you would like it dealt with by arbitration ☐

7 Signed
Plaintiff('s solicitor)
(or see enclosed particulars of claim)

Form F 1105 (County Court Form N201)   Fourmat Publishing 133 Upper Street London N1 1QP Tel (071) 226 7497   October 1992

Request for issue of default summons (cont.)

Notes

1 Plaintiff *the person making the claim*

Fill in the plaintiff's full name and address or place of business. If the plaintiff is:

- **a company registered under the Companies Act 1985,** give the address of the registered office and describe it as such.

- **a person trading in a name other than his own,** give his own name followed by the words 'trading as' and the name under which he trades.

- **two or more co-partners suing in the name of their firm, 'A Firm'.**

- **an assignee,** say so and give the name, address and occupation of the assignor.

- **a minor required to sue by next friend,** state this, and give the full names, address or place of business, and occupation of next friend. You will also need to complete and send in Form N235 (which you can get from the court office).

- suing in a representative capacity, say in what capacity.

2 Address for service and payment

If this request is completed by a solicitor or by your legal department, the name, address and reference of the solicitor or legal department should be in Box 2. The court will use this address for sending documents to you (service). (If the address is the same as shown at Box 1, please write 'as above' in Box 2).

- **A plaintiff who is not represented by a solicitor or legal department must not use Box 2** except for an address to which payment may be made. In this case you must delete the word 'service' in the title to Box (2).

3 Defendant *the person against whom the claim is made*

Fill in the defendant's surname and (where known) his or her initials or names in full. **It is essential that the defendant should be identified as fully and as accurately as possible.** Also give the defendant's address or place of business (if the owner of a business). Say whether defendant is male or female and, if under 18, state 'minor'. If the defendant is:

- **a company registered under the Companies Act 1985,** the address given can be the registered office of the company (you must describe it as such) or its place of business. If the summons is not sent to the registered office, there is a risk that it will not come to the notice of an appropriate person in the company. As a result, the court may be asked to set aside any judgment on that case that has been made. **For fixed amount cases only** - Bear in mind that if the company you are suing defends the case, the case will automatically be transferred to his local court. If the registered office and place of business are not in the same court area, you may decide to choose the address which is most convenient to you.

- **a person trading in a name other than his own** who is sued under that name, add 'A Trading Name'.

- **two or more co-partners** sued in the name of their firm, add 'A Firm'.

- **sued in a representative capacity,** say in what capacity.

4 What the claim is for

Put a brief description of your claim in the box (eg price of goods sold and delivered, work done, money due under an agreement).

5 Particulars of your claim

Give a brief statement of the facts of your claim and the amount for which you are suing. Include any relevant dates and sufficient details so that the defendant understands what your claim is for. He is entitled to ask for further details. If there is not enough space or the details of your claim are too complicated, you should enclose a separate sheet for the court and a copy for each defendant. The court can help you in setting out your particulars of claim.

6 Amount claimed

Fill in the total amount you are claiming. The court fee and solicitor's costs are based on this and you should enter these too. A leaflet setting out the current fees is available from the court.

7 Signature

The person filling in the form should sign and date it, unless enclosing separate details of claim (in which case the enclosed sheets should be signed).

8 Personal injury claims

In these cases you must include a medical report for the court and for each defendant. If you are also claiming special damages (eg loss of income, medical expenses etc) an up to date statement, to include details of any future expenses or losses, must also be included for the court and for each defendant. If you cannot provide these you should apply to the court for directions.

9 Unliquidated claims for more than £5000

If your claim is not for a fixed amount and you expect to recover more than £5000 (excluding interest and costs), you must state this in your particulars of claim.

10 Where to send the summons

- **If the summons is for a fixed amount,**
  you can ask any county court in England and Wales to issue the summons but you will usually choose your local court or the court for the area where the defendant lives or carries on business. Bear in mind that if the person you are suing defends the case, the case will automatically be transferred to the defendant's local court.

- **For a personal injury or other unliquidated claim,**
  you may prefer to choose the court where the cause of action arose. The case will not be automatically transferred if a defence is filed.

To be completed by the court	
Served on:	
By posting on:	
Officer:	

Further information on how to issue a default summons and what happens after issue can be obtained from any county court office.

54

County Court Summons

County Court Summons

Case Number	*Always quote this*	

In the

County Court

The court office is open from 10 am to 4 pm Monday to Friday

Telephone:

Plaintiff's full name address

Plaintiff's Solicitor's address

Ref/Tel No.

Defendant's full name including title, eg Mr, Mrs or Miss and address

Seal

This summons is only valid if sealed by the court.
If it is not sealed it should be sent to the court.

Keep this summons; you may need to refer to it.

What the plaintiff claims from you

Give brief description of type of claim

Particulars of the plaintiff's claim against you

Amount claimed	see particulars
Court fee	
Solicitor's costs	
Total amount	

Summons issued on

What you should do

You have 21 days (16 days if you are a limited company served at your registered office) from the date of the postmark to either
* **defend the claim** by filling in the back of the enclosed form **and sending it to the court;**
OR
* **admit the claim** and make an offer of payment, by filling in the front of the enclosed reply form and **sending it to the court.**
If you do **nothing** judgment may be entered against you.

Please read the information on the back of the form. It will tell you more about what to do

My claim is worth   £5,000 or less ☐   over £5,000 ☐

All cases over £1,000
I would like my case decided by   trial ☐   arbitration ☐

Signed
Plaintiff('s solicitor)
(or see enclosed "Particulars of claim")

55

County Court Summons (cont.)

Please read this page; it will help you deal with the summons

If you dispute all or part of the claim
You may be entitled to help with your legal costs. Ask about the legal aid scheme at any county court office, citizens' advice bureau, legal advice centre or firm of solicitors displaying the legal aid sign.
• Say how much you dispute in the part of the enclosed form for defending the claim and return it to the court. The court will tell you what to do next.
• If you dispute only part of the claim, you should also fill in the part of the form for admitting the claim and pay the amount admitted into court.
• If the court named on the summons in not your local county court, and/or the court for the area where the reason for the claim arose, you may write to the court named asking for the case to be transferred to the county court of your choice. You must explain your reasons for wanting the transfer. However, if the case is transferred and you later lose the case, you may have to pay more in costs.

How the claim will be dealt with if defended
If the claim is worth £1,000 or less it will be dealt with by arbitration (small claims procedure) unless the court decides the case is too difficult to be dealt with in this informal way. Costs and the grounds for setting aside an arbitration award are strictly limited. If the claim is for £1,000 or less and is not dealt with by arbitration, costs, including the costs of help from a legal representative, may be allowed.
If the claim is worth over £1,000 it can still be dealt with by arbitration if either you or the plaintiff asks for it and the court approves. If your claim is dealt with by arbitration in these circumstances, costs may be allowed.

If you want to make a claim against the plaintiff
This is known as a counterclaim.
Fill in the part of the enclosed form headed 'Counterclaim'. If your claim is for more than the plaintiff's claim you may have to pay a fee - the court will let you know. Unless the plaintiff admits your counterclaim there will be a hearing. The court will tell you what to do next.

If you admit the claim or any part of it
• **You may pay an appropriate amount into court** to compensate the plaintiff (see **Payments into Court** box on this page), accompanied by a notice (or letter) that the payment is in satisfaction of the claim. If the plaintiff accepts the amount paid he is also entitled to apply for his costs.
• **If you need time to pay,** complete the enclosed form of admission and give details of how you propose to pay the plaintiff. If your offer is accepted, the court will send an order telling you how to pay. If it is not accepted, the court will fix a rate of payment based on the details given in your form of admission and the plaintiff's comments. Judgment will be entered and you will be sent an order telling you how and when to pay.
• **If the plaintiff does not accept the amount paid or offered,** the court will fix a hearing to decide how much you must pay to compensate the plaintiff. The court will tell you when the hearing, which you should attend, will take place.

General information
• If you received this summons through the post the date of service will be 7 days (for a limited company as its registered office, the second working day) after the date of posting as shown by the postmark.
• You can get help to complete the enclosed form and information about court procedures at any county court office or citizens' advice bureau. The address and telephone number of your local court is listed under 'Courts' in the phone book.
• Please address forms or letters to the Chief Clerk.
• Always quote the whole of the case number which appears at the top right hand corner of the front of this form; the court is unable to trace your case without it.

Registration of judgments
If the summons results in a judgment against you, your name and address may be entered in the Register of County Court Judgments. **This may make it difficult for you to get credit.** A leaflet giving further information can be obtained from the court.

Interest on judgments
If judgment is entered against you and is for more than £5,000 the plaintiff may be entitled to interest on the total amount.

Payments into Court
You can pay the court by calling at the court office which is open 10 am to 4 pm Monday to Friday.
You may only pay by:
  • cash
  • banker's or giro draft
  • cheque supported by a cheque card
  • cheque (unsupported cheques may be accepted, subject to clearance, if the Chief Clerk agrees).
Cheques and drafts must be made payable to HM Paymaster General and crossed.
Please bring this form with you.

By post
You may only pay by:
  • postal order
  • banker's or giro draft
  • cheque (cheques may be accepted, subject to clearance, if the Chief Clerk agrees).
The payment must be made out to HM Paymaster General and crossed.
This method of payment is at your own risk.
And you must:
  • pay the postage
  • enclose this form
  • enclose a self addressed envelope so that the court can return this form with a receipt.
*The court **cannot** accept stamps or payments by bank and giro credit transfers.*
Note: You should carefully check any future forms from the court to see if payments should be made directly to the plaintiff.

To be completed on the court copy only

Served on:

By posting on:

Officer:

This summons was returned by the Post Office marked "Gone Away" on:

Form F 1192 (N2): Default Summons (amount not fixed)
© Fourmat Publishing, Tolley House, 2 Addiscombe Road, Croydon, Surrey CR9 5AF November 1993

Affidavit of service

Affidavit of Service

<table>
<tr><td colspan="2">In the</td></tr>
<tr><td></td><td align="right">County Court</td></tr>
<tr><td>Case No. always quote this</td><td></td></tr>
<tr><td>Plaintiff including reference</td><td></td></tr>
<tr><td>Defendant</td><td></td></tr>
</table>

(1) Insert full name, address and occupation of deponent

I, (1)

make oath and say as follows:

1.   That I am over 16 years of age and
(a)   acting as agent for plaintiff (OR
(b)   employed by
    of
    (solicitor, acting as agent for

    of   ) solicitor for the above-named plaintiff

(2) insert date of service

2.   That on the (2)   I served the summons,
    a true copy of which is attached and marked "A", on (3)

(3) insert name of person served

Postal service (personal injury claims only)

(a)   by posting it to (3)   by ordinary
    1st class post in a prepaid envelope on (5)
    The letter or envelope has not been returned by the Post Office as undelivered.

(4) state place of service

Individual

(b)   by delivering it to (3)   personally
    at (4)

(5) insert date of posting

Firm

(c)   by delivering it to (4)
    to (3)
    who stated that he was a partner in the defendant firm (or who carried on)(or who stated that he carried on) business
    in the name of the defendant firm, OR
(d)   by delivering it at (4)
    to a person who did not give his name but stated he (was a partner in)(or carried on business in the name of)
    the defendant firm,OR

Limited Company

(e)   by posting to (leaving it at) (4)
    the address stated on the summons to be the place of business of the defendant company.
(f)   by leaving it (or by sending it by 1st class post on the previous day)(or by 2nd class post on
    in a pre-paid envelope addressed to the defendant company at (4)

    the address stated in the summons to the registered office of the defendant company.

Substituted service

(g)   by sending it on the previous day by registered post together with a sealed copy of the order for substituted service of the summons,
    addressed to the defendant at (4)

                  in accordance with the order.

3.   That at the same time I paid or offered to (3)
    the sum of £   for his/her expenses (and loss of time).

Sworn at   in the

of   this   ....

   day of   19   Before me   Officer of a court, appointed
                                      by the Circuit Judge to take affidavits

Indorse the copy summons as follows: This paper marked "A" is the copy summons referred to in the attached affidavit.

This affidavit is filed on behalf of the plaintiff.

Instructions for personal service
Service must be effected by delivering the summons to each defendant personally. If the defendants are sued as partners, service may be effected
by delivering the summons to any one or more of the defendants personnally. If the defendant is a person carrying on business in a firm's name,
service may be effected by delivering the summons to him.
ALL OTHER SUMMONSES MUST BE SERVED PERSONALLY

Affidavit of service (o.7, r.6(1)(b)) **Form LF 1142 (N215)**   © Fourmat Publishing Tolley House 2 Addiscombe Road Croydon CR9 5 AF

Issuing proceedings

Application to set aside judgment obtained in default

IN THE BARCHESTER COUNTY COURT   **Case No 941234**

(Case heading)

TAKE NOTICE that the Defendant will apply to the District Judge of the Barchester County Court at 9, High Street, Barchester on   day the day of   1994 for an Order that the judgment in default entered on behalf of the Plaintiff herein on 2nd September 1994 be set aside and that the Defendant be at liberty to defend the said action.

AND that the costs of this application be paid by the Defendant in any event

DATED this   day of   1994.

Application to extend the validity of a summons

IN THE BARCHESTER COUNTY COURT   **Case No 941234**

(Case heading)

TAKE NOTICE that the Plaintiff will apply to the District Judge of the Barchester County Court at 9, High Street, Barchester on   day the   day of   at   am/pm for an Order that the period of service of the summons issued herein on 3rd August 1994 be extended for a period of 4 months from 3rd December 1994.

AND for an Order that the costs of this application be costs in the cause.

DATED this   day of   1994

Affidavit in support of application to extend validity of summons

(Case heading)   Plaintiff
                                                  No 1
                                                  Sworn 11/11/94

I, Joseph Jones, Solicitor of Jones and Co, 72 High Street, Barchester,
MAKE OATH and say as follows:

1. I am a solicitor of the Supreme Court and am conducting the claim of
   Mr K Brown against Mrs P Smith. I am authorised by my client to make
   this affidavit on her behalf and save where otherwise stated, I depose
   to facts within my own knowledge.

2. The Plaintiff's claim is for damages for personal injury following an
   accident which occurred on 12th May 1992. The Plaintiff was then
   resident with the Defendant, when he slipped on a carpet and fell,
   sustaining back injuries. The Plaintiff alleges that the carpet had not
   been properly secured to the floor by the Defendant.

3. Proceedings were issued against Mrs Smith in this Court on the 3rd
   August 1994. I attempted to effect postal service on the 5th August,
   but the summons was returned to my office by the dead letter post
   system on 7th August 1994. The letter was marked 'gone away' and
   is now shown to me and produced marked JJ1.

4. I immediately made enquiries as to the whereabouts of Mrs Smith and
   instructed the Jarvis and Co form of investigators to find the
   Defendant. A copy of the firm's preliminary report is now shown to me
   and produced marked JJ2. As can be seen from the report, it seems
   that Mrs Smith moved in July of this year to the Bridgwater area.
   Smith and Co are continuing their enquiries and hope to trace her
   reasonably quickly.

5. I am concerned that due to the difficulties which I have experienced
   in tracing Mrs Smith, I will not be able to find her within the four
   months allowed for service of the summons. I therefore humbly
   request that an order be made in the terms of the application to allow
   for the extra time involved in tracing Mrs Smith.

SWORN etc.

Application for approval of settlement reached on behalf of minor (where proceedings already commenced)

(Case heading)

TAKE NOTICE that the Plaintiff will apply to the District Judge of the Barchester County Court at 9, High Street, Barchester on   day the   day of   1994 for an Order that the following terms of settlement between the parties be approved by this Honourable Court.

Under the terms of settlement, it is proposed that the Defendant pay the sum of £4,000 together with the Plaintiff's costs in settlement of the claim.

DATED this   day of   1994.

Particulars of claim seeking approval of settlement reached on behalf of a minor (where proceedings have not been issued)

(Case heading)

1. The Plaintiff is a minor having been born on the 17th day of January 1990 who sues by her mother and next friend Mrs Virginia Kemp.
2. The Plaintiff's claim is for damages for personal injury sustained when she fell from a wooden chair supplied by the Defendant on 12th April 1992.
3. It is alleged that the said chair was defective in that one of its legs was not properly attached to its seat and that the Plaintiff's fall occurred by reason of this defect.
4. The Plaintiff suffered a broken ankle in the said accident. Full details of the injury are set out in the medical report of Mr Smith FRCS served herewith.
5. The proposed settlement is set out (*overleaf*). By way of settlement it is proposed that the Defendant pay the sum of £4,000 in full satisfaction of all causes of action for which the Plaintiff claims.

AND the Plaintiff requests that this Honourable Court do approve the said settlement.

Dated etc.

NB. It is often helpful to District Judges if the terms of settlement are set out over the page from the application. Many District Judges prefer to form their own view of quantum on reading the medical report. If they were to see the terms of settlement before doing so, their judgment could be influenced. Putting the figure on the next page gives the District Judge an opportunity, should he wish, to avoid seeing the figure before he forms a view.

Chapter 8

Defence and other pleadings

In the county court, the defence should be sent to the court, although a copy is often sent, in addition, to the plaintiff's solicitors to keep delay to a minimum. The time limit for service of the defence is 14 days from service of the Particulars of Claim.

1. Time for service of defence

It is often extremely difficult to serve a defence in time, especially if the case is new to the defending solicitor and some investigation is needed. Because of this, it is quite normal to agree an extension of time with the plaintiff's solicitors. A specific date should be agreed and diarised by both sides.

If the plaintiff's solicitor is unwilling to grant any, or any further, extensions, the defendant's solicitor will have to apply under O 13 r 4 CCR for a time extension. This will have the effect of extending the time in which the defence must be served. Just serving the summons automatically extends the time for service and the defendant need not serve the defence before the summons is heard (*Hobson* v *Monks* [1884] WN 8).

2. Contributory negligence

This defence is used widely in personal injury actions. It must be expressly pleaded before any finding can be made. If it is successfully raised, the plaintiff's damages will be reduced by a percentage decided by the trial Judge.

Allegations of contributory negligence are used not only in cases based on negligence, but also in cases concerning allegations of breach of statutory duty.

The danger presented to the plaintiff by allegations of contributory negligence occurs when a payment in is made by the defendant. The damages award against which the payment in will be measured, will be the award after subtracting the element of contributory negligence found to be appropriate. It is often difficult to predict a court's approach to the question of contributory negligence and this can make advising on whether to accept a payment in hazardous. The best the solicitor can do is consider the risks and advise the client fully of the situation.

3. Third party proceedings

If the defendant's case is that someone else is responsible for the accident, he will normally bring third party proceedings against the person concerned. He does this by issuing a third party notice in the form shown at the end of this chapter. As automatic directions are now made in personal injury cases, leave will be required under O 12 r 1 CCR before a third party notice is issued. The reason for this is simply that directions will be required for service of the notice and defence thereto. Application is made to the District Judge, and the plaintiff should be notified.

Under the third party notice, the defendant will claim a contribution or indemnity, or other remedy, from the third party. A contribution is essentially a claim to a partial indemnity.

Once a third party notice is issued, the third party is in effect a defendant to the defendant in the main action. He should come into the picture only if the defendant is found liable to the plaintiff, but to simplify matters, his case is normally dealt with at the same time as the trial between plaintiff and defendant.

The defendant should be especially careful to ensure that his claim against the third party is fully pleaded and includes any separate claim which he might have arising out of the accident. This was demonstrated in *Talbot* v *Berkshire County Council* [1993] PIQR 319 where the plaintiff suffered injuries in a car accident. He was sued by his passenger, B. The defendant's case was that the accident was caused by the highway authority and he issued third party proceedings against the authority. The difficulty, however, was that he claimed only in respect of any liability to B, and did not claim compensation for his own injuries. B joined the authority as second defendant and succeeded at trial on the basis of two-thirds liability against the plaintiff and one-third against the highway authority. The plaintiff then sought to bring fresh proceedings against the highway authority for his own injuries, but was unsuccessful on the basis that he was barred under the principle of *action estoppel* from bringing a fresh claim against the highway authority.

Although, as seen earlier, the third party is a defendant to the defendant, he cannot make a payment in. Instead, there is a procedure under O 12 r 7 by which he can make a written offer of contribution. This offer is made to the defendant who seeks to make him liable and is, in effect, an offer to contribute to a specified extent to the damages. Like a payment in, the offer is served on the party concerned, and a copy filed with the court. The offer is not brought to the attention of the court at the hearing until all questions of liability and damages have been decided. The court can take account of the offer when looking at the question of costs.

The immediate question for the plaintiff's solicitor, on receiving notice that the defendant wishes to bring third party proceedings, will be whether to sue the third party direct. The risk is that if the third party is wholly to blame for the accident, the defendant would not be found liable. The plaintiff would have no claim directly against the third party and would therefore fail. If, as is more common, both third party and defendant must bear part of the blame, the plaintiff could recover all of his damages against the defendant and leave him to sue the third party. However, in doing so, some costs will be wasted. In practice, unless the allegation by the defendant is obviously unfounded, it is often prudent to join the third party as a second defendant.

4. Loaning servants

This is a situation to watch out for in the industrial accident scenario. In cases where the accident was caused by an employee in the course of his employment, it will be sensible to sue the employer of the tortfeasor on the basis of vicarious liability. What happens, though, if the servant in question had been loaned to another employer at the relevant time?

A delicate question arises as to who is the true employer. Unfortunately, there is no clear cut answer. The starting point seems to be that the servant remains in the employ of his permanent employer, but that this burden can be discharged in certain circumstances. A discussion of this problem took place in the House of Lords in *Mersey Docks and Harbour Board* v *Coggins & Griffith (Liverpool) Ltd* [1947] AC 1, [1946] 2 All ER 345. A 'control' test was applied by the House of Lords, in which regard was had to factors such as who paid the tortfeasor, how long he was working for the temporary employer, who had the power to dismiss him, and so on. If the employee is lent together with machinery, and some skill and discretion is needed in the operation of such machinery, it seems that he will remain under the control of his original employer.

In such a situation, the sensible solution must be to issue proceedings against the original employer. If the claim is defended on the basis that the employee was under the control of the temporary employer (who may well be brought in as a third party) this latter employer should be added as a second defendant so that all eventualities are covered.

5. Counterclaim

The defendant may include a claim against the plaintiff in his defence — in other words, a counterclaim. This happens most frequently in cases arising out of road traffic accidents, where the defendant will claim that the accident occurred because of the plaintiff's own negligence, and counterclaim the cost of repairs to his vehicle. There is nothing, however, to stop a counterclaim being made in other situations — indeed, it need not even arise from the accident in question.

If a counterclaim is made by the defendant it is vital that the plaintiff's insurers are informed. This is easy to forget but can result in cover under the policy being refused. In addition, a reply and defence to counterclaim will be needed within 14 days or the defendant can obtain judgment in default on his claim.

6. Reply

We have seen that the plaintiff must serve a reply and defence to counterclaim if a counterclaim is made.

He may also consider serving a reply if the defence raises new or unexpected allegations. In the county court, a reply will not normally be expected to straightforward allegations of contributory negligence, but if a very specific allegation is made (for example, that the plaintiff had been warned on three separate occasions not to use the equipment concerned), a reply may well be appropriate to clarify the issues before the court.

7. Request for further and better particulars

It is often the case that a pleading is vague or begs further questions. In this situation, reference should be made to O 6 r 7 CCR (further and better particulars of the particulars of claim) and O 9 r 11 (further and better particulars of the Defence). The starting point is that a party to litigation is entitled to such particulars as will give him the information which a reasonable man would require respecting the matters in question.

If this information is not given, the opposing party should file a request for further and better particulars of the particulars of claim, or of the defence, as appropriate. This should firstly be made by way of a written request. This is in the form of a pleading and should normally be settled by counsel if the original pleadings were prepared in this way. If the particulars required are not given, application should be made to the District Judge.

In making a request, one should bear in mind that whilst a litigant is always entitled to know the nature of the case against him, he is not entitled to find out the evidence which will be used in support of that case. This is in accordance with the general principle that facts, not evidence, are pleaded. Whilst the distinction between the two is normally straightforward, difficulties do sometimes arise and it must be said that the practices of District Judges do vary.

8. Automatic directions

The court will make automatic directions under O 17 r 11 in all personal injury actions except for Admiralty actions, third party proceedings and arbitrations. There follows a summary of the most important directions which will be made on close of pleadings (ie 14 days after the delivery of a defence, or 28 days if the defence is accompanied by a counter-claim):

- discovery of documents within 28 days and inspection 7 days thereafter. In a road accident case, or where liability is admitted, discovery need extend only to quantum;
- no expert evidence unless the substance of this has been disclosed in the form of a written report within ten weeks;

- number of expert witnesses to be limited to two medical experts and one of any other kind;
- written statements of oral evidence to be adduced to be served within ten weeks;
- photographs, sketch plans, and police accident report book to be receivable in evidence and agreed if possible;
- the plaintiff must within six months of close of pleadings request a day for the hearing, supplying a time estimate and the number of witnesses to be called. If no request is made within 15 months of close of pleadings (or within nine months of the expiry of a period set by the court to make such a request) the claim is automatically struck out.

These directions should be all that is required in most cases, but if they do not suffice, an application for a specific direction can always be made. In a case concerning complicated injuries, for example, it may often be necessary to call more than two doctors. If this is so, an application should be made well before trial.

Checklist

1. Defence is due within 14 days of receiving Particulars of Claim, unless extension agreed.
2. If no extension, apply by way of time summons to District Judge.
3. On receiving defence, consider whether reply is required.
4. Reply and defence to counterclaim will certainly be needed if the defendant includes a counterclaim in his defence.
5. If third party proceedings are brought by the defendant, consider making the third party a second defendant.
6. If pleadings from either side are vague, make a request for further and better particulars.
7. Consider whether the automatic directions will suffice for the case.

IN THE BARCHESTER COUNTY COURT   **Case no**

(Case heading)

THIRD PARTY NOTICE

TO THE THIRD PARTY, BARCHESTER DISTRICT COUNCIL of Barchester House, Barchester BR2 2LP.

TAKE NOTICE that this action has been brought by the Plaintiff against the Defendants. In it the Plaintiff claims against the Defendants damages arising out of an accident on 27th March 1994 as appears from the Particulars of Claim a copy of which is served herewith.

The Defendants deny that they are liable to the Plaintiff as appears from their defence, a copy whereof is served herewith, but if contrary to that contention the Defendants are found liable to the Plaintiff, the Defendants claim against you to be indemnified against the Plaintiff's claim and the costs of this action, alternatively they claim a contribution to such extent as is deemed just.

AND the Defendant's claim against you is made on the following grounds:

1. At the time of the said accident, the Plaintiff was working under the direction of the Third Party, and such injuries loss and damage as the Plaintiff may prove were caused by the negligence of the Third Party, their servants or agents in the direction of the Plaintiff and the Third Party's own employees in their work.

PARTICULARS

   i.   Directing one Joseph Smith, an employee of the Third Party, to operate a crane in the vicinity of the Plaintiff when the said Smith was unqualified to carry out such work.
   ii. Allowing the said Smith to carry out his work in a way which presented an obvious danger to the Plaintiff.
   iii. Failing in the circumstances to take reasonable care for the Plaintiff's safety.

AND TAKE NOTICE that within fourteen days after service of this Notice on you, counting the day of service, you must acknowledge service and state in your acknowledgment whether you intend to contest the proceedings. If you fail to do so, or if your acknowledgment does not state your intention to contest the proceedings you will be deemed to admit the Plaintiff's claim against the Defendants and the Defendants claim against you and your liability to indemnify the Defendant to such extent as may be deemed just and will be bound by any judgment or decision given in the action and the judgment may be enforced against you in accordance with the County Court Rules.

Served, etc.

Chapter 9

Tactical moves for the plaintiff

The plaintiff's solicitor should be concerned with obtaining the largest sum of money reasonably due to his client in the shortest possible time. It is fairly easy, in a strong case, to obtain money for a plaintiff, but the real skill comes in getting such sums as quickly as possible.

The key to successfully pursuing a claim on behalf of a plaintiff is to keep maximum pressure on the defendants at all times. Nothing is more disconcerting for an insurance company lawyer than to find one's defence almost instantly responded to by a list of documents, an application for specific discovery and then an application to set down for trial.

To this end, maximum use should be made of the diary. Review dates should be set up each time any action is taken. The file should be neat and in order, and a strip on the outside should show the dates of all important steps.

In addition to these basic points, there are some more specific ways of progressing the plaintiff's case, and these are outlined below.

1. Summary judgment

Under O 9 r 14 CCR, summary judgment can be sought in any personal injury claim worth £500 or more in which there is no real defence. The judgment will be interlocutory and a date can then be assigned for the assessment of damages.

It has always been difficult to obtain summary judgment, as the plaintiff must show that there is no defence. This is especially difficult where allegations of contributory negligence are raised, as, perhaps illogically, these are treated as constituting a defence rather than simply affecting the quantum of damages. But application can still be made in certain circumstances, for example where one vehicle reversed into another.

Application for summary judgment is made to the District Judge and must be supported by an affidavit. Sample forms are given on pages 73 to 74. The affidavit should be made by the plaintiff or his solicitor (preferably, the plaintiff). It must specify the facts upon which the claim is based and state the deponent's belief that there is no defence. It should be filed with the court and a copy served not less than seven days before the hearing (O 9 r 14(3)). The same time limit applies to service of the application itself.

If the application is contested, the defendant should file an affidavit in reply, showing that he has a defence to the claim. This is defined in O 14 RSC as being:

- a good defence to the claim on the merits;
- a difficult point of law is involved;
- a dispute as to the facts which ought to be tried;
- a real dispute as to the amount due (this may well not apply in personal injury cases as such questions can be dealt with at the assessment of damages hearing);
- other circumstances showing reasonable grounds for a *bona fide* defence.

The defendant's affidavit must contain particulars of his case and should be filed and served not less than three clear days before the day of the hearing.

In certain cases, the District Judge may grant leave to the defendant to defend the claim, but make this conditional upon his paying a specified sum of money into court. The approach of District Judges to conditional leave has relaxed over the years and it is worth suggesting conditions if there is anything suspicious or shadowy about the defendant or doubt as to his good faith. Realistically, though, such an argument will not be successful where the defendant is insured by a reputable company.

2. Interim payments

Interim payments were introduced following the recommendations of the Winn Committee on *Personal Injury Litigation* (Cmnd 3691). The County Court Rules incorporate O 29 rr 10–17 in relation to interim payments. An application for an interim payment should be considered in all but those cases which look likely to be settled in the very near future.

An interim payment is defined in the RSC as 'a payment on account of any damages, debt or other sum which he may be held liable to pay to the Plaintiff'.

Whilst an interim payment should not affect the eligibility of the plaintiff for legal aid, it may well affect his position so far as income support is concerned. In the long run, however, this should make no difference, as income support payments will be deducted from the final damages award.

(a) Eligibility

The plaintiff will need to be able to show that the defendant:

- is insured in respect of the plaintiff's claim; or
- is a public authority; or
- is a person whose means and resources are such as to enable him to make the interim payment.

In addition, the plaintiff must show that he has either had judgment entered in his favour, or that if the action proceeded to trial, would obtain judgment against the defendant for a substantial sum of money.

(b) The application

Application is made to the District Judge by summons and an affidavit must be filed. Sample forms are set out on pages 73 to 76. This is much simpler under the new rules, as the special damages element of the claim will already have been prepared and reference can simply be made to the statement. If the position on special damages has changed, an updated statement should be provided. The medical report will also have been served at the time of service of the particulars of claim, and reference should be made to it in the supporting affidavit.

The affidavit must verify the damages — in other words, explain how the figures are arrived at. It should also show that the defendant falls into one of the categories referred to above, and explain why the plaintiff needs an interim award.

Once the threshold conditions for an award of interim damages are met, the Judge should not concern himself with the use to which it is planned to put the money — *Stringman* v *McArdle* The Times 19 November 1993.

The defendant should file an affidavit if he does not agree to making the payment. He may argue that he has a good defence, or that he is not a defendant against whom an order for an interim payment should be made. Alternatively, he may argue that there is a serious doubt whether the plaintiff will receive anything.

(c) Two or more defendants

If the court is satisfied that each of the defendants bears some liability, an order for an interim payment can be made against both defendants — *Schott Kem Ltd* v *Bentley* [1991] 1 QB 61, [1990] 3 All ER 850, [1990] 3 WLR 397. However, the court must be satisfied of the liability of each particular defendant before making an order against it — *Ricci Burns Ltd* v *Toole and Another* [1989] 3 All ER 478, [1989] 1 WLR 993.

The court has the power to order which defendant shall bear a particular proportion of the interim award. The insurance company will prefer the award to be made from the special damages element of the claim as this attracts the higher rate of interest.

(d) Amount of the award

It was acknowledged in the *Schott Kem* case that a practice had developed whereby an order for an interim payment would be limited to sums for which the plaintiff could show a need. However, there is no such limitation in the rules and Neill LJ felt that there was no need for such a limitation, as O 29 gave the court a wide discretion to award 'such amount as the court thinks just', on the basis that the amount 'is not to exceed a reasonable proportion of the damages which in the opinion of the court are likely to be recovered by the plaintiff'.

The effect of this is that the courts tend to agree to awards to compensate the plaintiff for lost wages and other items of special damage already incurred, but are less willing to make awards which dig significantly into general damages. The order will normally expressly state whether the payment is in respect of general or special damages; this clarifies the position when interest is calculated at the end of proceedings.

(e) The relationship of an interim payment to a payment into court

Like a payment in, an interim payment is not referred to in the pleadings. Reference to it will not be made in the trial unless the defendant consents or the court directs.

Under O 29 r 16 RSC, if the defendant makes a payment into court after making an interim payment, the notice of payment in should state that the defendant has taken into account the interim payment in making the payment in. If, on the other hand, the interim payment is ordered after a payment in has been made, the defendant can ask for the money to be paid from the sum in court.

(f) Interim payment and the application for summary judgment

If the defendant obtains unconditional leave to defend on an application for summary judgment, is the plaintiff prevented from obtaining an interim payment? The Court of Appeal has made conflicting decisions on the point in two cases, coincidentally reported on adjacent pages in the All England Reports. In *Ricci Burns Ltd* v *Toole and Another* (above) it was held that the court could make an interim payment order in such circumstances given the difference in the standard of proof required of the plaintiff's chances of success on each application. The case was heard in September 1988.

However, in *British Holdings plc* v *Quadrex Holdings Inc* [1989] 3 All ER 492, it was held that the *Ricci Burns* decision was incorrect, being at variance with an earlier Court of Appeal decision in *Shanning International Ltd* v *George Wimpey International Ltd* [1988] 3 All ER 475. It was held by Browne-Wilkinson V-C that it would be impossible for the court to be satisfied that the plaintiff would succeed at trial and at the same time hold that the defendant had an arguable defence justifying the grant of unconditional leave to defend.

The latter decision must, of course, prevail, but it may well be argued that the two decisions against an interim payment in such circumstances both concerned contractual disputes. There does seem to be scope for arguing that the plaintiff in a personal injury action is in a different position — especially where the only real defence is one of contributory negligence.

(g) Adjusting the interim payment after trial

When the case has been concluded, the court will, under O 29 r 17 RSC, adjust the interim payment in such manner as it thinks just. Where the award made exceeds the interim payment, the payment already made will simply be deducted from the relevant quantum of general or special damages. If the plaintiff is in the unfortunate position of losing, or being awarded a sum less than the interim payment, he can be ordered to repay all or part of the sum to the defendant.

3. Split trials

In the light of r 17 of the County Court (Amendment No 4) Rules 1989, the county court now has the power to make an order for one or more questions or issues to be tried before the others. Application is made under O 13 r 2 CCR. A form is set out at page 76. This allows a court to order a trial on, say, liability, leaving the question of quantum for a later day when, perhaps, the prognosis is clearer.

Before the House of Lords decision in *Thomas* v *Bunn* [1991] 1 All ER 193, [1991] 2 WLR 27, there was a real advantage in obtaining an early judgment either in this way, or by making an application for summary judgment. The reason was that the plaintiff was entitled to interest at the full judgment rate on his eventual award of damages from the date of judgment. The effect of the House of Lords decision is that interest now runs from the date of the judgment measuring the damages payable to the plaintiff.

A split trial may still be useful in certain circumstances. Psychologically, it is always helpful to have a judgment, and it forces insurers to get on and deal with the case. It is still a valuable way of applying pressure, even if the case is not quite strong enough for summary judgment.

4. Provisional damages

Under O 22 r 6A, the county court now has the power to make an award of provisional damages. Under O 6 r 1B CCR, the Particulars of Claim must contain a statement that the plaintiff makes such a claim. The facts which are relied upon in support of the claim for provisional damages must also be pleaded.

The power to award provisional damages stems from s 51 of the County Courts Act 1984. A provisional award will be held to be appropriate if there is proved or admitted to be 'a chance that at some definite or indefinite time in the future the injured person will, as a result of the act or omission which gave rise to the cause of action, develop some serious disease or suffer some serious deterioration in his physical or mental condition'.

If there is such a chance, the court is empowered to award damages assessed on the assumption that the injured person will not develop the disease or suffer the deterioration, whilst leaving the door open for the plaintiff to be awarded further damages in the future should the chance materialise.

Provisional damages have been available in the High Court for several years, and the extension of the county court's jurisdiction in this respect simply mirrors s 32 of the Supreme Court Act 1981.

Some guidance in interpreting the provisions relating to provisional damages is given in *Willson* v *Ministry of Defence* [1991] 1 All ER 638. It was held that use of the word 'chance' connoted a wide range of possibilities ranging from the minimal to the probable, but there had to be a possibility that was measurable rather than fanciful.

'Serious deterioration' was held to imply a clear and severable risk, as distinct from an ordinary deterioration in the plaintiff's condition. The question of whether the deterioration was serious could differ according to the plaintiff — an example was given of a deterioration in the hand of a concert pianist being more serious than an identical situation involving somebody else.

Medical experts should be asked to advise whether there is such a risk of serious deterioration. If so, a suitable paragraph should be included in the Particulars of Claim.

Checklist

1. Summary judgment — apply under O 9 r 14. Affidavit in support will be required. Service of application and affidavit must be not less than ten days before hearing. Consider asking for conditional leave.

2. Interim payments — check that defendant is eligible to make payment. Application should be supported by affidavit — should be served at least ten days before return day.

   NB. Beware of combining an application for summary judgment with an application for an interim payment unless you are sure of success on the former.

3. Split trials — useful to apply pressure on defendants. Make application under O 13 r 2. Rules do not require affidavit, but is a good idea to file one.

Application for summary judgment

(Case heading)

TAKE NOTICE that the Plaintiff will apply to the District Judge of the Barchester County Court at 9, High Street, Barchester, on   day the   day of   1992 for interlocutory judgment in this action for damages to be assessed and costs to be taxed.

AND take notice that a party intending to oppose this application should send to the opposite party or his solicitor, to reach him not less than three days before the date above mentioned, a copy of any affidavit intended to be used.

DATED this   day of   1992.

Affidavit in support of application for summary judgment

(Case heading)

I, Mrs J Smith, MAKE OATH and say as follows:

1. I am the Plaintiff herein and make this affidavit in support of my application for summary judgment against Mr Desmond Jones, the Defendant to this action. Except where otherwise stated, I make this affidavit from facts within my own knowledge.
2. On 19th November 1991, I was involved in a car accident whilst I was at the junction of Old Street and Mill Lane, Barchester. I was travelling north, and had stopped at the traffic lights alongside the railway station. I had been stationary for about a minute when my car, a Vauxhall Cavalier, was hit from behind by a Ford Escort, which I subsequently discovered was driven by the Defendant.
3. I suffered a whiplash injury of the neck in the accident and refer to the medical report of Mr P White, FRCS served with these proceedings.
4. Because the Defendant drove into the back of my stationary vehicle, I believe that there can be no defence to this action and I therefore make this application for interlocutory judgment.

SWORN etc.

Application for interim payment

(Case heading)

TAKE NOTICE that the Plaintiff will apply to the District Judge of the Barchester County Court at 9, High Street, Barchester, on   day the   day of   1992 for an Order that the Defendant do make to the Plaintiff as an interim payment such sum as the court shall think just (together with interest thereon) and that such payment shall be made on account of any damages which the Defendant may subsequently be held liable to pay to the Plaintiff,

AND that the costs of this application be costs in the cause.

DATED this   day of   1992.

Affidavit in support of application for interim payment

(Case heading)

I, Janice Jones, MAKE OATH and say as follows:

1. I am the Plaintiff herein and make this affidavit in support of my application for an interim payment. Except where otherwise stated, I depose to facts which are within my own knowledge.
2. On 19th November 1990, I was involved in an accident whilst I was walking along High Street, Barchester. As I was walking along the street, a bucket of water fell onto me from above.
3. I looked up shortly afterwards and saw the Defendant, Mr Edwards who was cleaning the windows of the shop outside which my accident occurred. He shouted 'Sorry love – I dropped the bucket. Are you OK?'
4. Apart from being soaked, I received a blow to my head which made me very dizzy. Although I managed to get home, the dizziness got worse and I called my GP out that night. He arranged for me to be admitted to the Barchester hospital where it was discovered that I had sustained a sub arachnoid haemorrhage.
5. A medical report from Mr James Smith FRCS has been filed with the Court and served on the Defendant and it can be seen that unfortunately, complications set in and I was in hospital for three months after the operation.
6. At the time of the accident, I was employed as a secretary with Barchester Council. I refer to the Schedule of Special Damages served by my solicitors on the Defendant and filed with this Court. The Schedule indicates that I received full pay from my employers for four weeks, but have not received any further payments whilst I have been away from work.
7. As can be seen from the Schedule, at the time of the accident I was receiving £850 net per month. From this, I need to pay my mortgage, food, clothing and other bills. In fact, my outgoings are only £20 less than my income each month.
8. Because I have not received any pay for the last two months, I have been put into some financial difficulty. I have been advised and verily believe that I have a strong case against the Defendant, who is insured through the Provident Insurance Company, and that the claim will be for a substantial amount of money.
9. I understand from my doctors that I will be able to return to work in three months time. With this in mind, I seek an interim payment from the Special Damages element of my claim, to compensate me for the total of five months without pay which I am currently suffering.

SWORN etc.

Tactical moves for the plaintiff

Application for a split trial

(Case heading)

TAKE NOTICE that the Plaintiff will apply to the District Judge of the Barchester County Court at 9, High Street, Barchester on   day the   day of   1992 at   am/pm for an Order that the question of the liability of the Defendant to the Plaintiff in this action be tried as a preliminary action before the issue of damages be tried; and that subject to the Defendant being found liable to the Plaintiff, the issue of damages be tried subsequently as may be directed by the trial judge.

AND that the costs of this application be costs in the cause.

DATED this   day of   1992.

Chapter 10

Tactical moves for both parties

1. Interrogatories

Interrogatories are written questions put by one party to the other. The answers are admissible in evidence and are given on oath.

Under the County Court (Amendment No 4) Rules 1989, interrogatories can be administered without a court order. The County Court Rules adopt O 26 RSC. Under O 26 r 3, interrogatories may be served on a party not more than twice without order. The onus is then on the party receiving the interrogatories to apply for them to be varied or withdrawn.

(a) Use of interrogatories

Order 26 allows for interrogatories 'relating to any matter or question between the applicant and the other party in the cause or matter' which are necessary either:

- for disposing fairly of the cause or matter or
- for saving costs.

So, for instance, an interrogatory will generally not be allowed if it is concerned with establishing an admission which can be dealt with by a witness who is going to be called at the trial in any event.

Oppressive interrogatories are not allowed. In previous cases, this has been interpreted as meaning interrogatories which exceed the legitimate requirements of the particular occasion, for example, those requiring a search through books for many years. However, few District Judges have objections to interrogatories concerned with previous incidents over a reasonable period of time.

In addition, 'fishing' interrogatories are not allowed. It is often difficult to establish whether an interrogatory falls into this category — indeed, it could be said that all interrogatories are essentially fishing expeditions. Although the interrogatory must, of neccessity, relate to information not within the knowledge of the party applying for it, the party must have some suspicions about it.

(b) Objecting to interrogatories

Objection can always be made on the ground that the interrogatories are fishing, or do not relate to the matters in question, or are not necessary.

In addition, the side interrogated can claim that the answers are privileged. The rules on this are the same as those relating to the disclosure of privileged information on discovery. These are examined in Chapter 12; see page 97.

(c) Drafting interrogatories

The drafting of interrogatories is a fairly difficult task as it is important to put the questions in a way which forces the party interrogated to answer them constructively. It is somewhat specialised, and for this reason, is often left to counsel.

Examples of interrogatories and answers are given on pages 80 and 81.

2. Notices to admit

These are closely related to interrogatories and if a point can be covered by the use of a notice to admit, interrogatories will not be allowed.

Notices to admit are served under O 20 rr 2 and 3. The admissions sought can be either of facts or documents. Notices to admit facts are dealt with in r 2 which states that:

> 'A party to an action or matter may, not later than 14 days before trial or hearing serve on any other party a notice requiring him to admit, for the purposes of that action or matter only, such facts, or such part of his case, as may be specified in the notice.'

The other party cannot be forced to reply to such a notice, but if he does not deliver a written admission of the facts within seven days of the service of the notice, he (unless the court directs otherwise) will bear the costs of proving the facts occasioned by his failure to admit.

A similar rule exists under O 20 r 3 with regard to admitting the authenticity of documents. However, the party served must act if he wishes to challenge the authenticity, or else he is deemed to have admitted it.

Under O 20 r 3(4) one party can also serve a notice requiring the other party to produce a document. If the document is not produced, the party calling for it may then give secondary evidence of it.

Specimen forms are set out on pages 81 to 83.

3. Exchange of witness statements

The automatic directions now provide for the exchange of written statements of all oral evidence which parties intend to adduce at trial. This has made an enormous difference to the conduct of personal injury actions — not the least important development being that it has in many cases promoted settlements as each party is in a better position to understand the strength or weakness of its opponent's case.

Detailed provision on the form and use of statements can be found in O 20 r 12A CCR. Essentially, statements must be dated and signed by the maker (unless there is good reason why signature is not possible) and contain a statement that the contents are true to the best of his knowledge or belief.

The trial will still be heard on oral evidence, although the Judge can order that the witness statement should serve as the examination in chief. The witness will not normally be allowed to give evidence outside the ambit of the statement, although the Judge can give leave if new matters arise, or if the statement had been exchanged only in relation to specific issues of fact. This means that great care will need to be taken in relation to the drafting of witness statements. The statement will need to be full, and should only contain admissible evidence. However, the drafter of the statement must at all costs avoid the temptation to gild the lily — if the witness fails to come up to proof, the difficulties will be painfully obvious.

In addition, the ramifications of *Black & Decker Ltd* v *Flymo Ltd* must be borne in mind. This case is examined in Chapter 12, but the effect of the decision is that documents referred to in the statement may be examined even if they would otherwise be privileged.

Checklist

1. *Interrogatories*

— in the light of the County Court (Amendment No 4) Rules 1989, a court order will not be necessary for the first two sets of interrogatories;
— the onus is now on the defendant to object.

2. *Notices to admit*

— can be used to gain admissions of either facts or documents;
— must be served no later than 14 days before hearing.

3. *Exchange of witness statements*

— now ordered as part of the automatic directions;
— the statement will be admitted only if the person who made it is at court to give evidence;
— the statement can be ordered to stand as examination in chief;
— the witness will not normally be permitted to go outside the ambit of his statement;
— considerable care will be needed in the drafting of statements, which must be comprehensive and accurate, and must not refer to privileged documents.

Tactical moves for both parties

Interrogatories

In this case, it is assumed that the plaintiff was involved in an accident in which she was pushing a loaded pallet of goods in a supermarket. The goods were secured by a webbing retaining strap which had been tied around the outside of the pallet. The strap broke under the strain, and the items fell out, injuring the plaintiff. The client is the plaintiff and the purpose of the interrogatories is to establish what became of the strap, and whether the defendant agrees that it was broken.

(Case heading)

INTERROGATORIES

On behalf of the above named Plaintiff for the examination of the above named Defendant.

1. At the time of the Plaintiff's accident on 12th October 1990, was a Mr John Smith employed by the Defendant as the manager of the branch of the Defendant's supermarket where the Plaintiff's accident occurred?
2. If the answer to (1) above is in the affirmative, did not the Plaintiff inform Mr Smith of the happening of the said accident?
3. Did not the Plaintiff show Mr Smith a broken piece of webbing strap?
4. Did not the Plaintiff indicate to Mr Smith that the accident had been caused by the breaking of the said strap.
5. Did not the said Mr Smith take possession of the said strap?

DATED etc.

Affidavit answering interrogatories

(Case heading)

AFFIDAVIT OF JOHN SMITH IN ANSWER TO INTERROGATORIES SERVED BY THE PLAINTIFF ON 2ND JANUARY 1992

In answer to the said interrogatories, I Raymond Brown, of 32 Acacia Close, Barchester, Managing Director of the Defendant company MAKE OATH and say as follows:

1. TO the first Interrogatory, namely

   At the time of the Plaintiff's accident on 12th October 1990 was a Mr John Smith employed by the Defendant as manager of the branch of the supermarket where the Plaintiff's accident occurred?

   Yes.

2. TO the second Interrogatory, namely

    If the answer to (1) above is in the affirmative, did not the Plaintiff inform Mr Smith of the happening of the said accident?

    Yes.

3. TO the third Interrogatory, namely
    Did not the Plaintiff show the said Mr Smith a broken webbing strap?

    Not entitled. As the Plaintiff will no doubt give evidence at the trial, she can deal with such an allegation in her evidence.

4. TO the fourth Interrogatory, namely
    Did not the Plaintiff indicate to Mr Smith that the said accident had been caused by the breaking of the said strap?

    Not entitled. The Plaintiff can give evidence herself if she wishes to make such an allegation.

5. TO the fifth Interrogatory, namely,
    Did not the said Mr Smith take possession of the said strap?

    Yes.

    SWORN etc.

NB. It may well be open to the plaintiff to attack the refusal to answer Interrogatories 3 and 4 on the basis that no objection was made when they were served.

Notice to admit facts

(Case heading)

TAKE NOTICE that the Plaintiff (or Defendant) in this action requires the Defendant (or Plaintiff) to admit, for the purposes of this action only, the several facts hereunder specified.
And the Defendant (or Plaintiff) is hereby required, within 7 days after receiving this notice to admit the said several facts, saving all just exceptions to their admissibility, as evidence in this action.

DATED this   day of   1992

To etc.

The facts, admission of which is required are:
1. That at the time of the said accident, the Defendant's vehicle had the following defects, namely:
    − defective front brakes
    − defective steering.

Tactical moves for both parties

Admission of facts pursuant to notice

(Case heading)

The Defendant (or Plaintiff) in this action for the purposes of this action only, hereby admits the several facts hereunder specified, subject to the qualifications or limitations, if any, hereunder specified, saving all just exceptions to the admissibility of such facts, or any of them, as evidence in these proceedings.

DATED this   day of   1992

. . . .
Solicitor for the
Defendant

To the solicitor for the Plaintiff

Facts admitted	Qualifications or limitations if any, subject to which they are admitted
1. It is admitted that the front brakes and the steering of the Defendant's vehicle were found to be defective after the accident.	

Notice to admit documents

(Case heading)

TAKE NOTICE that the Plaintiff (or Defendant) in this action proposes to adduce in evidence the several documents hereunder specified, and that the same may be inspected by the Defendant (or Plaintiff) or his solicitor at   on   between the hours of   and the Defendant (or Plaintiff) is hereby required within seven days to admit that such of the said documents as are specified to be originals were respectively written, signed or executed as they purport respectively to have been; and that such as are specified as copies are true copies, and that such documents as are stated to have been served, sent or delivered, were so served, sent or delivered respectively; saving all just exceptions to the admissibility of all such documents as evidence in this action.

AND further take notice that if you do not within the aforementioned seven days give notice that you do not admit the authenticity of the said documents (or any of them) and that you required the same to be proved at the trial or hearing you shall be deemed to have admitted the said documents unless the court shall otherwise order.

Dated the   day of   1992

. . . .

Solicitor for

To:

_____

ORIGINALS
_____

Description of document   Dates

– –

– –

– –

COPIES

– –

Description of document   Dates   Original or duplicate
                                                served, sent or
                                                delivered, when,
                                                how and by whom

– –

– –

Notice to produce documents at hearing

(Case heading)

TAKE NOTICE that you are hereby required to produce and show to the Court on the hearing of this action all books, papers, letters, copies of letters, and other writings and documents in your custody, possession or power, containing any entry, memorandum or minute relating to the matters in question in this action, and particularly

(insert details)

DATED this day of   1992

. . . .

Solicitor for

To:

Chapter 11

Tactical moves for the defendant

1. Striking out a claim

A pleading can be struck out under O 13 r 5 if:

- it discloses no reasonable cause of action or defence;
- it is scandalous, frivolous or vexatious;
- it may prejudice, embarrass or delay the fair trial of the action; or
- it is otherwise an abuse of the process of the court.

The ground of no reasonable cause of action or defence is used reasonably often and merits further brief consideration. There are two ways in which this situation comes about. If the action is entirely misconceived, application can be made under this rule. It is not enough simply to show that the claim stands little chance of success, or even that it is statute barred (*Ronex Properties Ltd v John Laing Construction Ltd* [1983] QB 398, [1982] 3 All ER 961, [1982] 3 WLR 875). Even in a situation where the case appears to turn on a point of law, the court may well be loath to strike out a claim without the enquiry into the facts brought about by a trial — see *Lonrho plc v Tebbit and Another* The Times 24 September 1991.

The other situation in which an application might be thought to be appropriate arises where no claim is apparent through a defect in the pleading. The court has the power to give leave to amend such a defect — *CBS Songs Ltd v Amstrad* [1988] Ch 61, [1987] RPC 417 & 429.

2. Striking out for want of prosecution

Regard should be had to O 13 r 2, which allows the court to dismiss the claim for want of prosecution. This arises in two situations:

- where the plaintiff's default has been intentional and contumelious; proof of this will, in itself, give rise to an application to strike out;
- more commonly, where there has been inordinate and inexcusable delay on the plaintiff's part giving rise to a substantial risk that a fair trial would not be possible or would cause serious prejudice to the defendant, an application to strike out may be made.

The most common example of contumelious behaviour is disobedience to a peremptory order of the court.

As to the meaning of inordinate and inexcusable delay, in *Birkett* v *James* [1978] AC 297, [1977] 2 All ER 801, [1977] 3 WLR 38, it was held that the power to dismiss an action for want of prosecution should not normally be exercised within the currency of the limitation period as the plaintiff could simply issue a new writ, causing further delay. Until recently, there was some debate as to whether this meant that delay occurring before the limitation period had expired could not be taken into account in determining an application to strike out.

Such an interpretation was rejected, albeit *obiter*, by two members of the Court of Appeal in *Hollis* v *Islington London BC* [1989] CA Transcript 67. The Court of Appeal was finally able to rule on the matter in *Rath* v *CS Lawrence & Partners* [1991] 3 All ER 879, [1991] 1 WLR 399, where it was held that whilst no account could be taken of delay within the limitation period before the issue of a writ, the court could take into account delay which occurred once proceedings had been issued, but before the limitation period had expired. Further support was given to this approach in *Trill* v *Sacher* [1993] 1 All ER 961, where Neill LJ set out the governing principles where the application is brought on the second limb — ie inordinate and inexcusable delay giving rise to prejudice:

- the burden of proof in such an application is on the defendant;
- 'inordinate delay' must depend on the facts of the case, but it must exceed, probably by a substantial margin, the times prescribed by the rules of court for the taking of steps in the action. Delay in issuing proceedings cannot be inordinate if proceedings are issued within the limitation period;
- delay which is inordinate is *prima facie* inexcusable. It is for the plaintiff to provide a reasonable excuse, which may include difficulties with regard to obtaining legal aid;
- where the plaintiff delays issuing proceedings until towards the end of the limitation period, he should then proceed with the case with reasonable diligence;
- a defendant cannot rely upon a period of delay if he was responsible for it;
- a defendant cannot rely upon a period of delay if he conducts himself as to induce the plaintiff to incur costs in the reasonable belief that the defendant intends to proceed to trial;
- save in exceptional cases, an action will not be struck out for want of prosecution within the limitation period;
- once the limitation period has expired, the court can take account of periods of inexcusable delay since the issue of proceedings;
- a defendant cannot rely upon any prejudice to him by the late issue of proceedings;
- prejudice to the defendant can take different forms, including the impairment of witnesses' memories, or their moving away and becoming untraceable;
- the prejudicial effect of delay may depend on the nature of the issues in the case;

- the court will look for a causal connection between the period of delay and prejudice alleged by the defendant;
- an appellate court should only interfere where the Judge has erred in principle.

Whilst the question of delay is examined from the defendant's point of view, reasons and explanations given by the plaintiff's solicitors will be taken into account.

In addition, the defendant will have to show that he is prejudiced by the delay. The degree to which this can be shown will vary according to the circumstances of the case. In a case which turns upon expert evidence gathered years ago, it will be difficult to show prejudice. However, in *Antcliffe* v *Gloucester Health Authority* [1993] PIQR 47 it was held that in a medical negligence action, a change in the defendant's insurance arrangements whereby the health authority would have to meet claims itself up to £300,000 could amount to prejudice. It was accepted that had the claim been prosecuted with due diligence, it would have been dealt with before the change of arrangements, in which case the health authority would have had the benefit of a full indemnity from insurers.

Some retreat appeared to be made from this approach, though, in *Gascoine* v *Haringey Health Authority and Others* [1994] PIQR 416 in which it was held that it would be proper to take into account the change of arrangements but that prejudice resulting from this should not be a determinative factor in itself.

If witnesses are having difficulty remembering the accident (although their memories can, of course, be refreshed by their statements), or have become untraceable, an application to strike out the plaintiff's claim can be something of a double edged sword. The defendant must file an affidavit stating how the prejudice arises, and the obvious risk is that by doing so, he will put the plaintiff on notice of the problems which he is experiencing in dealing with the case. After *Hornagold* v *Fairclough Building Ltd and Industrial Development (Norwich) Ltd* The Times 3 June 1993 the defendant must produce some evidence of the prejudice alleged to have been suffered — simply to assert prejudice in itself is not enough.

A form of application to strike out for want of prosecution and an affidavit in support are set out on pages 90 to 91.

(a) Can the plaintiff argue that the defendant is estopped from complaining of delay by his own conduct?

In *Culbert* v *Westwell & Co* [1993] PIQR 54 it was held that an *estoppel* could be created if the plaintiff could establish that he had been induced to act to his detriment, in a way that was more than minimal, by a clear and unambiguous representation by the defendant (the representation in this case being that the defendant intended to proceed to trial notwithstanding the delay and prejudice which it had sustained). In this case, although the obtaining of an 'unless' order amounted to such a representation, it could not be regarded as binding the defendant to accept further delay and prejudice.

A further discussion of *estoppel* took place in *Draper* v *Ferrymasters Ltd and Others* [1993] PIQR 356 where it was held that neither negotiations nor a payment in would create an *estoppel* where there had been inordinate and inexcusable delay unless there was an express promise by the defendant not to seek to dismiss the action. In *Armstrong* v *Glofield Properties Ltd* [1992] PIQR 358 serving a request for further and better particulars, on the facts of the case, was not conduct to induce a reasonable belief that the action would proceed to trial. Further, in *Harwood* v *Courtaulds Ltd* [1993] PIQR 284 and *Roebuck* v *Mungovin* [1993] PIQR 444 it was held that where the defendant has acquiesced in a period of delay and seeks to rely upon a later delay on the part of the plaintiff, he must show additional prejudice, which was more than merely minimal, arising from this subsequent delay.

3. Payment in

Order 11 allows the defendant to pay into court a sum sufficient to meet the plaintiff's claim. If this sum is accepted within 21 days, the plaintiff is entitled to his costs. If the plaintiff rejects the payment in, but receives less at trial, he will normally be liable for the costs of the action since the payment in was made. This is not an absolute rule — all that the rules say is that a payment in can be taken into account by the trial Judge when deciding the question of costs.

(a) Making a payment in

In Chapter 15 it will be seen that the rules relating to the recovery of State benefits paid by reason of the accident have changed and that, with the exception of small awards, relevant benefits will be deducted from the final award of damages. The compensator (ie the defendant) is responsible for making the repayment to the DSS, and does so by making a deduction when he sends the damages cheque to the plaintiff. The defendant will know how much to deduct because the DSS will provide him with a 'Certificate of Total Benefit', specifying the appropriate figure.

It is wise to obtain this certificate before making a payment in. It will allow for the payment in to be made withholding the benefits to be refunded. The court should be given a statement of the amount withheld so that the plaintiff can be notified of the gross amount offered. The actual payment in and certificate are together treated as the payment in under the new rules.

If the defendant has not obtained a certificate, he may make a full payment in and apply for a certificate on the day that the payment in is made. He remains liable to pay the Compensation Recovery Unit, even though nothing is withheld and no deduction can be made.

To make the payment in, a cheque, made payable to HMPG, should be sent to the county court, together with a letter giving details of the case and asking that the sum be paid in. A notice of payment is not strictly required under the rules, but is useful. The court will serve the notice on the plaintiff. For a form of notice, see page 92.

(b) Time limits for acceptance

The plaintiff has 21 days from receipt of the notice of payment in to accept it, but in any event, notice of acceptance must be given at least three days before the hearing.

The payment in should thus be made as soon as possible and in any event not less than 21 days before trial. However, in certain circumstances, a late payment in can be effective — *King* v *Weston Howell* [1989] 2 All ER 375, [1989] 1 WLR 579. In this case, the defendant made a late payment in as he was unable to get details of the plaintiff's claim for special damages in time. The Court of Appeal held that in the circumstances, the late payment in could be taken into account when looking at the question of costs.

(c) Accepting the payment in

A notice of acceptance (see page 93) should be filed. If the acceptance is made within 21 days of receipt of the notice of payment in, leave will not be required. All that will be needed is a letter to the chief clerk of the court, explaining the situation.

(d) Costs after a payment in

In *Legal Aid Board* v *Russell* [1991] 2 WLR 1300, it was held by the House of Lords that where the plaintiff gave notice of acceptance in the High Court, he became automatically entitled to his costs without having to obtain an order of the court. He would not, however, be entitled to interest on those costs.

If the payment in was made in respect of only one of several causes of action which the plaintiff was pursuing in the same proceedings, and the plaintiff abandons the other causes of action when he accepts the payment in, he will still be entitled to all his costs of the entire action, including the costs of the abandoned claims (*Hudson and Another* v *Elmbridge Borough Council and Others* The Times 29 November 1990).

(e) Late acceptance of payment in

It is always possible to accept the payment in after the time limit for acceptance has expired, with the agreement of the defendant. Often such agreement can be obtained and in such circumstances, application can be made for a consent order. On this note, regard should be had to *Proetta* v *Times Newspapers Ltd* [1991] 4 All ER 46, [1991] 1 WLR 337 in which it was held that the court should not make an order extending the time for acceptance if there has been a substantial change in the risks.

4. Video evidence

Recent years have seen a considerable increase in the use of video evidence, particularly by defendants. They are used extremely effectively where there is a dispute about whether or not the plaintiff's injuries are genuine, or whether he is malingering. Video evidence which shows a man who is allegedly unable to walk because of his injuries playing in the park with his children, for instance, can be devastating.

(a) The decision to seek video evidence

Video evidence is expensive to acquire. It will require the discreet attendance of the filmer over a period of several days at possibly unsocial times. For these reasons, the bill is likely to be reckoned in terms of thousands rather than hundreds of pounds. There is no question that, in the right case, video evidence can justify its costs many times over. What needs to be carefully considered is whether the case in hand is one in which video surveillance is likely to come up trumps.

First, video evidence should only be considered where the claim is substantial. Generally, this will be a case where permanent injury is alleged and where damages will be in the region of at least £20,000.

Secondly, the defendant's consultant must have some realistic doubts as to whether the injuries are genuine. The type of case in which such doubts are often found is that of serious back injury. It is generally accepted by doctors that a patient can be suffering from genuine back problems, even though no physical cause for the symptoms can be found. Where this is alleged, the plaintiff's case will stand or fall on his credibility. If the consultant feels that there is a chance that he is shamming serious injury, and that no physical cause for his symptoms can be found, video surveillance should be considered.

(b) Admissibility

Video evidence is treated as documentary evidence. As such, the party using it must show a *prima facie* case that it is authentic. This is achieved by calling the person who took the film to confirm that it is an accurate recording of the events in question.

(c) Disclosure

Defendants were formerly assisted by the case of *McGuinness* v *Kellogg Company of Great Britain* [1988] 2 All ER 902, [1988] 1 WLR 913 in which it was held that the court could allow the production of video evidence without prior warning to the plaintiff. Where there was a suspicion as to the *bona fides* of the plaintiff, such a surprise could be devastating.

However, the power of the court to allow this evidence without prior notification was severely curtailed in *Khan* v *Armaguard Ltd* The Times 4 March 1994 in which it was held in the Court of Appeal that in the new era of 'cards on the table', an order for non-disclosure would be made in only the rarest of circumstances. Disclosure, it was held, would allow for earlier disposal of the case by settlement, and would be in the interests of the parties, the Legal Aid Fund and the efficient conduct of business.

Checklist

1. Application to strike out — O 13 r 5.
2. Striking out for want of prosecution — intentional or contumelious delay; or inordinate and inexcusable delay causing prejudice to the defendant.
3. Payment in

   • obtain CRU certificate first
   • send notice form and cheque to court
   • plaintiff has 21 days to accept, otherwise leave will be required.

4. In serious cases, consider video evidence.

Application to strike out for want of prosecution

(Case heading)

TAKE NOTICE that the Defendant will apply to the District Judge of the Barchester County Court at 9, High Street, Barchester on   day the   day of   1992 for an Order that the Plaintiff's claim herein be struck out for want of prosecution and that the Defendant be awarded the costs of the action to be taxed if not agreed.

AND that the costs of this application be the Defendant's costs in any event.

DATED this   day of   1992

. . . .

Solicitor for the
Defendant

Affidavit in support of application to strike out

(Case heading)

I, James William Smyth, Solicitor and partner in the firm of Smyth and Co. of Little Chambers, High Street, Barchester, MAKE OATH and say as follows:

1. I have the conduct of the above matter on behalf of the Defendant and am duly authorised to make this affidavit on its behalf. Save where otherwise stated I depose to facts within my own knowledge.

2. The Plaintiff's accident occurred on 14th May 1982. The cause of action arose out of a road accident in which it is alleged that the Defendant, John Brown, pulled out in front of the Plaintiff's car at a road junction in Barchester town centre.

3. The claim is defended on the basis that as the Plaintiff came up to the junction at which the Defendant was waiting, she waved at him, indicating that he should pull out in front of her. The Defendant did so, but the Plaintiff's car jerked forward as he was carrying out the maneouvre.

4. Proceedings were commenced in April 1983. There is now produced and shown to me marked JWS 1 a schedule of the steps which have been taken in the litigation since then. As can be seen from the schedule, pleadings closed in January 1984 and no steps have been taken in the litigation since then.

5. The Defendant is a man of 78 years of age and, inevitably, his memory of the events in question is beginning to dim. Further, we have obtained eye witness accounts of the accident from a Mrs Mary Brett and a Mrs Gladys Pink which support the Defendant's case. Unfortunately, Mrs Brett moved from the town some ten months ago and we have not been able to trace her. Mrs Pink is being expected to recall events which are now almost ten years distant and her memory, despite being refreshed by her statement, is dimming.

6. On the 6th May 1991, I wrote to the Plaintiff's solicitor, Messrs Slope and Co, expressing my worries about the pace at which the litigation was progressing. A copy of this letter is now shown to me and produced marked JWS2. No reply was received to it.

7. I am not aware of any reason for the delay in the conduct of these proceedings and cannot think of any excuse for such delay in the conduct of a claim based on straightforward issues of fact. Because the evidence is concerned so heavily with eye witness accounts of the accident, it seems to me that the Defendant is now severely prejudiced by reason of this inexcusable delay and I therefore seek an order that the Plaintiff's claim be struck out for want of prosecution.

Sworn etc.

Notice of payment in

LF1153: Notice to accompany payment into court

In the   **County Court**

Case no:

Between

Plaintiff

and

Defendant[s]

TAKE NOTICE that the defendant [1]

of

makes payment into court of the sum of £   [in satisfaction of] [on account of] [the amount admitted to be due in respect of][2] the plaintiff's cause[s] of action [namely] [3]

Dated this   day of   19

Signed

Solicitors for the defendant[s]

Address

To the District Judge and to the Plaintiff

Notes
(1) Where the defendant is one of several, insert the name of the defendant making the payment. Where more than one defendant makes payment a separate notice for each must be lodged. (2) Delete as appropriate (3) If there is more than one cause of action specify the cause or causes in satisfaction of which payment is made.

© July 1993   Fourmat Publishing Tolley House 2 Addiscombe Road Croydon Surrey CR9 5AF

Notice of acceptance of payment in

LF1149: Notice of acceptance or refusal of defendant's admission and offer for payment (O.9 r.6)

In the   **County Court**

Case no:

Between

Plaintiff

and

Defendant

TAKE NOTICE:

[1. that the plaintiff accepts the defendant's admission of [the claim] [the amount admitted in satisfaction of the claim] and the offer for payment and requests the court to enter judgment accordingly.] *or*

[2. that the plaintiff accepts the defendant's admission of [the claim] [the amount admitted in satisfaction of the claim] but refuses the offer as to payment and requests the court to fix a date for the disposal of this matter.] *or*

[3. that the plaintiff refuses the amount admitted in satisfaction of the claim and requests the court to fix a date for the trial of the matter.]

Dated this   day of   19

(Signed)

Solicitor for the plaintiff

Address

To the District Judge

© July 1993   Fourmat Publishing Tolley House 2 Addiscombe Road Croydon Surrey CR9 5AF

Chapter 12

Discovery

As the automatic directions indicate, discovery should take place within 14 days of the close of pleadings. In the first instance, discovery takes place by the exchange of lists of documents. A standard list is set out on page 100. It will be seen that the form divides up the documents to be disclosed into three groups. Schedule 1 part 1 deals with documents for which no privilege is claimed. In a personal injury claim, this section will consist largely of letters between the parties, accident reports, the pleadings and so on.

Schedule 1 part 2 is reserved for documents for which privilege is claimed. The circumstances in which documents may be privileged from production is dealt with on page 97. If a document is privileged, it should be mentioned in this section so that the opponent may consider whether to challenge its classification and ask for it to be disclosed.

Schedule 2 deals with documents which the party concerned had at one stage but has no longer. These will almost always be simply the originals of the letters referred to in the earlier part of the list.

1. Documents to be elicited

The importance of obtaining full discovery on behalf of the plaintiff in a personal injury case cannot be over-emphasised. It is sometimes argued that a particular document is of no relevance to the claim. A helpful authority on this point is *The Captain Gregos* The Times 21 December 1990, in which it was held that the test of relevance is not the probative value of the document but the question of whether the documents might or could reasonably be expected to provoke a line of enquiry which would be of assistance to a party.

Any documents which show that the defendant was aware of the problem which caused the plaintiff's accident will be of immense value and it is surprising how often such documents can be found. In particular, those acting for the plaintiff should make sure that the following are disclosed:

(a) Accident book

An employer of more than ten people is required by law to keep a book giving details of all accidents which befall its employees. The book is kept in a standard form and the date and a brief description of the accident should be provided. When asking for the book, entries for the three years before the plaintiff's accident should be requested to ascertain whether similar problems have arisen in the past.

(b) Form B176

If a person claims benefit following an industrial accident, the DSS will issue form B176 to the employer. It is useful in that it requires the employer to give an account of how the accident occurred. However, it is less common today than a few years ago, as employers must now pay the first eight weeks of sickness benefit to the employee.

(c) Form 2508

An employer must notify the Health and Safety Executive on form 2508 of any accident causing death or major injury. 'Major injury' is defined as a fracture of the skull, spine, pelvis, arm or leg (but not wrist or ankle), amputation of hand or foot, loss of sight of an eye or any other injury requiring hospital in-patient treatment for more than 24 hours.

(d) Works Safety Committee minutes

If the factory has a works safety committee, ask for copies of its minutes for the three years before the accident. It may be that the committee expressed concern about the very problem which caused the plaintiff's accident.

(e) Complaints book

Many employers keep a complaints book for the use of their employees. Obtain a copy of this and check for any comments relevant to your case.

(f) Statements

The employer may well have taken a statement from the plaintiff and from other witnesses to the accident. The plaintiff's statement should be disclosed, and, as will be seen later, if the dominant purpose in taking the statement was not just the investigation of the claim, it will be discoverable.

(g) Factory memorandums

Notices may have been circularised dealing with methods of working. In addition, the happening of the accident may have precipitated a new notice recommending a different way of working. This should be carefully scrutinised for any implied admissions.

(h) Equipment invoices etc

If there is an issue over the existence or suitability of safety equipment, ask for all documentation relating to its alleged purchase. If the accident arose because of a defect in a vehicle or other equipment, ask for all service records.

(i) Sick notes and medical records

Ask for all sick notes if the employee took time off after the accident. In addition, many companies employ medical staff who may well have records relating to the plaintiff. It is surprising how often such records contradict the defendant's medical expert at trial!

(j) Comparable earnings

If the plaintiff is claiming loss of earnings over a reasonably long period of time, obtain details of comparable earners at this stage (see page 9).

(k) Trade union accident forms

Most trade unions will require the potential plaintiff to fill in a standard form setting out how the accident occurred. This is the initial document used by the union solicitor. Is this discoverable by the defendant? Traditionally, there is a convention that the defendant does not ask for the union form, and that the plaintiff does not ask for the defendant's insurance claim form. However, there must be some doubt about the enforceability of the convention in the light of *Guinness Peat Ltd* v *Fitzroy Robinson Partnership* [1987] 2 All ER 716, [1987] 1 WLR 1027.

2. Obtaining the documents

The automatic directions provide that once lists have been exchanged, discovery should take place within seven days. Traditionally, this meant that each solicitor would visit the office of its opposing firm and would see, and copy, all disclosable documents. This can still happen in complicated cases, but in the vast majority of situations, the solicitors agree to send each other copies of any documents which they require. This is obviously considerably cheaper, especially if the solicitors practise in different areas of the country. If there is likely to be a significant disparity in the photocopying costs, each side can agree to meet the other's bill in this respect.

If one party refuses to serve a list, the opponent can apply for its pleading to be struck out and for judgment in its favour.

If, on the other hand, the documents are disclosed, but there are suspicions that there are other papers which have been kept back, there are two options available — seeking an affidavit verifying the list, and making an application for specific discovery.

3. Affidavit verifying list

It is reasonably easy to obtain an order from the District Judge that a party should swear an affidavit verifying his list. The effect of this is that it causes him to have a second look for documents, and then gives an assurance, on oath, that either there are no further documents, or that the only other documents are now disclosed. It will then be extremely embarrassing for the other party should further documents arise during the trial. The situation where this will be useful is where there are suspicions that the opponent will produce documents at trial which have not been disclosed in the list. A precedent application for an affidavit can be found on page 102.

4. Specific discovery

If the nature of the documents which are required is known, application should be made for specific discovery under O 14 r 2. This is made to the District Judge and the documents required should be set out in the application. The application should be accompanied by an affidavit explaining why the documents are relevant and why they are likely to be in the possession, custody or power of the party concerned. A precedent is provided at the end of this chapter.

5. Privilege

It is normally reasonably straightforward to determine whether a document is privileged or not. In the context of personal injury actions, the following are the most important grounds upon which privilege may be claimed:

(a) Legal professional privilege

Communications between a solicitor and his client are privileged if they take place in ordinary professional dealings between the party and his solicitor or counsel during or with a view to litigation. This last requirement should be emphasised — its importance was shown in *Ventouris* v *Mountain* [1991] 3 All ER 472, [1991] 1 WLR 607 where the Court of Appeal emphasised that to qualify, the document must have come into existence for the purposes of the litigation. It would not suffice simply for the document to have been obtained with the litigation in mind.

(b) 'Without prejudice' documents

Negotiations entered into by the parties with the intention of settling the cause of action are inadmissible should the trial subsequently go ahead. Solicitors generally head offers made during such negotiations 'without prejudice' to underline the fact that they are not disclosable. However, merely heading a letter in this way will not confer privileged status automatically, and the letter can be examined so that its nature can be ascertained — *Shropshire District Council* v *Amos* [1987] 1 All ER 340.

(c) Documents prepared with a view to litigation

Parties should be free to prepare their cases away from the scrutiny of the court and their opponents. Because of this, enquiries and other work carried out with a view to litigation are privileged. This rule tends to cause problems when enquiries are made both with a view to the impending litigation and with a view to safety or other matters. In such a situation, the document is privileged only if its dominant purpose was the preparation for litigation — *Waugh* v *British Railways Board* [1980] AC 521, [1979] 2 All ER 1169, [1979] 3 WLR 150.

(d) Witness statements

Regard should be had to the case of *Black & Decker Ltd* v *Flymo Ltd* [1991] 3 All ER 158 in which there was a short discussion of the relationship between discovery and witness statements. A witness statement served on behalf of the plaintiffs referred to the fact that a new lawnmower was designed around 'the concept of a dish-like chassis'. The defendants asked for discovery of design documents and drawings relating to the mower. The plaintiffs objected on the basis that the information was privileged, but it was held by Hoffmann J that 'once the statement has been disclosed pursuant to the rule, there can no longer be any question of privilege'. It was further held that witness statements, once disclosed, are admissible for the purposes of specific discovery.

The case was not being appealed, and carries important ramifications for all cases in which witness statements are exchanged. It may be that it will be challenged in the future, bearing in mind O 38 r 2A(8) RSC which provides that 'Nothing in this rule shall deprive any party of his right to treat any communication as privileged or make admissible evidence otherwise inadmissible'.

However, as it stands, the decision underlines the need for extreme care in drafting statements. Any documents referred to in the statement can be examined, even if they appear to be privileged. Such documents must therefore be considered in their entirety before reference is made to them in the statement.

(e) Public interest immunity

In certain circumstances, the defendant can argue that there is a public interest in not disclosing documents; this must be balanced against the plaintiff's interest in having all relevant papers available. Such arguments have tended to arise quite frequently in relation to social work records (see *Re M (a minor) (Disclosure of Material)* [1990] 2 FLR 36). In addition, the argument was successfully raised in *Goodwill* v *Chief Constable of Lancashire Constabulary* [1993] PIQR 187 in relation to a police public order manual which dealt with strategy for dealing with public order offences and the appropriate training for officers in this area.

6. Accidental disclosure of privileged documents

Occasionally, one party accidently reveals documents which are privileged to its opponents. Can the opponents then rely upon these papers? Some assistance can be gained from *Derby & Co Ltd and Others v Weldon and Others (No 8)* [1990] 3 All ER 762, [1991] 1 WLR 73. Discovery in the case had been voluminous and the plaintiffs had listed files of documents simply as files, without giving details of the contents. Fourteen documents were included in one of the files which came within the scope of legal professional privilege. The defendants' solicitors asked for, and were given, copies of these privileged documents, and the mistake only came to their attention when copies of the documents were exhibited to an affidavit by the defendants.

The test applied by the Court of Appeal in its judgment in *Guinness Peat Properties Ltd* v *Fitzroy Robinson Partnership* [1987] 2 All ER 716, [1987] 1 WLR 1027 was approved and applied. In the *Guinness Peat* case, it was held that in the ordinary course of events, a party who sees a particular document referred to in the opponent's list without discovery being claimed is entitled to assume that privilege was being waived. There are, however, three exceptions to this rule:

- where the error is discovered before inspection takes place;
- where a party has procured inspection of the document by fraud;
- where the party realises that he has been permitted to see the document only by reason of an obvious mistake.

Checklist

1. Always ensure that discovery is full. Resist suggestions that lists are not required.
2. If there are problems with discovery apply for either an affidavit verifying the list in a case where the suspicion is that the opponent will produce documents not referred to; or make an application for specific discovery if documents are required for later use.
3. Be aware that any document referred to in a witness statement can be examined by the opponent.

Discovery

List of documents

List of Documents	In the
Plaintiff:	County Court
	Case No. *Always quote this*
Defendant:	

* Delete words in brackets if list is sent in response to automatic directions *(O.17 r.11)*

The following is a list of documents which contain information about matters in dispute in this case which are or have been in my possession. *[They are sent in response to your request dated *(insert date)*
                     19   ]

Schedule 1 *Part I*

List and number here in a convenient order the documents (or bundles of documents, if of the same nature, eg invoices) in your possession which you do not object to being inspected. Give a short description of each document or bundle so that it can be identified and say if it is kept elsewhere, ie at a bank or by a solicitor.

I have in my possession the documents numbered and listed here. I do not object to you inspecting them.

Schedule 1 *Part II*

List and number here, as above, the document in your possession which you object to being inspected.

I have in my possession the documents numbered and listed here but I object to you inspecting them:

Say what your objections are.

I object to you inspecting these documents because:

List of documents *(O.14, r.1(5))*

Form F1107 (N265)
© Fourmat Publishing
133 Upper Street
London N1 1QP
December 1992

PTO

100

List of documents (cont.)

Schedule 2
I have had the documents numbered and listed below, but they are no longer in my possession.

List and number
here the documents
you once had in your
possession but
which you no longer
have when this list is
served.
For each document
listed say when it
was in your
possession and
where it is now.

All the documents which are or have been in my possession and which contain information about the matters
in dispute in this case are listed in Schedules 1 and 2.

Signed: ....

Dated: ....

Plaintiff/Defendant

Application for affidavit verifying list of documents

(Case heading)

TAKE NOTICE that the Plaintiff will apply to the District Judge of the Barchester County Court at 9, High Street, Barchester, on   day the   day of   1992 for an Order that the Defendant do make and serve an Affidavit verifying the List of Documents served on 1991.

AND that the costs of this application be costs in the cause.

Dated etc

Application for specific discovery

(Case heading)

TAKE NOTICE that the Plaintiff will apply to the District Judge of the Barchester County Court at 9, High Street, Barchester, on   day the   day of   1992 for an Order that the Defendant do within 14 days make and serve an affidavit stating whether any of the documents specified in the schedule hereto are or have been in his possession custody or power and if such documents are not in his custody at present, stating when he parted with them and what has become of them

AND that the costs of this application be costs in the cause.

THE SCHEDULE

1. Accident report dealing with Plaintiff's accident on 30.6.91
2. Minutes of Works Safety Committee meeting on 19th July 1991.

Dated etc

Affidavit in support of application for specific discovery

(Case heading)

I, JOHN SMITH, of Smith and Co, Solicitors of 54 High Street, Barchester, MAKE OATH and say as follows:

1. I am a Solicitor and partner in the firm of Smith and Co and have been conducting the above named Plaintiff's claim against the Barchester Corporation. I am authorised to make this affidavit on my client's behalf, and, save where otherwise stated, depose to facts within my own knowledge.

2. Mr Smith's accident occurred on 30th June 1991 when he slipped on some oil which had been left on the floor of the Defendant's bus garage. Proceedings were issued in October 1991 and a List of Documents filed by the Defendant on the 1st February 1992.

3. I was concerned to note that the list did not contain any reference to the accident book which the Defendant is under obligation to keep. In addition, I have been informed by my client and verily believe that a few days after the accident there was a meeting of the Works Safety Committee at which the general problem of oily floors was discussed.

4. I am confident that the Defendant has these documents and believe that they are relevant to the Plaintiff's claim.

5. There is now produced and shown to me marked JS1 a bundle of correspondence between myself and the Defendant's insurers. It can be seen from the correspondence that apart from a brief acknowledgment on 16th February, I have received no response from the insurers.

6. For this reason, I seek an order that the Defendant do give specific discovery of the documents set out in the schedule to my application.

Sworn etc

Chapter 13

Preparing to set down

After discovery has taken place, the next important step in the proceedings will be to file certificates of readiness and set the case down for trial.

(a) The 15-month rule

The plaintiff's solicitor should never forget the provisions of O 17 r 11(9) CCR:

> 'If no request is made pursuant to paragraph 3(d) [ie to fix a date for hearing] within 15 months of the day on which pleadings are deemed to be closed (or within 9 months after the expiry of any period fixed by the court for making such a request), the action shall be automatically struck out.'

This draconian provision was examined by the Court of Appeal in *Rastin* v *British Steel plc and others* [1994] The Times 18 February 1994. Debate had raged as to the nature of the power — if an action was struck out under the rule, could it be reinstated, or was the position akin to where a successful application had been made to strike out for want of prosecution?

It was held in *Rastin* v *British Steel* that the action could be reinstated under the provisions of O 13 r 4 CCR, which gives the court power to extend the period within which any act in the proceedings is required to be done. However, reinstatement is an act of judicial discretion, and an application to reinstate will not succeed unless the plaintiff and his advisers can show that he had otherwise prosecuted his case with at least reasonable diligence. He will have to show that his failure to comply with the 15-month rule was excusable, and the more technical his failure, the more readily he will be excused. The court can also take into account prejudice to the defendant, but the absence of prejudice is not a potent reason for exercising discretion in the plaintiff's favour.

The moral of this is very clear — plaintiff solicitors should ignore this rule at their peril. If it is not complied with, the onus will be on the plaintiff to persuade the court to reinstate the action, and the test looks considerably tougher than the test applied when an application to dismiss for want of prosecution is made.

Although the 15-month rule should never be forgotten, it is unlikely that the plaintiff's solicitor will be ready to apply for a hearing date immediately after discovery. It may be that the prognosis is not yet clear, or that, in any event, a further medical report will be needed. Expert opinion may be required on various points, and this may result in the need to amend pleadings. This chapter is essentially a checklist of the various steps that may need to be taken between discovery and setting down.

1. Expert evidence

(a) Medical evidence

By this stage, the plaintiff will probably have only a preliminary report from his medical expert. This is the time to send the client back for a full report. The doctor should be pressed for as firm a prognosis as possible. In addition, thought should be given to whether another medical expert should be consulted. The automatic directions allow for two medical experts and it is always possible to apply for leave to call more should the need arise.

If the injuries sustained by the client cross the traditional medical boundaries, it will be obvious that more than one medical report will be required. A less obvious case in which another expert should be used is that concerning serious back injury. The classic combination in this situation is an orthopaedic surgeon and a neurologist. In a case which will be decided on the basis of which expert is preferred by the Judge, it obviously does no harm to back up the client's claim by supplying agreeing evidence from two consultants of different specialities.

The plaintiff's solicitor should also consider whether he will require non-medical expert evidence. The most likely options in this respect will be engineers, employment consultants and pension experts.

(b) Engineering evidence

There are several well-known firms of consulting engineers with considerable experience of giving evidence about how an accident arose and whether an employer should shoulder the blame for it. Authority for the expenditure should be obtained from the union or insurer, or from the legal aid area office.

Once instructed, the engineer will almost certainly need to visit the scene of the accident. The client should, if possible, also attend. The engineer will be told how the accident occurred and will carry out an inspection of the premises and of any equipment alleged to be involved. He will also take photographs which will form part of his eventual report.

If the accident occurred at the premises of the defendant, the plaintiff's solicitor will need to obtain the defendant's permission for the inspection. This is rarely refused, although many defendants like to be present at the inspection, or even arrange for their own expert to be present at the same time. The official reason for this is that it minimises disruption to the defendant. In addition, it is often helpful to both sides to see what their opponent's expert is concentrating on.

If the defendant objects to an inspection, application to the District Judge can be made under the rules discussed in Chapter 5.

(c) Employment consultants

It may well be the case that before the accident, the plaintiff was employed in a physically hard, but reasonably remunerative, job. If he sustained permanent injury, he may be capable of performing some employment, but not his old job. He will therefore suffer a continuing loss of earnings which must, as far as possible, be quantified.

An employment consultant will be extremely helpful in this situation. He should be given the medical information relating to the plaintiff, and will probably want to interview him to assess the extent of his disability. He will then consider the plaintiff's education and experience and look at what employment would be a realistic option. His report should then set out the plaintiff's chances of getting such a job, and the likely level of his wages should he succeed in doing so. Whilst such a report will essentially be based on guesswork, it will allow a reasoned quantification of the plaintiff's claim for future loss of earnings.

Further consideration was given to the use of such experts in *Larby* v *Thurgood* [1993] PIQR 218 where the defendant sought a stay pending interview of the plaintiff by the consultant. The application was refused, and a timely reminder was given that such matters as the plaintiff's general suitability for employment, willingness and motivation to work were matters of fact for the Judge.

It may be that after considering the options, the employment consultant will decide that the plaintiff stands very little chance of obtaining new employment. If this is the case, a claim for total loss of earnings should be pursued. The expert's report will still be vital in dispensing with any arguments from the defendant that the plaintiff could find himself another job.

(d) Pensions experts

A matter of growing importance in dealing with personal injury claims is quantifying a plaintiff's loss of pension. In many occupations today, the provision of a pension forms an important part of the plaintiff's remuneration. If he is deprived of this by reason of the accident, he is entitled to claim it.

There are two basic ways of claiming the loss of a pension. They were set out in the case of *Auty* v *National Coal Board* [1985] 1 All ER 930, [1985] 1 WLR 784:

Approach A

(a) Calculate the pension and any lump sum had the plaintiff's accident not occurred and had he worked on to pensionable age.

(b) Calculate what he will actually receive by way of pension and lump sum in the light of the accident and his reduced contributions.

(c) Put forward quotations for the cost of topping up this reduced pension to the pension which he would have obtained had the accident not occurred.

(d) Although there does not seem to be authority on this point, it would seem only fair that any contributions which would have been made by the plaintiff to his pension should be deducted from the award to avoid over-compensation.

Approach B

This is a considerably more complex formula. The starting point is the annual loss of pension suffered by reason of the accident. The Judge then applies to this a multiplier, which is then discounted to take account of early payment and the contingencies of life.

Once the parties have all the reports they require, each side should consider whether they will need to obtain leave to call more experts than are allowed under the automatic directions. There should be no problems in obtaining leave unless the application is wholly unreasonable. A form of application is given on page 112.

2. Amending pleadings

It may well be that on obtaining expert evidence, it becomes apparent that the pleadings no longer fully demonstrate the plaintiff's case against the defendant. This is the stage at which to consider whether the Particulars of Claim should be amended.

(a) Amending the particulars of claim

Amendments can be allowed under O 15 of the CCR. There are three basic categories of amendment — the correction of clerical errors, amendments without leave and amendments with leave.

Clerical errors can be corrected easily and quickly under O 15 r 5 — known as the 'slip rule'. This allows the court to correct a genuine slip. It can be invoked simply by writing to the chief clerk of the relevant court.

Pleadings can be amended without the consent of the court where all parties consent. In such a situation, the amended pleading should be filed with the court.

In most situations, however, it will be necessary to seek leave to amend. Order 15 r 1 allows the court to direct that any pleading or other document be amended, or that any person be added, struck out or substituted as a party to the proceedings.

The court has a wide power to allow amendment, and it will use such power unless to do so would cause injustice to the other side. In most cases, the opponent can be adequately compensated for any inconvenience by an award of costs.

It is also useful to note that an amendment will be allowed to correct a defect caused by a *bona fide* mistake of law.

Application to amend is made to the District Judge. A form of application to amend is set out at page 112. A copy of the proposed amended pleading should be provided with the application. Additional parts of the pleading should be underlined in red (or green if they are re-amendments) so that the District Judge and all parties can see what they are.

(b) Amending after the limitation period has expired

Order 15 r 1(2) refers to the conditions and restrictions imposed by s 35 of the Limitation Act 1980, and to the provisions of the RSC. Under s 35(3) of the Act, the court will not allow a new claim, other than an original set-off or counterclaim, to be made in the course of any action already proceeding after the expiry of any time limit imposed under the Act which would affect a new action to enforce that claim.

Provision is made under the Act for rules allowing exceptions to this principle, but such exceptions may only be made if the conditions set out in s 35(5) and O 20 r 5 of the RSC are satisfied. These conditions are:

(i)   A claim involving a new cause of action must arise out of substantially the same facts as are already in issue on any claim made in the original action. Further, it must be considered to be just in the circumstances to do so. This latter requirement was emphasised by the Court of Appeal in *Hancock Shipping Co Ltd v Kawasaki Heavy Industries Ltd* The Times, 16 July 1991, where amendments were disallowed, as to allow them would deprive the defendants of an accrued defence. This in itself would not mean an automatic bar on amendments after the limitation period had expired, but it was one of the factors which the court should take into account.

(ii) In a claim involving the addition of a new party, the addition is necessary for the determination of the original action.

3. Pleading the injury

A check should also be made at this stage to ensure that the injuries pleaded are still in accordance with the medical evidence. It was made clear in *Owen v Grimsby & Cleethorpes Transport* The Times, 14 February 1991, that there is no need to amend the pleadings each time there is a fresh medical report which shows the development of the injuries. However, the injuries as pleaded should reflect the case which the plaintiff will put at trial.

4. Organising the evidence

By this stage, the evidence should fall into three groups — proofs (which should be updated if necessary) from the witnesses who will be called; experts' reports, and documents. It is important at this stage to consider any potential problems relating to the admissibility of the evidence.

(a) Civil Evidence Act notices

The Civil Evidence Act 1968 can be used in two potential problem areas. Firstly, if a witness is dead, abroad or unfit to attend court, the Act allows his statement to stand as his evidence. Secondly, the Act allows records kept in the course of a trade or business to be admissible in certain circumstances.

If evidence under either of these categories is to be given, it will be necessary for the side wishing to use it to serve a notice on its opponents. The county courts are governed by the RSC on this point, and the notice must contain details of:

- the time, place and circumstances at or in which the statement was made;
- the person by whom, and the person to whom, the statement was made;
- the substance of the statement.

In addition, a copy of the statement must be annexed to the notice. The notice should also state why the maker of the statement is not being called as a witness. A form of notice is given on page 113.

Note also that the notice must be served not less than fourteen days before the day fixed for trial (O 20 r 17). However, this time limit can be disapplied under r 20 in appropriate cases.

If the opponent objects to the use of the statement, he can do so by serving a counter notice within seven days of service of the notice on him. See page 113 for a form of counter notice. If this occurs, application should be made before trial for the issue to be determined.

(b) Affidavit evidence

Order 20 r 7 provides a useful alternative to the Civil Evidence Act procedure. It allows evidence to be given by affidavit provided that, no less than 14 days before hearing, notice of such intention is given and the affidavit served on the opponent. If no objection is made within 14 days, the opposing party will be presumed to have consented to its use and the affidavit will be admissible.

(c) Evidence by deposition

Order 20 r 13 allows the court to order the examination on oath of a person 'at any place in England and Wales'. This is only made where there is good reason why the witness cannot attend court — ill health, or age (where the witness is over 70, the order is likely to be granted), for instance. If the order is made, the witness will be examined before a nominated officer of the court or other person. The witness's evidence will be put into the form of a deposition, authenticated by the signature of the examiner, which will be filed with the court.

Application is made to the District Judge and should be supported by an affidavit.

Preparing to set down

(d) Experts' reports

Under the automatic directions, the exchange of experts' reports should be effected within ten weeks of the close of pleadings. This is achieved very rarely in practice, as reports are often simply not available at this early stage.

In the past, this caused something of a dilemma for solicitors. Obviously, it was important to serve all experts' reports to be relied upon well before the trial to avoid their being ruled inadmissible. However, if one's opponents did not forward their own reports by exchange, they could be placed in an advantageous position. This is because their own reports could be quickly prepared or amended to deal with the points raised in the reports served on them. This tended to lead to a situation where, if reports were not exchanged by agreement, each side would defer serving its report until as late as possible.

To some extent, matters are now assisted by r 13(5) of the County Court (Amendment No 4) Rules 1989. This provides that '... where [the provisions relating to disclosure] requires disclosure to be made by more than one party the reports shall be disclosed by mutual exchange, medical for medical and non-medical for non-medical, within the time provided'.

Thus, before sending the opponents his experts' reports, the solicitor should check with them that they will send their own reports to you by way of mutual exchange. If they are not willing to undertake to do so, the reports should be kept for the time being, but an immediate application to the District Judge for an order for mutual exchange should be made. In *Croft* v *Jewell* [1993] PIQR 270 the defendant unsuccessfully sought to adduce new expert evidence less than one month before trial — a reminder that mutual exchange is now very much the order of the day.

The automatic directions also provide that expert evidence should be agreed if possible. There are very good reasons for avoiding calling experts if at all possible, in that considerable sums of costs will be saved, and there will be greater flexibility in the listing of the case as it will not be necessary to fit in with the schedules of busy experts. However, it is wise to think very carefully before agreeing evidence. The directions provide that if this is to be done, the evidence shall be presented in the form of a written report. You should therefore agree that only one of the reports go forward.

(e) Documentary evidence

Remember that, under the automatic directions, photographs, a sketch plan and the contents of the police accident report book are receivable. These should be agreed if possible.

Check that all the documents upon which you propose to rely have been included in your list of documents. If more have since appeared, serve a supplementary list.

110

If the originals of the documents are kept by the opponents, remember to serve a notice to produce.

5. Obtaining counsel's advice

By this stage, all the evidence which will be put before the judge should be available. Each side will know if it is likely that the pleadings will have to be amended and the case will be ready to be set down for trial.

In all but the most straightforward cases, it will be helpful at this stage to obtain counsel's advice. In a legally aided case, the certificate may only cover the solicitor as far as obtaining counsel's advice on liability. It will only be extended to cover the trial if counsel's advice is positive. In a privately funded case, it is still worth considering whether to obtain an advice on liability and/or evidence. The latter can be particularly helpful. It is surprising how easy it is to miss an important point when one is dealing with all the aspects of a case. Having a fresh mind can assist in this respect. In addition, if counsel is to be instructed to present the case, obtaining his or her advice at this stage should avoid too much last minute hurry to obtain evidence which is felt to be relevant.

6. Setting down

The onus is on the plaintiff to request that the action be listed for hearing. Unlike a High Court action, the court will already have the pleadings. The only formal requirement, therefore, is that the plaintiff should give a time estimate for the trial at this stage. In giving this estimate, the solicitor should remember that the chances of getting the case into court at 10.30 am are remote in the extreme, as the court will probably have several urgent injunctions to deal with first. The estimate should therefore err on the side of pessimism.

The only potential difficulty now relates to the question of obtaining a fixed date for the hearing. In most personal injury actions, experts will be required to attend. They will need considerable notice of a court date; in the past it was always reasonably easy to obtain a fixture for this reason. However, unfortunately, many courts are becoming less accommodating in this respect. If a fixture is refused and a date is ultimately given which is unsuitable, all that can be done is to agree an adjournment with the opponents and obtain a fresh date.

Checklist

1. Update medical evidence.
2. Consider whether other expert evidence – eg from engineers, employment consultants and pensions experts – is required.
3. Amend pleadings to accurately represent the party's case on liability and quantum.

4. Consider any potential problems with evidence and witnesses and make appropriate applications.
5. Obtain counsel's advice on evidence (and liability if required).
6. Set down for trial with time estimate.

Application for leave to call further witnesses

(Case heading)

TAKE NOTICE that the Plaintiff will apply to the District Judge of the Barchester County Court at 9, High Street, Barchester, on   day the   day of   1992 for an Order that the Plaintiff be at liberty to call three medical expert witnesses and two non-medical expert witnesses, and that the reports of such witnesses be disclosed within 28 days of the Order herein

AND that the costs of this application be costs in the cause.

Served etc

Application to amend Particulars of Claim

(Case heading)

TAKE NOTICE that the Plaintiff will apply to the District Judge of the Barchester County Court at 9, High Street, Barchester, on   day the   day of   1992 for an Order that the Plaintiff do have leave to amend the Particulars of Claim as marked in red on the copy supplied with this Notice of Application and that the Defendant do have leave to serve an Amended Defence if so advised within 14 days thereafter

AND that the costs of this application be costs in the cause.

Served etc

Civil Evidence Act notice

(Case heading)

TAKE NOTICE that at the trial or hearing of this action the Plaintiff desires to give in evidence the statement contained in the following document namely a written statement dated . . . .
A copy of the same document is annexed hereto.

AND FURTHER TAKE NOTICE that the Particulars relating to the said statement are as follows:

(1) The said statement was compiled on 21st March 1990 at the offices of Slope & Co, solicitors for the Plaintiff.
(2) The statement was made by Mr John Smith and was given during the course of an interview with Mr Robert Williams, the Plaintiff's solicitor.
(3) The statement gives an account of the accident which befell the Plaintiff herein on 15th February 1991.

AND FURTHER TAKE NOTICE that the said John Smith is unable to attend at the trial herein as he is beyond the seas, namely in Zambia.

DATED the   day of

Counter notice to Civil Evidence Act notice

(Case heading)

TAKE NOTICE that the Defendant herein requires you to call as a witness at the trial or hearing of this action Mr John Smith particulars of whom are contained in your Notice dated

AND FURTHER TAKE NOTICE that the Defendant contends that the said John Smith returned from beyond the seas in March 1992 and should be called as a witness at the trial of this action.

DATED the   day of

Chapter 14

Preparing for trial

1. The statement of special damages

In the High Court, the plaintiff is under a duty to file a statement of special damages at least 28 days before trial. There is no such express duty in the county court. However, there is an increasing tendency to file a statement setting out the plaintiff's claim for special damages. The advantage of doing so is that it clarifies the issues before the court and concentrates everyone's mind.

The statement should be set out in the form of a pleading. Apart from this, there are no rules about what form it should take. Perhaps the most sensible approach to take is to set out the heads of damage in this order:

1. Loss of earnings to trial
2. Projected future loss of earnings
3. Other items of special damage
4. Pension loss.

It is often helpful to the court to include appendices setting out the calculations in detail, so that the actual statement looks uncluttered. An example is given on page 121.

2. Interest

It should be remembered that, in the event of obtaining judgment, the plaintiff will be entitled to interest on both general damages and special damages. Whilst s 69 of the County Courts Act 1984 gives the court a wide discretion to award interest for such period and at such rate as it thinks fit, various practices have grown up in this area. The first point to be aware of is that the rate of interest awarded under each category is different. The plaintiff will normally be entitled to interest at the rate of 2 per cent on his general damages from the date of the service of the summons. The reason for this relatively low rate is that the award of general damages should take account of inflation in any event. Interest on special damages is normally calculated on the basis of the court's own short term investment account rate. This fluctuates from time to time but is generally in the region of 9–15 per cent. When special damages have accrued fairly evenly over the period to trial, interest is normally awarded at one half of the short term investment rate. This avoids having to calculate the interest from the date that each separate item of loss arose. If, however, most of the special damages occurred early in the proceedings, interest at the full short term investment rate should be requested. Note too that interest on special damages is due from the date that the accident occurred.

It is as well to have a calculation of interest before trial. However, in all but the most straightforward cases, it is likely that the level of damages awarded will not be completely predictable. It is wise to take a calculator to court to carry out a quick assessment of interest after judgment.

3. State benefits (system for injuries occurring after 1 January 1989)

(a) Deductions

Under the Social Security Administration Act 1992, State benefits paid to accident victims will be deducted from the plaintiff's damages cheque. The benefits which will be taken into account in this way are listed below:

- attendance allowance
- constant attendance allowance
- disablement benefit
- family credit
- income support
- invalidity benefit (due to become incapacity benefit)
- mobility allowance
- Old Cases Act benefits
- reduced earnings allowance
- retirement allowance
- severe disablement allowance
- sickness benefit (due to become incapacity benefit)
- statutory sick pay (but not after 6 April 1994)
- unemployment benefit
- dependency increase payable with the above

The new rules considerably simplify the drafting of the statement in that it is no longer necessary to calculate the benefits and give credit for half of most benefits under the Law Reform (Personal Injuries) Act 1948.

Instead, the question of benefits can be completely ignored in the statement. The system descends once the case is settled or judgment obtained. By this stage, the defendant should have obtained a Certificate of Total Benefit from the Compensation Recovery Unit. The plaintiff will have been sent a copy of this certificate so that the figures can be checked. This certificate tells the defendant how much to deduct from the damages agreed or awarded. The defendant sends the relevant amount to the CRU and sends the plaintiff his reduced damages cheque.

In *Re R* [1993] PIQR 252 it was held that benefits must be deducted up to the period of acceptance of a payment in, even though the payment in itself was calculated on the basis of six months' loss of income whilst the benefits related to a nine-month period.

(b) Exemptions

In certain situations, the benefits will not be recoverable by the State. These are as follows:

- small payments. If the award of damages is below £2,500, no benefits are repayable. However, in this situation, the defendant can still use the Law Reform (Personal Injuries) Act 1948 to offset half of the benefits paid for a period of five years (see (c) below);
- payments made under s 35 of the Powers of Criminal Courts Act 1973 (payments awarded against a person found guilty of criminally injuring another);
- payments under the Fatal Accidents Act 1976;
- payments that would have been made under the Fatal Accidents Act 1976; (this is to cover the situation where a claim is made in part for the losses of the deceased. If such a claim is made in addition to the dependant's losses, it cannot be made under the Act. In such a situation, the dependant's claim will be exempt);
- payments made under the Vaccine Damage Act 1979;
- awards made by the Criminal Injuries Compensation Board;
- payments made out of disaster funds where more than half is made up of public donations;
- payments made out of the Macfarlane Trust (a fund set up to compensate the families of haemophiliacs infected with the HIV virus in blood transfusions);
- payments made under an insurance policy taken out by the claimant before the date of injury;
- redundancy payments taken into account in assessing the compensation;
- payments made under the Pneumoconiosis Compensation Scheme;
- payments for noise-induced hearing loss where the hearing loss is less than 50 decibels in one or both ears;
- periodic payments made under the terms of a structured settlement;
- contractual payments made to an employee by his or her employer in respect of a day of incapacity for work.

Remember that recoupment is made from all elements of the claim — general damages as well as specials.

(c) Injuries occurring before 1 January 1989

Claims arising before this date will continue to be governed by the Law Reform (Personal Injuries) Act 1948. This provides that, when calculating the special damages sustained by a plaintiff, credit will be given for one half of the following benefits for the five years beginning with the date when the cause of action arose:

- sickness benefit;
- invalidity benefit;
- non-contributory invalidity pension;
- severe disablement allowance;
- injury benefit;
- disablement benefit.

Note that these benefits will only be offset against a claim for loss of earnings.

In addition, the following benefits will be wholly deductible from a loss of earnings claim in respect of an accident before 1 January 1989:

- unemployment benefit directly attributable to the injury;
- income support;
- industrial rehabilitation allowance;
- tax rebates;
- savings due to the plaintiff's maintenance at public expense in a hospital, nursing home, etc;
- payments from job release scheme;
- family income supplement;
- payments under the employer's health insurance scheme — but not if the payment was made gratuitously, or as a benevolent act.

Remember to take sick pay into account in assessing the loss of earnings. The employer or insurer should provide details of this at an early stage.

Note that after *Smoker* v *London Fire and Civil Defence Authority* [1991] 2 All ER 449, [1991] 2 WLR 1052, pension monies paid to the employee because of his injury by the defendant are not deductible from the damages.

When dealing with a claim arising before 1 January 1989, the benefits received and deductions made must be set out in the schedule. Details of the benefits paid should now be obtained from the Compensation Recovery Unit, rather than individual social security offices, as used to be the case. The Compensation Recovery Unit is at the DSS, Reyrolle Building, Hebburn, Tyne and Wear, NE31 1XB; Tel (091) 225 8030 or (091) 225 8542.

4. Witness summonses

The solicitors for both sides should always arrange for witness summonses to be issued to all lay witnesses. Even if there is a suspicion that the witness may not give the evidence set out in his proof, he should be summonsed and a further proof taken at court, unless it is quite clear that the case can get by without him.

The solicitor should check with each expert whether a summons is required. Some experts find it easier to arrange leave of absence from their normal work if a summons is issued — others can be slightly offended to receive one.

Application for a summons is made under O 20 r 12. There is a standard form available and this should be issued not less than seven days before the date when attendance is required. Once issued, it will either be served by post by the court, or will be returned to the solicitor for him to carry out service. Service must be effected not less than four days before the date when the witness is required to attend court.

Conduct money should always be proffered when the summons is served. The sum given must be enough to cover the witness's expenses in getting to court. In addition, O 20 provides that the sum of £8.50 should be tendered to the witness (or £6 to a police officer). If the court is asked to effect postal service, the correct monies must be sent to the court or a delay will ensue.

5. Booking and briefing counsel

It is of course highly desirable that the barrister who prepared the pleadings should present the case in court. With this in mind, his or her clerk should be contacted as soon as a hearing date has been set (or if a fixture is unobtainable, as soon as the case is set down).

The clerk will almost certainly take the case, even if the barrister concerned appears to be booked on the day in question as, in civil cases, there is always a substantial chance that a case will settle before the hearing date. If it becomes apparent that the first choice barrister will definitely not be available, it is generally felt preferable to keep the brief in the same set of Chambers if possible. There is inevitably a fair amount of interaction between barristers in the same set of Chambers and a considerable amount of time can be spared if the barrister originally instructed is in a position to go through the case with counsel who is to conduct it.

The brief should be prepared and delivered in good time for the hearing. Precisely when this should be will vary according to the nature of the case — the more complex the case, the earlier delivery should be. There is a good argument for delivering the brief before the schedule of special damages is filed, to allow for amendments to be made before service, should counsel require.

At the time of delivering a brief, the solicitor should also consider whether a conference is appropriate. In most cases, a conference will help enormously, as there will almost always be new developments or queries from counsel. It is also often helpful to the client to meet the barrister who will conduct the case a few weeks or days before the hearing.

When drafting the brief, the solicitor should always bear in mind that he will know far more about the case than counsel. The brief should therefore be full and should set out the relevant points in every area. It is helpful to counsel if the brief is divided into sections dealing with liability, loss of earnings, reports and so on. The brief should also summarise which witnesses are to be called on each point and whether any of the expert evidence is agreed.

It is extremely helpful to provide a chronology dealing with the conduct of the litigation from the date of the accident. This should set out, for example, the dates on which pleadings were served, discovery entered into and reports made. It should also set out the nature and result of interlocutory applications (including the costs orders made).

Once the nuts and bolts of the case have been described to counsel, the solicitor should set out his views as to the weak and strong parts of the case. In addition, he may be able to advise the barrister of any 'off the record' comments of experts, or experts' letters setting out how the opposing expert may be challenged.

Counsel should be warned of any points of law anticipated by the parties, and of any attempts at settlement which have been made. Lastly, the position on special damages should be explained, and how the calculations have been made should be set out.

6. Preparing bundles

Order 17 r 12 of the CCR contains important new provisions dealing with providing the court with the documentation which will be used at the trial. The defendant must now, at least 14 days before the hearing date, tell the plaintiff which documents he wishes to have in the trial bundle. The plaintiff must, at least seven days before the hearing date, file one copy of a paginated and indexed bundle, comprising the documents upon which either of the parties proposes to rely or wishes to have before the court. In addition, the plaintiff must file two copies of the following documents with the court at the same time:

- requests for further and better particulars, together with the particulars given and any answer to interrogatories;
- witness statements which have been exchanged and experts' reports which have been disclosed. The solicitors should indicate whether these documents are agreed;
- legal aid documents.

Obviously, further copies of the trial bundle and reports should be provided for the use of both sides and the witnesses at trial. It is often helpful to arrange for a copying firm to prepare the bundles as this relieves pressure on the office photocopier. In addition, the copying firm should bind the bundles which will give them a neat and professional look.

Checklist

1. Prepare the statement of special damages.
2. Carry out a provisional calculation of interest.
3. Calculate the impact of the rules on State benefits. If some are to be recovered by the State, remind the client accordingly.

4. Arrange for witness summonses to be served on all lay witnesses that you require.
5. Book counsel and prepare the brief in good time. Consider whether a conference is required.
6. Prepare the bundles for trial, in accordance with the new O 17 r 12 CCR.

Statement of special damages

(Case heading)

STATEMENT OF SPECIAL DAMAGES

1. Loss of earnings to medical retirement

Earnings prior to accident (See Appendix 1)	£100 pw (net)
Absent 3rd February 1990 – 2nd February 1991 when retired = 52 weeks	
Potential loss therefore	£5,200
Sick pay received (see Appendix 2)	£2,000
Loss is therefore	£3,200

2. Loss of earnings from medical retirement to trial (5.6.93)

(i) Loss 1st Feb 1991 – 5th April 1991

Should have earned £110 pw (net) × 9 weeks (see Appendix 3 for calculation based on comparable earners)	£990

(ii) Loss 6th April 1991 – 5th April 1992

Should have earned £150 (net) pw × 52 weeks (see Appendix 4)	£7,800

(iii) Loss 6th April 1992 – 5th April 1993

Should have earned £200 (net) pw × 52 weeks (see Appendix 5)	£10,400
Since 1st February 1993, the Plaintiff has been employed as a lift operator earning £150 net pw. Wages to 5th April are therefore 150 × 9 weeks =	£1,350
Loss is therefore	£9,050

3. Future loss of earnings

Plaintiff will suffer annual shortfall of £50 pw × 52 = £2600 Multiplier of 3 =	£7,800
TOTAL CLAIM FOR LOSS OF EARNINGS:	£21,820

4. Other items of special damage

Orthopaedic bed	£200
Painkillers	£50
TOTAL CLAIM FOR SPECIAL DAMAGES	£22,070

Chapter 15

The trial, appeals and costs

If the preparations listed in the previous chapters have been made, the actual trial should proceed relatively smoothly, allowing the solicitor time to concentrate on any last minute surprises and deal with them accordingly.

Shortly before the trial, it will probably be sensible to have a conference with counsel. This will be useful in that there are bound to be questions that the barrister instructed will have of the client. This will also be a good time to discuss any late offers made by the defendant. In addition, it will no doubt be helpful to the client to meet the barrister who will present the case before the day of the hearing (the disadvantage of this, of course, is that the client may well be more upset if the first choice barrister is forced to return the brief).

1. Trial day

On the day of the trial, the client should be asked to arrive at court in good time for the hearing. If he is unused to court proceedings, it is helpful to explain to him what he can expect to encounter in terms of the court layout, the order of witnesses and so on. He (and all witnesses to be called) should be given a copy of his statement to refresh his memory, but it should be emphasised that he will not be able to refer to this in the witness box.

Both sides should be ready at court to look into any last minute points that counsel raises. Remember that he or she will not be permitted to speak to any witnesses apart from the client, and may therefore need the solicitor to take some last minute supplementary statements.

It may be that an improved offer will be made before the trial starts. The traditional advice is to be very wary of such offers since there will be little saved by way of costs by settling at this very late stage. The client may well be mentally prepared and ready to give evidence. However, the risk of turning down a good offer in the heat of the moment is to be avoided. The situation should be explained to the client, and if it is a good offer, it should be recommended that he accept it.

A problem which frequently occurs in the county court is that last minute cases are inserted in the list. Often, these take up the best part of the morning and this can create time problems. In most county courts, if the case is not concluded within the time allotted to it, it will be adjourned to the next date on which the court has time. This may be several months in the future, when the case will obviously not be as fresh in the Judge's mind as it could have been. If it appears inevitable that the case will not finish in time, and a new date will not be available for some time, it is probably better to adjourn the case and start afresh another date. This is always upsetting for all parties, not least the client, but it is one of the problems of practising in the county court.

2. The trial

If the case does get on without problem, it will be opened by the plaintiff's barrister. He or she will tell the Judge what the case is about, and the nature of the evidence which will be called. He will take the Judge through relevant parts of the pleadings and the agreed bundle of documents.

The plaintiff will then be called. Traditionally, he will explain how the accident occurred, and the extent of his injuries. In the light of recent developments relating to the exchange of witness statements, there is an increasing tendency simply to read the plaintiff's statement in place of examination in chief. This should reduce the time spent in this part of the trial.

After the plaintiff has given his evidence, he will of course be cross-examined by counsel for the defendant. The same pattern of evidence will be applied to all of the plaintiff's witnesses. It is normal to deal with the witnesses as to liability first, and medical witnesses last. When the medical and engineering witnesses are called, the court will be referred to their reports which should be in the trial bundle.

Once the plaintiff's case has been closed, the defendant calls his witnesses, who give evidence and are cross-examined in the same way. At the end of his evidence, counsel for the defendant makes a closing speech. The plaintiff's counsel gets the last word in that he is allowed to sum up the plaintiff's case after the defendant's speech.

It is important to keep a full note of all the evidence which is given. This is never more important than when one's own counsel is dealing with a witness as he is unable to keep his own note at such times. However, a note should be kept at all times, as even when counsel is sitting down, his note will be concerned with detailing points for cross-examination in addition to keeping a note of the evidence. It will probably therefore not be totally complete.

After the case has been summed up in this way, the Judge will probably retire to consider his decision. When judgment is given, once again a full note should be kept so that an appeal can be properly considered.

3. Costs

The question of costs will be considered once judgment has been given. The normal approach is that costs follow the event, and the winner should therefore be awarded costs, to be taxed if not agreed.

As we saw in Chapter 2, however, special rules apply to legally aided litigants who may not be ordered to pay an amount other than one which is reasonable in the circumstances. This is often limited to the contribution which the Legal Aid Board has required of the litigant. If, however, there still seems to be doubt about the assisted person's means, it is possible to have the case adjourned so that the court can make its own enquiry.

If the assisted person was the plaintiff it should be remembered that a successful defendant may be able to claim his costs from the legal aid fund under s 18 of the Legal Aid Act 1988. Application should be made at the end of the trial for an appropriate order.

Normally, an unassisted plaintiff will not be entitled to claim any of his costs from the legal aid fund under s 18. However, if the legally aided defendant had included a counterclaim in his defence, the plaintiff will be regarded as a defendant to this part of the proceedings and it is possible to obtain an order for costs under s 18 for the expense of defending the counterclaim.

In addition, careful note should be made of the date on which an assisted party's legal aid certificate was granted, as the protection afforded under the Act applies only from this date. It is therefore possible to have an order for costs up to the date on which the certificate was granted. This principle was accepted by the Court of Appeal in the case of *Dugon* v *Williamson* [1964] Ch 59, [1963] 3 All ER 25, [1963] 3 WLR 477.

If there are two defendants and both are found liable, there will be no problem in making an order for costs against them. The position only becomes more complex if the plaintiff is successful against one defendant only. The starting point in such a situation is that if it was reasonable for the plaintiff to join both defendants, the unsuccessful defendant can be ordered to pay the successful defendant's costs. One common situation in which it is normally considered reasonable to add a second defendant is where the first defendant argues that another person was responsible for the accident.

If it is held that it was reasonable for the plaintiff to join both defendants, there are two basic mechanisms for making an appropriate order. The first is the so-called *Sanderson* order, after *Sanderson* v *Blyth Theatre Co* [1903] 2 KB 533, in which the unsuccessful defendant is ordered to pay the other defendant's costs direct. This tends to be used where the plaintiff is legally aided or financially incapable of paying the successful defendant.

The second mechanism is the *Bullock* order (after *Bullock* v *London General Omnibus Co* [1907] 1 KB 264), where the plaintiff is ordered to pay the successful defendant's costs himself. The plaintiff then includes these costs in his own claim for costs against the unsuccessful defendant.

4. Taxation

This is the process by which the court protects the unsuccessful party to litigation by scrutinising the winner's quantification of the costs due to him.

It is often possible to agree the costs and avoid the time and further expense of a taxation. If this is not possible, the bill of costs and supporting documentation should be filed with the county court. The allowable costs are determined according to the scales which relate to the amount recovered in the claim.

Drafting the bill of costs is a time-consuming and technical matter in which a detailed knowledge of the various rates and allowances is required. Most solicitors are happy to leave this task to a specialist costs draftsman who will normally charge a percentage of the total bill.

Once the bill has been prepared, a copy should be sent to the solicitors representing the loser. It is likely that at this stage a *Calderbank* offer will be made. This is an offer made "without prejudice save for the question of costs". The maker states a sum which he is prepared to pay. If less is awarded at the end of the taxation procedure, the taxing officer will be referred to the offer and will probably be persuaded to order that the costs of the taxation itself be paid by the winner.

5. Appeals

The most common appeals are to the county court Judge from the decision of a District Judge; and to the Court of Appeal from the decision of the county court Judge.

(a) Appeals from interlocutory decisions

These will be appeals from the District Judge to the county court Judge. It is important to note the extremely limited time for making the appeal — five days from the decision. In this time, the appeal must be filed and served on the opposite party.

In deciding whether the decision was indeed interlocutory, recourse should be had to O 59 r 1(A) RSC which sets out a list of decisions which will be regarded as final, and a further list of interlocutory decisions. A useful working definition contained in the order is that a decision will be regarded as final only if the entire cause or matter would have been finally determined whichever way the court below had decided the issues before it. Thus, for example, a decision striking out a claim will be regarded as interlocutory — *Hunt* v *Allied Bakeries Ltd* [1956] 3 All ER 513, [1956] 1 WLR 1326.

The appeal, when heard, will take the form of a complete rehearing of the point in dispute, except that it is for the appellant to open the appeal. The Judge will not be fettered in any way by the decision of the District Judge and will look at the issue afresh, hearing all the evidence, even if this was not put before the District Judge.

(b) Appeals from final decisions of the District Judge

The time limit for making an appeal from a final decision of a District Judge is extended to 14 days from the date of the judgment or order.

Under O 37 r 8(2), the court may stay execution under the judgment or order pending the appeal.

This type of appeal is dealt with in a very different way from an appeal from an interlocutory order. The appellant must show grounds, and the jurisdiction of the Judge is regarded as an appellate jurisdiction rather than a power simply to rehear the case. The Judge can only allow the appeal in circumstances in which the Court of Appeal could grant a new trial — *Devenish* v *PDI Homes (Hythe) Ltd* [1959] 3 All ER 843, [1959] 1 WLR 1188.

Under O 37 r 6, the county court Judge is empowered to:

- set aside or vary the judgment or order or any part thereof;
- give any other judgment or make any other order in substitution for the judgment or order appealed from;
- remit the action or matter or any other question therein to the District Judge for rehearing or further consideration;
- order a new trial to take place before himself or another Judge of the court on a day to be fixed.

(c) Appeals from the county court to the Court of Appeal

Appeals to the Court of Appeal are made either as of right or by leave. Under the County Court Appeals Order 1991 (SI 1991 No 1877) and the Supreme Court (Amendment) Rules 1991, leave will be required in the following cases:

(i) where the value of the claim or counterclaim does not exceed £5,000. The value is arrived at in the same way as that provided under the High Court and County Courts Jurisdiction Order 1991;

(ii) where the determination to be appealed from was made by a Judge acting in his appellate capacity.

Where leave is required, application may be made either to the court which made the decision, or to the Court of Appeal. However, under O 59 r 14(4) RSC application should be made to the court below unless there are special circumstances.

The appeal itself will be made by a notice of appeal which should be served on all parties affected by it within four weeks from the order or judgment (although this may be extended or abridged). The notice must contain the following information:

- the precise form of order which is sought from the Court of Appeal;
- a prescribed statement as to the notification of the date of the hearing;
- the grounds of appeal.

Once the appeal has been served on all the parties, it must be set down within seven days. Notice that the case has been set down should be given to all parties.

If the respondent to the appeal wishes himself to ask for an order varying the order of the court below, or affirming it on different grounds from those put forward by the Judge, (or if he wishes to make a cross appeal) there is provision for him to serve a notice known as a respondent's notice.

Once the appeal is set down, papers should be lodged for use by the court. Reference should be had to the Practice Statements found in the notes to O 59 in *The Supreme Court Practice* about matters such as the preparation of bundles, estimates of the length of hearing, notes of evidence and judgment, skeleton arguments and so on. On this latter point, it should be noted that a timetable for skeleton arguments has been introduced as from 1 June 1990, and that these should be filed with the court 14 days before the hearing.

The Court of Appeal is empowered to affirm, set aside or vary the order of the court below. In addition, it can order a new trial. The grounds upon which it can do the latter are listed in *The Supreme Court Practice,* and include, for example:

- misdirection, where a substantial wrong or miscarriage has been thereby occasioned;
- improperly admitting or rejecting evidence, where some substantial wrong or miscarriage has been thereby occasioned;
- discovery of fresh evidence;
- irregularity in the trial.

Checklist

1. Arrive in good time for a pre-hearing conference.
2. Take a good note of all evidence and the judgment.
3. Costs — consider making application for costs against legal aid fund if legally aided opponent is unsuccessful.
4. Protection of legally aided party is only effective from the date on which his certificate was granted.
5. If there are two defendants and one successfully defends, plaintiff should be prepared to show why it was reasonable to join the successful defendant.
6. Taxation — have a bill of costs prepared by specialist draftsman. Consider use of *Calderbank* offer.
7. Appeals — note time limits:
   5 days from interlocutory decision of District Judge
   14 days from final decision of District Judge
   28 days from county court Judge — leave required in certain cases.

Successful negotiating — some practical tips

Only a tiny minority of personal injury actions find their way to court. In most cases, the outcome so far as liability is concerned is clear, and the only question between the parties will relate to how much the plaintiff should receive.

The key to successful negotiating lies in a realistic appraisal of all the aspects of the case. In the light of the new developments on the use of witness statements, it is quite feasible for each side to have a realistic idea of the strength of its case long before trial. Once the chances of success have been appraised, it is for the client to decide how he wishes negotiations to proceed. Obviously, if the case is hopeless, he should be advised accordingly and a notice of discontinuance filed. In less clear cut cases, many clients prefer to settle for an amount considerably less than that which they would receive on the basis of full liability. There can be no absolute rule as to how to negotiate in such cases, but it is important that the client is given a realistic assessment of his chances and is able to make his decision on a fully informed basis.

In a strong case, one should remember that by settling, the opponent will save himself the cost of a trial. It is all too easy to develop the attitude that all settlements should be at a rate less than that which the plaintiff could hope to achieve — the so called 'litigation risk' approach. Whilst this is appropriate in a case which is marginal, it is unfair to the client where the case is strong.

There are four stages at which cases tend to settle — before proceedings are issued; on service of pleadings; shortly before trial; and at the door of the court.

Settling before proceedings are issued: In this situation, negotiations may well be carried out between the plaintiff's solicitor and the local claims inspector for the insurance company concerned. He or she will visit the solicitor without the client being present. There will then be a frank discussion of the case on both sides, which will normally lead to an offer being put forward.

There is often some juggling about who makes the first offer. This is important as it defines a lower or upper parameter, depending on who goes first. Traditionally, the plaintiff's solicitor will insist that the insurer makes the first offer, on the basis that it is the defendant who wants to settle the case.

If it is possible to come to an agreement on the award, the plaintiff's solicitor will need to take instructions before committing his client. It is wise to send a letter to the insurer confirming the terms of the offer and indicating that instructions are being sought.

It is vitally important when settling a case in this way that the question of costs is dealt with. When proceedings have been issued, it is always possible to ask the court to tax the plaintiff's bill of costs if agreement proves impossible, but where there are no court proceedings, costs must be agreed as part of the settlement.

Settling after proceedings have been issued: In this instance, negotiations will normally be between the solicitors for each side. As more becomes known about the case, so the incentive to settle on the part of the party likely to lose increases, and the offers tend to increase in generosity. In such a situation, one should bear in mind that there is always something to be said for allowing the case to be settled at the earliest possible stage. If, however, the offers are likely to be more generous closer to trial, the tactic should really be to get the case to such a stage as quickly as possible.

If the case is settled, a consent order setting out the terms of the settlement should be drafted and approved by the District Judge. To make absolutely sure, the court office should also be informed that the case has been settled and the court should be asked to remove it from the list.

PART II:

THE ASSESSMENT OF DAMAGES

Chapter 16

Planning the claim

1. Setting a target

An action for damages for personal injuries should be dominated by one question from the initial interview to the last day of trial: how much is this claim worth? The correct answer to that question is the best guide to strategy. The award the plaintiff can reasonably expect will decide the forum. It will also decide how much it is sensible to invest in the case. Is it worthwhile instructing an expert? Does the case really merit two doctors' opinions, or will one do? Should the plaintiff open negotiations? How should the plaintiff react to a payment into court? And so on.

A case should never be launched without a clear target in mind. What, if I establish that the defendant was entirely responsible for this accident, do I expect to recover?

2. Jurisdiction

Under the new scheme for the distribution of business between the High Court and the county courts introduced from 1 July 1991 by the High Court and County Courts Jurisdiction Order 1991 (SI 1991/724) the value of a claim will determine the forum. In general all personal injury actions will be heard in the county court unless the value of the claim is £50,000 or more.

3. Valuing a claim

According to Article 9 of the Order, the value of a claim is 'the amount which the plaintiff reasonably expects to recover'. This ignores:

- contributory negligence, unless admitted by the plaintiff;
- where a claim for provisional damages is made, the possibility of a further application in the future;
- payments to be made to the Compensation Recovery Unit under Part IV of the Social Security Administration Act 1992;
- interest;
- costs.

4. Classification of damages

Damages in a personal injury action fall into four broad categories:

- general damages;
- special damages;
- damages for disability on the open labour market, generally known as *Smith* v *Manchester* damages;
- provisional damages.

Practitioners use these categories to give structure to their discussions. The categories also determine the rate at which interest will be awarded on the damages which fall under each head.

Special damages traditionally represent pecuniary loss, and general damages non-pecuniary loss. In *Daly* v *General Steam Navigation Co Ltd* [1981] 1 WLR 120, [1980] 3 All ER 696, however, Ormrod LJ said that special damage:

> '...represents "actual" as opposed to "estimated" loss. So far as general damage is concerned, that loss necessarily has to be estimated.'

Whatever the legal theory behind the distinction, it is better to regard as special damage those items of loss that a county court Judge would expect to find in the plaintiff's statement of special damage.

5. General damages

In a personal injury action general damages are what the Judge awards to compensate the plaintiff for pain, suffering and loss of amenity. Although damages for pain, for suffering and for loss of amenity fall into three distinct sub-categories, very few awards make any distinction in practice. The sub-categories are useful, however, for identifying the factors a Judge may be invited to take into account.

The award is said to be conventional. Pain, suffering and loss of amenity cannot be measured in money, but the courts aim for consistency. In *Wright* v *British Railways Board* [1983] 2 AC 773 at 777C, [1983] 2 All ER 698 at 699j Lord Diplock said:

> 'Such loss is not susceptible of measurement in money. Any figure at which the assessor of damages arrives cannot be other than artificial and, if the aim is that justice meted out to all litigants should be even-handed instead of depending on the idiosyncrasies of the assessor...the figure must be "basically a conventional figure derived from experience and from awards in comparable cases".'

(a) Pain

'Pain' has its normal meaning. According to Lord Scarman in *Lim Poh Choo* v *Camden and Islington Area Health Authority* [1980] AC 174 at 188G, [1979] 2 All ER 910 at 919a, the award for pain and suffering depends on:

'...the plaintiff's personal awareness of pain, her capacity for suffering.'

If the plaintiff is knocked permanently unconscious in the accident, he will recover nothing for pain. The same is true where the plaintiff dies within a few seconds of the beginning of the sequence of events which leads to his death: *Hicks and others* v *Chief Constable of the South Yorkshire Police* [1991] 1 All ER 690 (CA), [1992] 2 All ER 65 (HL). On the other hand, if he survives the accident for a few hours, his estate will recover for those few hours' pain.

The claim for damages for pain must be based on evidence. The plaintiff must give evidence in court of the nature and severity of the pain he has suffered or is suffering; on this point a doctor's evidence alone is not enough. If the plaintiff is incapable of giving evidence, but suffered pain before he became incapable, witnesses can give evidence of behaviour — screaming, for example — from which pain can be inferred.

(b) Suffering

'Suffering' refers to the other mental consequences of physical injury: a man may be tortured by the fear that he will become progressively more disabled, for example, while a young woman may be deeply embarrassed by scars on her legs.

This term does not include all the unpleasant consequences of injury. Damages are awarded for:

- shock '...not in the sense of a mental reaction but in a medical sense as the equivalent of nervous shock': Devlin J in *Behrens & Behrens* v *Bertram Mills Circus Ltd* [1957] 2 QB 1, [1957] 1 All ER 583. Nervous shock is a broad term; it includes both the physical effects of shock and the long-term psychological consequences, generally known as post-traumatic stress disorder;
- distress. In *Jefferson* v *Cape Insulation Ltd* [1982] CLY 835 the plaintiff recovered for the knowledge that death would soon part her from her children. In *Rourke* v *Barton* [1982] CLY 793, an injured woman recovered for the distress she had suffered owing to her inability to care for her husband, who was terminally ill at the time of her accident;
- embarrassment;
- suffering caused by the knowledge that the plaintiff's expectation of life has been reduced: s 1(1)(b) Administration of Justice Act 1982.

Damages are not awarded for:

- shock, in the popular sense, or shaking up: *Nicholls* v *Rushton* [1992] CLY 3252;

- grief: *Alcock* v *Chief Constable of South Yorkshire Police* [1991] 3 WLR 1057;
- loss of expectation of life: s 1(1)(a) Administration of Justice Act 1982.

Wherever the plaintiff is trying to establish a claim for suffering, he must give evidence about the cause. Where the claim is based on shock, or on suffering caused by the knowledge that the plaintiff's expectation of life has been reduced, medical evidence will be needed to prove the shock or the reduced expectation.

(c) Loss of amenity

'Loss of amenity' is loss of the enjoyment of life. A blind woman cannot see her children. A man who loses a leg can no longer take walking holidays in Scotland. A man whose back is injured finds sexual intercourse painful and his marriage begins to drift as a result. Unlike the award for pain and suffering, which is subjective, based on the plaintiff's own pain and suffering, the award for loss of amenity is objective, made wherever there has in fact been a loss of amenity, whether or not the plaintiff is aware of it: *Lim Poh Choo* v *Camden and Islington Area Health Authority* [1980] AC 174, [1979] 2 All ER 910.

Loss of amenity is often neglected by plaintiffs or supported only by the thinnest evidence. If, for example, a young man can no longer play the competitive rugby that used to be his main recreation before the accident, he should certainly give evidence himself of the pleasure he has lost, but he should also call other players to confirm that he played regularly and well.

6. Special damage

Defined as including those items of loss that a county court Judge would expect to find in the plaintiff's statement of special damage, this is a very wide category, ranging from the cost of replacing a pair of trousers torn in the accident to the cost of constant nursing care for the next 25 years. In all but the most trivial cases it represents the largest element in the overall award.

Special damages compensate the plaintiff for two types of loss: the money he has spent (or will spend) in meeting expenses caused by his accident, and the money that he has lost (or will lose) as a result of his accident. Past loss must be calculated precisely. Future loss has to be estimated as accurately as possible.

The cost of being involved in an accident can be high, and might include:

- the cost of replacing or repairing property damaged in the accident;
- the cost of medical treatment;
- the cost of travelling to and from hospital or to consult specialists;
- the cost of altering the plaintiff's house so that he can remain at home even though he is now confined to a wheelchair.

Those costs fall on the plaintiff just at the time when his income might be reduced as the result of:

- total loss of wages through inability to work at all;
- partial loss of wages through inability to work overtime, or at heavy manual labour, or on jobs which attract a bonus;
- loss of promotion prospects;
- loss of pension rights.

7. Damages for disability on the open labour market

If a plaintiff is unemployed when his case comes to trial, or secure in a job, but earning less than he would have been had he not been injured, the assessment of his future loss is straightforward. His damages must be calculated to represent the wages he will lose from the date of trial to the date on which he will return to his pre-accident work or to work paying as much as his pre-accident job, or (if he will never earn as much again) to the date on which he would have retired in the normal course of events.

Where, however, the plaintiff is a valued or long-standing employee, many employers will keep him on at his full pre-accident salary, even though they have to make some allowance for his disability. Though secure for the moment, an employee in this position is vulnerable: if his employers change their mind, or their financial position worsens, and they dismiss him, he is likely to experience greater difficulty in finding work than an able-bodied person of similar age, qualifications and experience.

To compensate the plaintiff for his disability on the open labour market, the court awards a lump sum. Sometimes this can be calculated to represent a genuine estimate of the loss the plaintiff is likely to suffer should he become unemployed, but very often it is little more than an intelligent guess. The leading case on this point is *Smith* v *Manchester Corporation* (1974) 17 KIR 1 — hence the expression '*Smith* v *Manchester* damages'.

8. Provisional damages

A young woman, on the threshold of a medical career with every prospect of high earnings, suffers an eye injury. Prompt treatment limits the damage to a small area of blindness, which will be a major inconvenience but will not prevent her from pursuing her career: according to the medical evidence, however, she runs a ten per cent risk of losing her sight altogether, though if at the end of the next five years her sight is no worse, that risk will have fallen to one per cent.

Here the plaintiff is clearly entitled to damages for the injury she has sustained. Compensation for her present disability is easy to assess: but how can the plaintiff be compensated for the risk of losing her sight altogether?

137

To award damages on the basis that the plaintiff will go blind would clearly be absurd, since she is much more likely to keep her sight. On the other hand, to award even ten per cent of the damages appropriate to total blindness would be unjust; for if the worst does happen, the plaintiff will be severely disabled, will be unable to continue practising her profession and will suffer perhaps 30 years' partial loss of earnings. Since 1985 the courts have been able to overcome this problem by making an award of provisional damages: the plaintiff is compensated for his present disability on the assumption that the worst will not happen, but is given the chance to return to court for a further award if it does.

9. The unborn and the dead

Under the Congenital Disabilities (Civil Liability) Act 1976 a child born disabled as a result of injuries sustained in the womb has an action against anyone but the mother in respect of disability caused by an occurrence which:

- affected either parent in his or her ability to have a normal, healthy child; or
- affected the mother during her pregnancy, or affected her or the child in the course of its birth, so that the child was born with disabilities which would not otherwise have been present.

On the other hand, a child has no claim for pain and suffering caused by a failure to abort the foetus: *McKay* v *Essex Area Health Authority* [1982] QB 1166, [1982] 2 All ER 771.

Under the Law Reform (Miscellaneous Provisions) Act 1934 the deceased's estate can sue for damages in respect of any injury sustained by the deceased. The estate cannot recover damages representing income that the deceased would have earned in the period after his death. His dependants' rights under the Fatal Accidents Act 1976 fall outside the scope of this book. See *Fatal Accident Claims* (Fourmat Publishing, 1993) by Mary Duncan and Christine Marsh.

Chapter 17

Assessing general damages

1. Defining the problem

The assessment of general damages for pain, suffering and loss of amenity is in theory a question of fact, not law. Until very recently a few old-fashioned Judges refused to allow advocates to cite authority in support of their submissions on the appropriate level of general damages — or indeed to put a figure on their clients' injuries. Since 1954, however, when Kemp and Kemp first published *The Quantum of Damages in Personal Injury and Fatal Accident Claims*, the practice has developed of putting forward a figure and supporting it with comparable cases. This practice is now universal.

2. Marshalling the evidence

A court can be asked to assess general damages only on the basis of evidence. In part this will be the plaintiff's own evidence about the pain he has been suffering, the disability he is experiencing, the ways in which he now finds his job more difficult than it was before the accident, the extent to which his social life has been curtailed. In the most trivial cases this will be the only evidence. In the vast majority, however, medical evidence will be required.

If the medical expert has been chosen well, his report will set out:

- the injuries sustained by the plaintiff;
- the immediate effect of those injuries;
- the treatment given to the plaintiff;
- the plaintiff's present level of disability, based both on his own complaints and on a clinical examination;
- unless it is entirely obvious, whether he considers the injuries are consistent with the accident described by the plaintiff;
- if the plaintiff has been off work, whether he considers the period of absence reasonable;
- if the plaintiff is still off work, when he considers the plaintiff will be fit to return;
- if the plaintiff will never be able to return to the work he was doing before the accident, the kind of job he will be able to do;
- the long-term consequences of the injuries;
- if there is a risk of some later complication — osteo-arthritis, for

example, in the case of a fracture — a percentage evaluation of the risk and an indication of the time within which it can be expected to occur.

These are all points on which the Judge will call for submissions in due course, and every submission must be based on evidence. A doctor who writes reports regularly for use in court will be well aware of the lawyers' requirements. Very often, however, the report fails to deal with a vital point, or fails to separate points which from the lawyers', if not the doctors', point of view give rise to separate questions.

Before doing anything, therefore, the legal practitioner should make sure that the report deals with every one of the points listed above. The simplest way to be sure is to write a summary of the report, using those headings. However complex the case, it should be possible to restrict the summary to a single sheet of paper; in most cases one paragraph should be enough. Where more than one doctor has reported, it will save time later if the source of each piece of information is indicated in the summary.

Medical expertise is expensive. Asking a doctor to deal with points he should have included in his original report is a waste of costs. This illustrates the importance of choosing the most appropriate expert in the first place. Those who write medico-legal reports regularly command high fees and often have waiting-lists as impressive as their fees; in most cases both the initial expense and the wait will prove worthwhile.

The doctor who has treated the plaintiff should in all but the most straightforward cases be regarded as the last resort. As the doctor responsible for the plaintiff's progress, he has a personal interest in reporting a good recovery.

3. Sources of information

Once the medical evidence has been assembled, the practitioner can then set about his assessment of the appropriate damages. There are two stages to this process: finding the bracket and choosing the figure.

There are six main sources of information about the level of awards being made for personal injury. The starting-point is *Kemp*. This book, now in three loose-leaf volumes and regularly updated, sets out awards under twelve headings:

A: injuries of maximum severity;
B: multiple injuries;
C: head;
D: senses;
E: spine;
F: internal organs;
G: sacrum, pelvis and hip;
H: upper limbs;
I: lower limbs;
J: skin;
K: minor injuries;
L: miscellaneous conditions.

Each section contains a table of the awards in that section giving the plaintiff's name, the reference in *Kemp*, the date of the award, the court which made it, the total award, the award made for pain, suffering and loss of amenity, and the award for pain, suffering and loss of amenity increased to take account of inflation between the date on which it was made and the date of the latest release of *Kemp*. The bulk of each section is devoted to the headnotes of a series of cases dealing with injuries of the same kind, and each section concludes with extracts from the judgments in the most significant cases.

The order of the cases, both in the table and the headnotes, is determined by the size of the award for pain, suffering and loss of amenity increased to take account of inflation: the biggest comes first. In all, the cases occupy the best part of two of the three volumes.

Butterworth's Personal Injury Litigation Service (*'PILS'*), first published in 1988 and edited by Goldrein and de Haas, also in three loose-leaf volumes, has two short sections reporting awards for personal injury. Division IX contains short case summaries grouped under classifications rather different from those used by *Kemp*:

- death;
- brain;
- multiple injuries;
- internal injuries;
- burns and scars;
- head;
- neck and shoulders;
- back and trunk;
- arms and hands;
- legs and feet;
- spinal injuries;
- miscellaneous;
- provisional damages awards.

Division X reproduces extracts from the judgments in important cases.

In each section the cases are set out in ascending order of magnitude. The figure comes first, marked either 'Total damages' or 'General damages'. Where the figure is for 'Total Damages', care must be taken to deduct the figure for special damages (which is given in the report) before using the case for the assessment of general damages. The awards are not updated for inflation.

Current Law, which appears monthly and is replaced at the end of each year by the *Current Law Yearbook*, contains in the section headed 'Damages' brief reports, usually contributed by a solicitor or barrister involved in the case, of decisions on quantum. These are grouped according to the classification adopted by *Kemp*. Although the reports are much briefer than those in *Kemp* or *PILS*, they are still useful, particularly for minor injuries.

Sweet & Maxwell publish a series of specialist reports, the *Personal Injuries and Quantum Reports*, which appear four times a year.

In addition to books, practitioners with access to *Lawtel* can find quantum reports under the *Decisions* heading.

Traditionally practitioners arrived at both the bracket and the figure by searching through *Kemp*, *Current Law* and, more recently, *PILS* to find cases involving injuries roughly comparable with their client's. An advocate whose client had sustained an injury to, say, his elbow would look at a number of cases involving elbow injuries to discover the range of awards made for injuries of this kind; that was the bracket. He would then look for one or more reported cases involving injuries as similar to his client's as possible and (provided that these injuries appeared to be of a similar level of severity to his client's — or, more commonly, that the injuries of his client fell between two cases, one of which was slightly more serious, the other slightly less serious) adopt those as the basis of the figure he would put forward as the appropriate award for his client.

At the end of 1991, however, the Civil and Family Committee of the Judicial Studies Board published its *Guidelines for the Assessment of Damages in Personal Injury Cases*. The second edition appeared in October 1994. Classified by the part of the body that has been injured, these guidelines attempt to lay down the bracket appropriate for each type of injury, ranging from the most minor to the most serious.

For example, Section G — 'Injuries to the elbow' — identifies three brackets:

'a. A Severely Disabling Injury
£16,000 to £21,500
b. Less Severe Injuries
£7,500 to £13,000
These injuries lead to impairment of function but do not involve major surgery or significant disability.
c. Moderate or Minor Injury
Up to £5,000
Most elbow injuries fall into this category. They comprise a simple fracture, tennis elbow syndrome and lacerations; i.e.those injuries which cause no permanent damage and do not result in any permanent impairment of function.'

Quite how these guidelines will be used in practice is not yet clear. Although based on an analysis of cases decided between 1981 and 1994, they have undoubtedly supplanted decided cases as the authority for the bracket in a given case: county court Judges no longer want to be referred to *Kemp* in deciding what the appropriate bracket should be. Even when he has decided on the appropriate bracket, however, a Judge must still decide where in that bracket a particular case falls: is a man with a 'less severe' elbow injury entitled to £7,500 or to £13,000? Here the practice varies from Judge to Judge. Some still welcome guidance from the cases, whilst others do not. Paragraph 4 of the introduction to the first edition of the *Guidelines* gave a broad hint that the Board hopes that advocates will not be so ready to cite cases in future:

'Counsel may continue to cite awards thought by them to be appropriate, but we hope that the qualifications and explanations of the brackets which we have extracted from our comprehensive analysis will assist the judge who is assessing damages to put any cited case into its proper context.'

The Criminal Injuries Compensation Board publishes its own guidelines. These used to provide a useful comparison, but in civil cases at least they have been superseded by the Judicial Studies Board's *Guidelines*.

4. Identifying the relevant factors

Far and away the most important factor in determining the level of award is the long-term consequences of the injury. A teenage boy may suffer multiple fractures severe enough to need surgery but, because he is young, fit and still growing, make a complete recovery. On the other hand, a woman in late middle-age who suffers an uncomplicated fracture, which needs nothing more than a plaster splint, may well find that even when her fracture has united she is left with impaired mobility and discomfort which will be with her for the rest of her life. It is a serious mistake to look just at the injuries: the more important factor is the level of pain and disability that the plaintiff is likely to experience in the future.

For any given level of permanent pain and discomfort, the younger the plaintiff the greater the damages he will recover; this rule reflects the grim actuarial truth that the older plaintiff is likely to suffer pain for a shorter period. That is not to say, however, that a younger person will recover more as a matter of course. If a woman of 30 and a woman of 70 both suffer a fracture which leaves them with a stiff and occasionally painful ankle, the effect on the older woman's life may well be the greater. The older woman may find that her mobility, her social life, even her ability to live alone are all destroyed, while the younger woman, being fitter and more adaptable, finds that she can cope with something that is little more than an annoyance. In every case the practitioner has to look at the particular consequences to the particular plaintiff of the particular accident.

All accidents are painful and most treatment is unpleasant. Where the pain was exceptional — for example, a plaintiff trapped in an accident may have suffered agony for several hours until released — or the plaintiff has had to undergo extensive surgery, those will be factors justifying an increase in the award of damages above normal.

Do not ignore functional overlay. Symptoms that are attributable to an organic cause attract a full award; symptoms that are the product of malingering attract nothing. In between, however, are those symptoms which cannot be ascribed to any organic cause but are nevertheless genuinely experienced by the patient. This, often called functional overlay, is very common. Provided that the plaintiff can establish that the symptoms are genuine, he will recover damages in respect of them.

Other terms for the same or closely related problems are post-traumatic syndrome, anxiety neurosis or (occasionally) compensationitis. Whatever the name, the principle is the same.

An extreme example of a case of this kind is *James* v *Woodall Duckham Construction Co Ltd* [1969] 1 WLR 903, [1969] 2 All ER 794. Mr James was physically fit to return to work three months after his injury, but was prevented by an anxiety neurosis for which there was no discernible physical cause. The medical evidence suggested that the neurosis, though genuine, would vanish once the claim for damages had been settled. The Court of Appeal accepted that Mr James was entitled to damages for loss of earnings in the meantime.

In cases of this kind a Judge often faces a conflict of evidence between the plaintiff's doctor, who diagnoses functional overlay, and the defendant's, who sees malingering. Faced with such a conflict, the Judge will tend to make up his own mind on the basis of the impression given by the plaintiff in the witness-box. Defendants, on the other hand, are increasingly employing private investigators to follow claimants whom they suspect of malingering. A minute's film of the plaintiff engaged in something he claims to be impossible is worth an hour's cross-examination.

5. Reaching a figure

For the moment at least, practitioners should use (a) the Judicial Studies Board's *Guidelines* to identify the appropriate range, and (b) decided cases to put a figure on their client's damages. Once a summary of the medical reports has been prepared, the category into which the plaintiff's injuries fall should be obvious.

Armed with that range, the lawyer should then turn to the table at the front of the appropriate section of *Kemp* and, looking at the column which lists the awards of general damages updated for inflation, make a note of the references of cases which fall within that range. He should then turn to the headnotes of those cases and find the one or two closest to his client's.

If the practitioner intends to cite a case from *Kemp* or *PILS* in court, he should always take a photocopy for the Judge; most county courts do not have these books. His opponent will appreciate a copy, too.

6. The special case of multiple injuries

Multiple injuries can be difficult to assess. The term can be applied to a crippling combination of two or three major injuries, or to a dozen or so minor injuries which, though each is trivial on its own, are in combination at least temporarily disabling. The Judicial Studies Board does not suggest guidelines for multiple injuries, so practitioners will have to continue using the traditional method of looking solely at comparable cases.

If a man loses his left eye, his left forearm and now despite treatment has a left leg two centimetres shorter than his right, he has three permanent injuries and his advisers will have to try to find a case which is directly comparable. They cannot, of course, simply add the damages appropriate to each of the three injuries.

In the great majority of cases, however, by the time the plaintiff is recovering from his injuries it will have become clear that one of the injuries is going to have much more serious permanent effects than any of the others. In such cases that injury can be used as the lead injury in determining the appropriate bracket, though the final figure will have to take into account the other injuries. This approach was recognised by the Judicial Studies Board itself in the first edition of its *Guidelines*:

> 'We have not endeavoured to put figures on "multiple injuries". It is usually the case that one element is identified as dominant and the award is so based. The subsidiary elements may, of course, merit additional damages but in such cases there is no substitute for the judge's own analysis of the evidence as it affects the individual claimant.'

7. Inflation

Inflation causes a steady increase in the level of general damages. Damages are always assessed at the level appropriate to the date of trial, not the date of the accident, even where many years have passed.

At the beginning of volume 2, *Kemp* provides a table of factors which can be used to inflate past awards to the present level. For each year since 1948 the table gives the figure which must be used to raise £1 in the January of that year to its value in the December of the last year given: thus if inflation was running at four per cent a year in the last year for which the table gives a figure, the figure for that year will be 1.04. The table is updated annually, to the December of the previous year.

Use of the table produces an approximate result. If an advocate presenting a case in November 1992 cites a case decided in December 1986, he will use a multiplier which raises January 1986 awards to the December 1991 level. That gives credit to which his client is not entitled for inflation between January and November 1986, but equally denies his client credit for inflation between January and November 1992. At present levels of inflation this is accurate enough, but for much of the year the column of awards updated for inflation at the beginning of each section in *Kemp* will in fact be more accurate.

The Judicial Studies Board will reissue its *Guidelines* to take account of inflation. It is aiming to do this once a year.

8. The fixed points

It is very helpful to make a mental note of the maximum awards which will be made for certain kinds of injury. These are not guidelines, but they help to put a scale on the map of general damages. They also give a very broad indication of the class of case likely to be heard in the county court:

- maximum award: £125,000
- worst brain damage: £100,000+
- total blindness: £90,000
- total loss of sexual function: £60,000
- colostomy: £55,000
- amputation of arm at elbow: £40,000
- worst knee injury: £37,000
- very bad ankle injury: £25,000
- wrist injury with permanent pain and stiffness: £10,000
- frozen shoulder lasting two years: £5,000
- dislocated thumb: £2,000
- loss of a front tooth: £1,250.

9. An example

The medical report ends as follows:

'SUMMARY
In a motorbike accident this 19-year-old sustained:

(1) a minimally displaced fracture of the right radius;
(2) a fracture of the right patella.

(1) was treated by reduction under general anaesthetic followed by immobilisation in a plaster splint, which was maintained for twelve weeks. (2) required fixation and partial patellectomy. The metalwork was removed under general anaesthetic three months later. He was on crutches for eight weeks.

The patient has made a complete recovery from the injury to his wrist. He is left with a surgical scar, 2 cm x 1 cm, over his right patella. The patient can squat only with difficulty and experiences aching after prolonged walking, driving or heavy lifting.

I have no doubt that by the time he reaches middle age he will have begun to suffer degenerative changes leading to increasing pain, discomfort and stiffness. There is a risk — which I put at 50 per cent — that further surgery will be required.

The patient was off work for 18 weeks. I regard this as entirely reasonable. I should not expect him to require further time off work unless further surgery is required; rehabilitation in that case could take three to six months.'

Although this is a case of multiple injuries, the injury to the leg is so much the more serious that it will undoubtedly determine the bracket. The starting-point is to decide into which of the categories suggested by the Judicial Studies Board this case falls. At first sight there are two candidates:

146

'(ii) A claim may be brought within this bracket by reason of such factors as significant damage to a joint or ligaments including instability, prolonged treatment or a lengthy period non-weightbearing, substantial and unsightly scarring, the likelihood of arthrodesis to the hip, the near certainty of arthritis setting in, the gross restriction of walking capacity and the need for hip replacement. A combination of such factors would be necessary to justify such an award. £16,000 to £22,500

(iii) This level of award still applies to relatively serious injuries, including severe, complicated or multiple fractures. The position of an award within this bracket will be influenced by the period of time off work and by the presence or risk of degenerative changes, imperfect union of fractures, muscle wasting, limited join movements, instability of the knee, unsightly scarring and permanent increased vulnerability to damage. £11,500 to £16,000.'

The plaintiff's case exhibits 'the near certainty of arthritis setting in' but a two-centimetre scar on a man's leg cannot be described as 'substantial and unsightly' and none of the other aggravating factors set out in (ii) is present. Since a case will fall into (ii) only where 'a combination of such factors' is present, the proper category is (iii).

The section dealing with knee injuries in *Kemp* is I2(v). A range of £11,500 to £16,000 covers around five cases. Of those the closest to this plaintiff's case is *Daniel* v *Platt* (1989) at I2–412. Mr Daniel was seventeen at the date of his accident. He sustained a fracture of the right wrist and left patella. The wrist was immobilised in plaster for one month and made a complete recovery. The kneecap was fixed and partially excised. The plaintiff underwent physiotherapy and rehabilitation; he was left with a noticeable surgical scar, audible crepitation on squatting, post-traumatic changes to the articulating surfaces and a 'real possibility' of further degeneration. If the degeneration were to occur, Mr Daniel would need further surgery, requiring a week in hospital and three months off work. Although there are minor differences between Mr Daniel's case and our plaintiff's, the cases are close enough for this to be a good guide.

In 1989 Farquharson J awarded £11,000 in general damages. The table of awards updates this to £14,190; the appropriate figure is therefore £14,000. (Incidentally, use of the inflation table would produce the slightly different figure of £14,080.)

10. Pre-existing disability

The general rule is, of course, that a tortfeasor has to take his victim as he finds him. Thus if the victim is already suffering from a disability which makes the effects of the tortious injury much worse for him than they would have been for an able-bodied person, the tortfeasor is liable for all the harm he has done.

The converse is also true. If the victim is already suffering from a disability which would have caused him pain and suffering in any event, the tortfeasor will not be liable even if his tort is the precipitating cause. Thus in *Cutler* v *Vauxhall Motors Ltd* [1971] 1 QB 418 the Court of Appeal refused to allow a claim for loss of earnings sustained while the plaintiff was in hospital undergoing treatment: although the defendants' tort had dictated the date of the treatment, the plaintiff's medical condition before the accident was such that he would have needed the treatment (and so would have lost the earnings) sooner or later even if the accident had not occurred.

Acceleration of a pre-existing disability presents a slightly different problem. The commonest example is that of a middle-aged person who suffers a whiplash injury. At the date of the accident degenerative changes were already well established in his neck but had produced no symptoms; as a result of the accident the plaintiff has symptoms which are likely to prove permanent. The medical evidence suggests that the accident has accelerated the onset of symptoms by (say) five years: in such a case the plaintiff will be entitled to compensation not for his present symptoms, which would have appeared eventually even if the accident had not occurred, but for the five years' pain-free life that he has lost.

11. Loss of amenity as a separate head

In most cases the claim for loss of amenity will be indistinguishable from the claim for pain and suffering. A young man breaks his leg: his inability to return to the rugby that was his principal recreation before the accident is an important factor which will tend to push his award further up the range of damages appropriate to his particular physical injury, but will not in itself merit a separate award or take the plaintiff's award into a higher category altogether. Loss of amenity is a broad term, however, and does include four heads of loss which effectively stand alone.

- Loss of job satisfaction;
- Loss of leisure;
- Loss of holiday;
- Loss of housekeeping ability.

(a) Loss of job satisfaction

A craftsman turned by his injuries into a machine-minder may well suffer no loss of earnings, but still feel that he has lost the main reason for going to work. The courts do award damages for loss of congenial employment, job satisfaction, or status, but the sums are small. Awards above £5,000 are rare and are generally much less.

Awards under this head can be difficult to trace, since the decisions are rarely reported. The best source is the table provided by *Kemp* at pp 5–251. Two decisions of the Court of Appeal which have been reported are *Morris* v *Johnson Matthey & Co Ltd* (1967) 112 Sol Jo 32, in which the court allowed a claim for the loss of pride which a craftsman had felt in the exercise of his craft, and *Hearnshaw* v *English Steel Corporation* (1971) 11 KIR 306, in which before the accident the plaintiff had been a skilled machine operator, but was now capable only of boring, unskilled work.

(b) Loss of leisure

If the plaintiff's working capacity is reduced so that he has to work longer hours to earn the same money, he can recover damages to compensate for the loss of his leisure: *Hearnshaw* v *English Steel Corporation* (above). Here, too, awards are small.

(c) Loss of holiday

If the plaintiff loses the enjoyment of a holiday as a result of the accident, he has a claim for general damages for loss of amenity. This applies whether the plaintiff was on holiday when the accident occurred (*Ichard* v *Frangoulis* [1977] 1 WLR 556, [1977] 2 All ER 461) or went on holiday afterwards (*Marson* v *Hall* [1983]CLY 1046). In the latter case Webster J held that the measure of damage is based not on the cost of the holiday but on the difference in value between the holiday the plaintiff would have enjoyed had he not been injured and the holiday he has in fact enjoyed.

(d) Loss of housekeeping ability

If the plaintiff's ability to perform the normal household chores of everyday life is reduced by his injuries, he has a claim for damages. A claim of this kind may be made in respect of the period between the date of the accident and the date of the trial, or in respect of the period after the date of trial (or, of course, both).

The Court of Appeal considered claims of this kind in *Daly* v *General Steam Navigation Co Ltd* [1981] 1 WLR 120 [1980] 3 All ER 696. It held as follows:

- If the plaintiff needs help with household tasks, and by the date of the trial has already employed someone to do the work that he can no longer do himself, he can recover the cost of employing that help. This is a straightforward claim for special damages.
- If the plaintiff needs help with household tasks, but at the date of the trial is struggling on without, he has instead a claim for general damages for loss of amenity. The measure of these damages is not necessarily the cost of employing someone else to do the work.
- If the plaintiff will need help with household tasks in the future, he has a claim for general damages for loss of amenity. The measure of these damages is the cost of employing someone else to do the work that he can no longer do himself; whether he in fact intends to employ someone is irrelevant.

- If the plaintiff's spouse takes time off work to do the household tasks that the plaintiff can no longer manage, and so suffers a loss of earnings, that loss can be claimed as special damages, but must be deducted from the plaintiff's claim for general damages for loss of amenity.

A claim of this kind is not limited to the cost of assistance with those tasks which before the accident the plaintiff would have done for his own benefit. It includes the cost of employing someone else to do those tasks which he would have done for his spouse and children: *Cutts* v *Chumley* [1967] 1 WLR 742, [1967] 2 All ER 89. Similarly, the claim need not be limited to household chores: it can include gardening, decorating and odd jobs of all kinds.

Checklist

1. Does the medical report deal with each of the topics listed above at pages 139–140?
2. If not, ask the medical expert for a supplementary report. Spell out precisely the points with which the medical expert should deal; if counsel has said further information is needed, enclose a copy of the relevant part of his advice.
3. Write a summary of the report. In a case of multiple injuries identify the lead injury.
4. Identify the appropriate range in the Judicial Studies Board's *Guidelines*.
5. Find within that range one or two cases as close as possible to the plaintiff's: remember to update for inflation.
6. Has the plaintiff lost the pleasure of some particular activity — sport, for example? If so, identify witnesses who can help prove to the court the importance of that activity to the plaintiff.
7. Does the plaintiff have a claim under any of the four heads of loss set out above on page 148? If so, identify relevant witnesses.
8. Is all the evidence in the form of witness statements each of which satisfies the requirements of O 20 r 12A(4) CCR in that it is dated; signed (unless there is a good reason set out in a letter accompanying the statement); includes a statement by the witness that the contents are true to the best of his knowledge and belief; and sufficiently identifies (by exhibiting, for example) any documents to which it refers?

Chapter 18

Provisional damages

1. The problem

Until 1985 the courts could make only a single award of damages. Where the long-term consequences of the plaintiff's injuries were clear at the date of trial, this worked no injustice — but grave injustice could be done to a plaintiff whose long-term future was uncertain. By waiting until the end of the limitation period before issuing the writ, and by taking full advantage of the period of one year then allowed for service of the writ once it had been issued, lawyers could give their clients the best possible chance of a clear prognosis, but there were some plaintiffs whose outlook was uncertain even five or six years after the accident.

Consider the case of a person who suffers an eye injury: the injury restricts his sight, but does not prevent him from returning to his pre-accident job three months after the accident. He is entitled to compensation for his injury and 12 weeks' loss of earnings. Now add a ten per cent chance that the plaintiff will go totally blind at some time in the five to ten years following the date of the trial. If he does go blind, not only will he have been deprived of the much greater award of damages that total blindness merits, but he will also suffer a total loss of earnings when he first goes blind and while he is being retrained, and almost certainly a partial loss of earnings for the rest of his working life; in addition he will probably require all kinds of special equipment.

To award, say, ten per cent of the damages that will be appropriate if the worst happens is grossly unjust to the plaintiff, since if the worst does happen, he will need every penny. To award the full amount, on the other hand, is grossly unjust to the defendant, since it is much more likely that the worst will not befall the plaintiff.

2. The solution

The solution is to confer on the courts power to make an immediate award of damages on the assumption that the worst will not happen, coupled with an order which allows the plaintiff to return to court for a further award if it does. Under such a scheme our imaginary plaintiff receives nothing at all now for the ten per cent risk of total blindness, but full compensation if the risk materialises. The order in such a case is called an award of provisional damages.

3. Power to award

The power to award provisional damages was conferred on the High
Court by s 32A of the Supreme Court Act 1981, which came into force
on 1 July 1985. The corresponding power in the county court is created
by s 51 of the County Courts Act 1984, which (in outline) provides:

'(1) This section applies to an action for damages for personal injuries
in which there is proved or admitted to be a chance that at some
definite or indefinite time in the future the injured person will, as a
result of the act or omission which gave rise to the cause of action,
develop some serious disease or suffer some serious deterioration in his
physical or mental condition.

(2) ... as regards any action for damages to which this section applies
in which a judgment is given in the county court, provision may be
made by county court rules for enabling the court, in such
circumstances as may be prescribed, to award the injured person —

(a) damages assessed on the assumption that the injured person will
not develop the disease or suffer the deterioration in his condition;
and

(b) further damages at a future date if he develops the disease or
suffers the deterioration ...

(5) In this section "personal injuries" includes any disease and any
impairment of a person's physical or mental condition.'

4. 'A chance'

In *Willson* v *Ministry of Defence* [1991] 1 All ER 638 at 642b Scott Baker
J held that the chance on which the plaintiff bases his claim for
provisional damages must be 'measurable rather than fanciful'.
Practitioners should therefore encourage their medical experts to assess in
percentage terms the risk they foresee.

5. 'Serious disease or ... deterioration'

In the same case Scott Baker J said that whether a prospective
deterioration is serious depends on the facts of the case: a hand injury is
more serious to a concert pianist than to the general run of plaintiffs. On
the facts of that particular case, however, he held that the future
development of osteo-arthritis would not amount to a 'serious
deterioration' in the condition of a man who had suffered a fracture, since
the development of osteo-arthritis is 'simply an aspect of a progression of
this particular disease'.

6. Procedure

The procedure to be adopted in cases involving an award of provisional
damages is laid down by O 37 rr 8–10 RSC, which apply (with minor
modifications) to the county court by virtue of O 22 r 6A CCR. The claim
for provisional damages must be expressly pleaded: O 37 r 8 (1)(a) RSC.

Rule 9 provides machinery by which the defendant can make an offer to submit to an award of provisional damages. Rule 10 lays down the procedure under which the plaintiff who has obtained an award of provisional damages applies for a further award: only one such application can be made in respect of each disease or type of deterioration specified in the order for provisional damages.

7. Refusal of provisional damages

If the court refuses to make an award of provisional damages, it should award immediate damages to compensate the plaintiff not only for his past and present pain, suffering and loss of amenity, but also for the chance that he will develop a disease or suffer a deterioration in the future. The plaintiff, too, has a right to refuse provisional damages. If he fails to make a claim for provisional damages in a case which apparently falls within the provisional damages provisions, he is still entitled as of right to damages which compensate for the future risk: *Cowan* v *Kitson Insulations Ltd* [1992] PIQR Q19.

Checklist

1. Does the medical evidence suggest that the plaintiff will: (a) develop a serious disease; or (b) suffer some serious deterioration in his physical or mental condition at some time in the future?
2. If so, does the medical evidence put: (a) a name to the disease or deterioration; (b) a figure on the chances of its occurring; and (c) a timescale on the period within which it is likely to occur?
3. If the answer to any of the questions in 2. above is no, obtain a supplementary report.
4. Consider whether the plaintiff should be advised to make a claim for provisional damages.
5. If this is a case for provisional damages, make sure it is correctly so pleaded.

Chapter 19

Pecuniary loss: heads of damage

1. Aim of award

In theory an award in respect of the plaintiff's pecuniary loss to the date of trial is special damages, while an award in respect of future loss is general damages. As suggested in Chapter 16, it is perhaps more helpful to regard as special damages whatever a county court Judge would expect to find in the plaintiff's statement of special damage. Past loss and future loss must still be calculated separately, however, since the techniques of assessment, and entitlement to interest, are different in each case.

In principle the aim of both awards is the same. *Per* Lord Scarman in *Lim Poh Choo* v *Camden and Islington Area Health Authority* [1980] AC 174 at 187E, [1979] 2 All ER 910 at 917h:

'The principle of the law is that compensation should as nearly as possible put the party who has suffered in the same position as he would have been in if he had not sustained the wrong.'

Chapter 21 deals with the special techniques used to calculate pecuniary loss to date of trial, while Chapters 22 and 23 deal with the calculation of prospective future loss. This chapter deals with the categories of loss that can be recovered and with the way in which the loss in each category is defined.

2. Heads of damage

Damages for pecuniary loss are in general awarded under 16 heads:

- medical expenses;
- travelling expenses;
- cost of professional nursing care;
- cost of amateur nursing care;
- cost of providing special accommodation;
- cost of special equipment;
- cost of modifying car;
- cost of special diet;
- increased cost of living;

- cost of household help;
- cost of employing professionals;
- loss of earnings;
- loss of expected pension;
- lost perks;
- marriage breakdown or loss of marriage prospects;
- Court of Protection fees.

This list is not exclusive; unless there is authority, or a statutory provision, to the contrary, the plaintiff can recover any financial loss caused by his injury. In practice, however, the list covers all the heads found in the vast majority of cases and illustrates the way in which a court will expect the plaintiff to break down his claim.

3. Medical expenses

The plaintiff can recover all medical expenses reasonably incurred as a result of the injuries he has suffered. In deciding whether expenses have been reasonably incurred, the court ignores the availability of treatment through the National Health Service: s 2(4) Law Reform (Personal Injuries) Act 1948. Provided that a plaintiff has acted reasonably and on medical advice, he can recover the cost of a course of treatment even though it proves with hindsight to have been unnecessary.

4. Travelling expenses

The plaintiff's own expenses in travelling to and from hospital, or to consult a specialist, can be recovered. In most cases the expenses incurred by his relatives in visiting him in hospital can also be recovered, since regular visits are often an important factor in a patient's recovery. If the visiting relative is the defendant himself, the plaintiff cannot recover the expenses the defendant incurs: *Hunt* v *Severs* [1994] 2 WLR 602 [1994] 2 All ER 385. An obvious example is the driver of the family car in which the plaintiff was travelling as a passenger.

5. Cost of professional nursing care

The plaintiff may need care full-time or only part-time. Care can be provided either in an institution or in the plaintiff's own home.

Full-time care in an institution is normally cheaper than similar care at home. That does not necessarily mean that a plaintiff must choose the cheaper option. In every case the question is the same: has the plaintiff, in the light of all the circumstances, acted reasonably? Where the plaintiff is living in an institution, his claim will be for the cost of staying in the institution less the cost, over the same period of living in his own home (as if he had not been injured).

In every case the plaintiff will need expert evidence to support his claim. Medical evidence will be needed to prove first that nursing care is required. The evidence must then go on to establish the nature of the care required. Does the plaintiff need attention night and day, or only at night? Does he need the services of a fully qualified nurse, or are an auxiliary's sufficient? Once the medical evidence has established the level of nursing care required, expert nursing evidence must be marshalled to prove the cost of providing that level of care. The British Nursing Association is often able to help; there are also a number of experts who offer their services commercially.

6. Cost of amateur nursing care

Professional care will be justified in only the most serious cases. In the majority of cases, however, the plaintiff's relatives will give up some time to care for him. That time may be working time or leisure time; in extreme cases a wife or husband, mother or father will give up work altogether to look after a spouse or child.

In such cases the plaintiff can recover, as trustee for the person who provides the care, the proper and reasonable cost of his relatives' services. If the person providing the services is the person whose negligence caused the orginal injury, the plaintiff cannot recover damages which represent the cost of those services: *Hunt* v *Severs* [1994] 2 WLR 602, [1994] 2 All ER 385. The commonest case of this kind is a road accident in which the driver has injured a member of his own family. Where the relative takes time off work to look after the plaintiff, the claim represents the relative's loss of earnings. Where the relative forgoes his leisure, the assessment is more difficult: a good guide is usually the cost of employing an unskilled person for the same hours.

Here, too, evidence is needed. The medical experts must give evidence about the type of care required. The relative must give evidence about the hours he spends on the plaintiff's care. If the relative has given up paid work to look after the plaintiff, he must be in a position to prove his loss of earnings in much the same way as the plaintiff will prove his own loss.

7. Cost of providing special accommodation

A plaintiff who is badly injured may be able to live at home provided his accommodation is adapted to his needs. If his pre-accident accommodation is suitable, it can be adapted; if not, the plaintiff will have to move house.

Where the plaintiff's own house can be adapted, assessment is easy. Suppose that a woman who lives in a two-storey terrace house is injured in a road accident and confined to a wheelchair. If she is to remain in her own home, she will need a lift, doorways wide enough to allow a wheelchair to pass, doorknobs at a height she can reach, a cooker, sink and working-surfaces she can reach, a ramp to her front door, and so on. The cost of all these modifications can be recovered in full. In addition, if the modification reduces the value of her house, that reduction can be recovered in full.

Where the plaintiff's own house cannot be adapted, the court adopts the approach laid down by the Court of Appeal in *Roberts* v *Johnstone* [1989] QB 878. As before, the plaintiff can recover in full the cost of modifications and the amount by which those modifications reduce the value of the house. In addition the plaintiff can recover the costs of sale, purchase and removal.

In general, however, to find a house suitable for alteration the plaintiff is forced to buy a more expensive house than the one in which he was living before the accident. If so, the plaintiff is said to suffer an annual loss represented by two per cent of the difference between the purchase price of the new house and the selling price of the old house. The rationale is that in the new house the plaintiff has an asset secured against inflation, but to acquire that asset has forgone the income the cash would have produced if invested in an asset yielding income: an index-linked, income-producing asset is unlikely to yield much more, after tax, than two per cent. How this decision will survive falling house prices remains to be seen.

Needless to say, evidence will be required in every case. The need for modifications, the type of modifications, the cost of carrying them out and the effect on the capital value of the house are all proved by expert evidence.

8. Cost of special equipment

If the plaintiff needs any special equipment as a result of his injuries, he can recover the cost in full. This includes not only the initial purchase, but also maintenance and replacement.

A man with a broken ankle may need a pair of crutches. A man who has lost the use of his legs will need a wheelchair. The court can be asked to infer that a man who cannot put weight on one leg needs crutches, but where plaintiff needs complex equipment, expert medical and nursing evidence will be needed to substantiate the claim.

The cost of buying, training, keeping and eventually replacing a guide dog can also be recovered under this heading.

9. Cost of modifying car

If the plaintiff is injured in such a way that he can drive a car only if it has been specially modified, he can recover the amount by which his motoring expenses have been increased. In general this is limited to the cost of installing the special equipment on purchase and of removing it before sale. Where the plaintiff also needs a bigger or more expensive car than he used to drive before the accident, however, he can recover the additional capital he will have to lay out each time his car is replaced.

10. Cost of special diet

If the plaintiff needs a special diet as a result of his injuries, he can recover the cost — less, of course, the cost of the everyday food he would have had to buy if he had not been injured. The need must be proved by medical evidence.

11. Increased cost of living

A plaintiff whose injuries keep him at home will spend more on heating than a man who is out at work all day. A plaintiff whose injuries make him incontinent will need to change his bed linen more frequently than normal. In each case the plaintiff can recover the amount by which his heating or laundry bills have been increased.

12. Cost of household help

As a result of his injuries the plaintiff may find it more difficult — or even impossible — to do his own heavy housework, washing, shopping and so on. If he has medical evidence to show that he cannot perform these tasks without subjecting himself to unreasonably severe pain or discomfort, he can recover the cost of employing someone else to do the work for him.

A claim of this kind can cover any household task which the plaintiff was accustomed to do for himself: the cost of employing a part-time gardener is a common claim, for example. Similarly, this head includes the cost of employing someone else to do those household tasks which the plaintiff would have done not for himself, but for the benefit of his spouse and children: *Cutts* v *Chumley* [1967] 1 WLR 742, [1967] 2 All ER 89.

If the plaintiff's spouse takes time off work to do the household tasks that the plaintiff can no longer manage, and so suffers a loss of earnings, that loss can be claimed as special damages. Any award under this head must, however, be deducted from general damages for loss of amenity awarded to the plaintiff for his own inability to perform those tasks.

13. Cost of employing professionals

Before the accident the plaintiff may have been in the habit of doing his own decorating or car maintenance. If as a result of his injuries he now has to employ a professional decorator, or have his car serviced at a garage, he can recover the cost of these services. This principle applies to any task which the plaintiff would have done for himself had the accident not occurred. These claims are often very substantial.

Before such a claim can be mounted the plaintiff will need cogent evidence. To the date of trial the plaintiff's claim is for the money he has already spent. As for the future, his solicitors should obtain from three or four sources an estimate of the annual cost of providing the service the plaintiff will need. The average of these estimates will form the basis of the plaintiff's claim.

14. Loss of earnings

(a) Employees

Where the plaintiff was employed at the time of the accident, his loss will be the difference between the wages or salary he would have earned if he had not been injured and the wages or salary he has in fact earned. The loss is total if the plaintiff has been unable to work at all; partial if he has been able to work, but not earn as much as before the accident.

The award tries to mirror exactly what would have happened if the accident had not occurred. Thus if the evidence shows that quite apart from the plaintiff's accident the factory in which the plaintiff was working would have closed down, making him redundant, immediately after his accident, the plaintiff will have no claim for loss of earnings, unless he can show that he would have been able to find another job. The same applies if he would have been prevented from working by an unrelated disease even if the accident had not occurred: *Cutler* v *Vauxhall Motors Ltd* [1971] 1 QB 418. On the other hand, if the plaintiff would have earned an increase in salary by winning promotion or moving to another job, his loss includes that increase.

The loss claimed must always be the real loss. Thus if an electrician who can no longer work was required to provide his own tools, the cost of buying, maintaining and replacing them must be deducted from his lost wages.

In many cases a plaintiff's employers will continue to pay him, for a time at least. If the money is paid as sick pay, which the employee is under no obligation to repay, whatever he receives from his employers must be deducted from his claim for loss of earnings. On the other hand, if the money is paid on the understanding that the plaintiff will repay it if he recovers damages from the person responsible for his injuries — and so is in effect a conditional loan — then it is not taken into account in assessing his loss. This is considered in more detail in Chapter 25.

(b) The self-employed

In principle there is no difference between a claim for loss of earnings made by an employee and one made by a self-employed person. In practice the differences may be important.

Self-employment can take one of two forms. A person who is self-employed in the strict sense incurs personal liability on contracts and pays income tax under Schedule D. The director of a company in which he holds 99 per cent of the shares is also effectively self-employed, however. He incurs no personal liability on his company's contracts, but he has complete control over the way in which he works.

The earnings of a self-employed plumber probably do not vary much: provided a long enough period is chosen, it will show a steady average income. At the other end of the spectrum a writer's income may be spectacular in the year in which his bestseller appears, but nil in the five years he spends writing it. A businessman's earnings in the three years before his accident may have been modest, but in the week before the accident he may have made the contact which would have opened up an entirely new market for his products.

Where earnings depend on a contingency in this way, the court has to decide what would have happened had the accident not occurred. The decision is made on the balance of probabilities. Is it, for instance, more likely than not that the author would have finished his book? That it would have been accepted for publication? That it would have been sold effectively? That it would have been one of the tiny percentage of books which become bestsellers? Each of these questions must be answered on the basis of solid evidence. In the example of a plaintiff who is a writer, he would have to call evidence of his past achievements to demonstrate his ability to complete what he has started; and expert evidence to assess his chances of success with the particular book he was writing at the time of his accident.

Where the plaintiff works through a one-man limited company, his remuneration may take the form of salary, director's fees, dividend or a combination of the three. On the other hand, the plaintiff may have been working to increase the value of his shares with a view to selling them to realise his profit. In each case the principle is clear: the plaintiff is entitled to recover a loss which is truly his, in the sense that he has lost money that would otherwise have come to him, but he is not entitled to recover money that would have remained the company's in any event.

On occasion the courts have been persuaded to look beyond the legal form to the underlying reality. In *Lee* v *Sheard* [1956] 1 QB 192, [1955] 3 All ER 777, for example, a plaintiff who held 490 of the 1,000 shares in a company run effectively as a partnership was held entitled to recover the amount by which his share of the company's profits had been reduced as a result of his accident.

In every case the overriding rule is that the claim must reflect the real loss. The plaintiff must always deduct from his claim what he would have spent to make the income or capital gain.

15. Loss of expected pension

This can arise in a number of ways. A plaintiff may be forced by his injuries to retire early, so he loses a number of years' contributions. He may be forced by his injuries to work less hard, so he earns less and makes correspondingly smaller contributions. He may miss promotion and so lose the opportunity of qualifying for a pension based on a much higher final salary.

In almost every case the loss will arise at some time in the future, normally at the plaintiff's expected date of retirement. An accident immediately before the plaintiff's retirement is unlikely to have any effect on the level of his pension.

The aim of the award under this head is to give the plaintiff now a capital sum which will make good the loss of capital or income he will suffer on retirement. This principle applies equally to loss of benefit under an employer's scheme, under an employee's or self-employed person's own pension contract, or under the State pension scheme.

16. Lost perks

In addition to a salary many employees receive fringe benefits. A salesman may, for example, have free use of his employer's car for private purposes. A railwayman enjoys free and reduced-rate travel. A farm worker has free accommodation. Employees in the financial sector qualify for loans at subsidised rates of interest. Provided that the fringe benefit can be valued in terms of money, its loss can be recovered.

Many kinds of self-employment also carry a fringe benefit. This can be direct or indirect. A dairy farmer, for example, has the direct benefit of free milk and eggs from his own farm. That same farmer also has an indirect benefit in that part at least of the cost of running a car used for the purpose of his business is an expense allowable against profit in calculating his taxable income. If that farmer can no longer farm, he can recover the cash value of both the fringe benefits he has lost.

17. Marriage breakdown or loss of marriage prospects

Injury can destroy a marriage. If it does, the injured party can recover damages. If the uninjured party was a husband or wife who stayed at home and looked after the family, the damages are best regarded as the money value of that party's lost services. A plaintiff whose marriage collapses as a result of his injuries cannot, however, recover compensation for the cost to him of the order for ancillary relief: *Pritchard* v *J H Cobden Ltd* [1988] Fam 22 [1987] 1 All ER 300.

The uninjured party has no redress. Section 2 of the Administration of Justice Act 1982 provides that a husband whose wife has been injured has no claim for loss of the services or society of his wife, while a wife has never had a claim for loss of her husband's services or society.

Injury can also prevent a marriage. Marriage may have been imminent at the time of the accident or (particularly where the plaintiff was young) just a possibility which in the nature of things was likely to materialise at some time in the future.

There are two elements to a claim for loss of marriage prospects: the plaintiff has lost a mate, but he or she has also lost financial support. The claim for loss of a mate is part of the claim for damages for loss of amenity, and so forms part of the general damages. Valuation of the lost financial support is a question of assessing what the plaintiff would have received had the marriage gone ahead.

In the past a woman whose fiancé broke off the engagement as a result of her injuries often claimed that she would have given up work altogether on marriage, and so recovered a capital sum to reflect the material support her husband would have given her: that, of course, depended on his means and prospects. Where that assertion reflects the truth, a claim can still be made in that way; and, of course, if the evidence supports it, the claim can equally well be made by a man.

These days, however, it is far more usual for the woman to continue working on marriage, stop work to raise a family, and then return to work. The courts adopt a rough-and-ready approach to this problem. On the assumption that the wife will be supported by her husband while she takes time off work, but will otherwise work full-time, her claim for loss of earnings is assessed as though the marriage was never going to take place; by the same token, she receives no general damages for loss of a mate: *Housecroft* v *Burnett* [1986] 1 All ER 332. This is, however, no more than a rule of thumb: if it is not supported by the facts, damages can be assessed in the traditional way. A claim for loss of financial support from some hypothetical marriage at some time in the future must be almost impossible to substantiate in modern conditions.

Sometimes the plaintiff's needs, or the changes in his personality, are such that the other party has to move into a second home. There are conflicting decisions of the Court of Appeal on whether the cost of the second home is recoverable.

18. Court of Protection fees

If the plaintiff is unable to look after his own affairs, his damages will be administered by the Court of Protection, which will charge for its services. These charges can be recovered by the plaintiff. Such cases are unlikely to find their way into the county court.

19. Categories not exhaustive

The heads of damage discussed above are not exhaustive, but they have two practical uses. They identify the items for which the vast majority of awards are made and they help practitioners to plan their client's claim systematically. It is helpful to run through the list every time and ask: has my client a claim under this head?

The fundamental rule remains, however, that the plaintiff can recover any financial loss that has been caused by his injury. In *Meah* v *McCreamer* [1985] 1 All ER 367, for example, Woolf J awarded damages for loss of liberty to a man who faced a lifetime as a Category A prisoner owing to a head injury, because the resulting personality change had led him to commit violent sexual assaults.

Checklist

1.   Run through with the plaintiff the possible losses listed above on pages 154–155. Has the plaintiff suffered loss under any head?
2.   If so, identify those which call for medical evidence — to prove,

for example, that the plaintiff's period away from work has been reasonable.

3. Does the medical expert deal with the points that need medical evidence? If not, commission a supplementary report.

4. Ask the plaintiff at the first interview for any documents he may have kept which substantiate his claims.

5. Remind the plaintiff to keep all documents which will help him to prove his claims. Nothing is too trivial: even bus tickets should be kept.

6. Advise the plaintiff at the first interview to start keeping a diary of his out-of-pocket expenses.

7. Think right from the outset how each item of loss is to be proved. Do not assume that the special damages will be agreed at the last minute: plaintiffs often have to abandon perfectly good claims because they are not in a position to prove them.

8. Is it necessary to take a proof from a third party to prove any head?

9. As trial approaches, consider whether all the evidence is in the form of witness statements which satisfy the requirements of the County Court Rules, and exhibit any relevant documents.

Chapter 20

Tax

1. Why tax is deducted

Damages for personal injuries are not subject to tax even when they represent compensation for loss of something which would have been taxable, for example earnings. The aim of compensation is to give the plaintiff what he would have had if the accident had never occurred: it follows that if damages are compensation for loss of something which would have been taxable, the damages must be reduced to take account of the tax the plaintiff would have had to pay. This principle was laid down by the House of Lords in *British Transport Commission* v *Gourley* [1956] AC 185, [1955] 3 All ER 796.

2. Which taxes are deducted

It is almost always the claim for loss of earnings that has to be reduced to take account of tax. In the vast majority of cases the relevant tax is income tax. In principle, however, the rule applies wherever the lost benefit would have been taxed: thus if the plaintiff was running a business through a company in which he was the majority shareholder, and claims that he would have enhanced the value of, and then sold, his shares rather than draw income, then he must give credit for the capital gains tax that would have been charged on the disposal.

Although National Insurance contributions are a tax, unlike any other tax they carry a corresponding direct benefit to the taxpayer. The contributions must be deducted from any claim for loss of earnings, but if the failure to pay contributions reduces the plaintiff's pension entitlement, it carries a corresponding claim for loss of pension rights.

3. How taxes are deducted

The need to deduct tax in making certain calculations has been mentioned in the sections of this book that deal with the particular calculations in which it arises. The aim of this chapter is to explain how those calculations take account of the tax element. There are four main points to bear in mind:

- Deduct only if the lost benefit was taxable.
- Look at the whole year.

- Look at the whole income.
- Use relevant rates and allowances.

4. Deduct only if the lost benefit was taxable

Compensation is reduced to take account of tax only if the lost benefit which it represents would have been taxed in the plaintiff's hands. Payment in money presents no problem, since that is always taxed. Most of the standard fringe benefits — company cars, for example — are taxed according to rules which are widely understood.

Some kinds of employments carry some kinds of benefits the tax effect of which is not always clear, however: a schoolmaster at a public school may, for example, be entitled to free education for his own children. In most cases whether a benefit is taxable can be decided by looking at the position immediately before the accident. In a few cases — where, perhaps, the plaintiff was injured just before starting a new job — the past will be no guide: in such cases the practitioner should consult *Tolley's Tax Guide* or *Tolley's Tax Service* or, in case of real difficulty, seek expert advice from a tax specialist.

5. Look at the whole year

Income tax is assessed over a year running from 6 April to the following 5 April. The plaintiff's tax position can be ascertained only by looking at the whole of the year; however short the period of lost earnings, therefore, the practitioner will need details of the whole of the plaintiff's income during the tax year in which the period falls.

Where the plaintiff pays under PAYE, tax will have been deducted on the assumption that his income was going to remain constant throughout the year. The drop in his income after the accident may falsify that assumption.

This can have one of two consequences. It may mean that the plaintiff's average net weekly or monthly pre-accident earnings cannot simply be multiplied by the number of weeks or months off work to produce a figure for his loss over that period, since (when the year as a whole is considered) the plaintiff was paying too much tax before the accident: in such cases his income, gross and net, has to be calculated for the whole year.

On the other hand, the plaintiff may be entitled to a tax rebate. If so, the rebate must be deducted from the claim for lost wages: *Hartley* v *Sandholme Iron Co Ltd* [1975] QB 600, [1974] 3 All ER 475.

6. Look at the whole income

Income is always lost first at the plaintiff's highest marginal rate: *Lyndale Fashion Manufacturers* v *Rich* [1973] 1 WLR 73, [1973] 1 All ER 33. The proportion of an individual's income taken in tax increases with his income, because each band of income is taxed at a progressively

165

higher rate. The first band, the personal allowance, which varies according to the individual's personal circumstances, is not taxed; for Tax Year 1994–95 the remaining, taxable, earned income is grouped into three bands, as follows:

Up to £3,000	20%
£3,001 – £23,700	25%
Over £23,700	40%

If a self-employed person earning £36,000 loses a month's work in Tax Year 1994–95 through injury, his gross loss will be £3,000. For the purposes of making a claim for loss of earnings tax must be deducted at 40 per cent, not 25 per cent, because his remaining income is still £33,000.

The rationale behind this rule is obvious where the whole of the plaintiff's income is earned and vulnerable to reduction through injury or illness. Some plaintiffs enjoy unearned income, however, which will not be affected by their inability to work. In calculating a claim for loss of earnings this income, too, must be taken into account.

Suppose a man with an investment income of £20,000 has a job which pays £18,000. His combined income of £38,000 takes him well into the higher rate tax band. On the other hand, because his earned income alone does not qualify for tax at the higher rate, tax will be deducted through PAYE only at the standard rate, the assessment to higher rate tax following once the total income from his investments in the relevant tax year becomes known. If that man is unable through injury to work for a month in Tax Year 1994–95, however, tax must be deducted from his gross loss of £1,500 at the rate of 40 per cent, not 25 per cent. This is a consequence of the rule that the claim for loss of earnings must look at the whole of the plaintiff's income for the whole of the relevant tax year: when he is finally assessed to tax for the whole of the year, £1,500 less of his investment income will bear tax at the higher rate than if he had been able to work throughout.

7. Use relevant rates and allowances

A calculation of past loss should use the rates and allowances in force during the tax year in which the loss was sustained. A calculation of future loss should use the current rates. Rates and allowances can be found in *Tolley's Tax Guide* or *Tolley's Tax Service*.

8. A special case: future unearned income

It is easy enough to take account of unearned income when calculating the plaintiff's loss to the date of trial: taking account of the future is much more difficult. Consider, for example, the higher-rate taxpayer who had a substantial unearned income from a few boom shares at the time he was injured in 1986. When his case came on for trial in 1988, the stockmarket was down, but his unearned income was slightly higher; by 1990 every one of his shares had stopped paying a dividend. If the court had assessed his future loss of earnings in 1988 on the assumption that his unearned income was going to continue at the same level, he could have been seriously under-compensated for his loss of earnings: for the assumption, justified in 1988, that the plaintiff's lost earnings would have been taxed at 40 per cent would have turned out in 1990 to be false.

In each case the court has to decide how secure the plaintiff's unearned income is. In *Gourley's Case* [1956] AC 185, [1955] 3 All ER 796 Lord Goddard said:

> 'If it is a life annuity under a will or settlement, it may well be expected to continue. If it is disposable investments which may be sold at any time or transferred to a child, less, perhaps little, regard should be paid to it.'

9. Changes in the tax position

In 1979 the top rate of tax was 98 per cent; it is now 40 per cent. Five years from now it may be higher or lower. Similarly the level of personal allowances varies with the passage of time. The calculation of the plaintiff's loss of earnings to the date of trial presents no problem, since the rate of tax for that period is known, but for the future the court simply has to assume (against reality) that it will remain unchanged.

In the absence of cogent evidence to the contrary, the same principle will apply to potential changes in a plaintiff's personal allowance owing to marriage, for example. Where, however, the plaintiff can show that it is more likely than not that his tax liability will change owing to some change in his personal circumstances, he should do so.

10. Proving the tax position

The defendant takes the benefit of any deduction for tax, but it is still part of the plaintiff's claim for loss of earnings, so it is for him to prove. Wherever possible, the parties should try to reach agreement, even if this means presenting the Judge with two alternative calculations. Say, for example, the plaintiff's claim for loss of earnings is either £16,000 or £29,500, depending on the way in which the Judge finds on one disputed fact: in such a case the parties should agree two separate, alternative calculations of the tax consequences.

The tax consequences are one of the matters put in issue by the plaintiff's claim for loss of earnings. It follows that the plaintiff must give discovery relating to, and can be ordered to give particulars of, the whole of his income.

11. Tax on damages

There is no tax on the damages themselves, but there will be tax on the income those damages yield. The system for calculating the claim for future loss of earnings described in Chapters 22 and 23 aims to produce a sum which, prudently invested, will be exhausted by the time the plaintiff would have retired but for the accident; in the meantime, however, the diminishing capital sum will have been producing a taxable income.

In the normal case the multiplier will be chosen to take account of that fact. This in itself is a rough-and-ready scheme, since the assumptions on which it is based could be belied by an increase in the level of tax, or a reintroduction of the investment income surcharge. The normal multiplier takes account only of tax at the standard rate, however; where the plaintiff has an existing income (earned or unearned) which will push the income produced by his damages into the higher rate, the multiplier should be increased to take account of this. Although such cases are rare, such an approach has been sanctioned by the House of Lords in respect of a claim under the Fatal Accidents Acts: *Taylor* v *O'Connor* [1971] AC 115.

12. Tax on interest awarded by court

There is no tax on interest awarded by the court: s 329(1) of the Income and Corporation Taxes Act 1988.

Checklist

1. In *Tolley's Tax Guide* or *Tolley's Tax Service* look up the rates and allowances for the tax year in which the plaintiff's losses fall.
2. Remember that a calculation of future loss uses the current rates and allowances.
3. Remember that the loss always falls first on the income taxed at the plaintiff's highest marginal rate.

Chapter 21

Pecuniary loss to trial

1. Need for two calculations

The calculation of the plaintiff's pecuniary loss falls into two distinct stages. The first calculation assesses the loss between the date of the accident and the date of trial: this is generally known as the 'past loss'. The second calculation assesses the loss from the date of trial as far into the future as the accident will continue to have a financial effect: this is known as 'future loss'. The calculation of past loss is by far the easier.

Chapter 19 identified 16 heads of loss. Of these, two, loss of expected pension and Court of Protection fees, give rise to a claim for future loss only. The other 14 give rise to a loss which may be past, future or both.

Each loss represents a loss of income: in each case owing to the accident the plaintiff is either not receiving income which he would have received or is incurring expenditure he would not have incurred. The compensation for losses of this kind takes the form of a capital sum. The aim of Chapters 21 to 23 is to explain how the various income losses identified in Chapter 19 can be converted into a corresponding lump sum. This chapter deals only with losses between the date of the accident and the date of trial; calculation of losses from the date of trial is dealt with in Chapters 22 and 23.

2. Basis of past loss calculation

The aim of this calculation is to compare in financial terms what has happened to the plaintiff since the accident with what would have happened if the accident had not occurred. In many cases part of the claim relates to expenses which, trivial in themselves, when taken together account for a substantial sum. The practitioner should always therefore advise a plaintiff at the first interview to keep a diary of his expenses; when a claim can be properly proved, the amount of money involved is often surprising.

3. Loss of earnings

This is by far the commonest claim for past loss. The basis of the calculation is very simple: what the plaintiff would have earned had the accident not occurred, less what he has in fact earned. If the plaintiff could have returned to work but has not, then (provided jobs within his capacity are available) his loss will be calculated as though he had gone back to work when fit.

(a) Employee paid weekly

The first task is to determine just what the plaintiff was earning, per week or per month, at the time of his accident. The aim is to discover the true net figure.

Where the plaintiff was an employee in a regular job, paid weekly, the task is straightforward. His earnings from week to week may have been dependent on overtime, but in most cases a workable figure can be reached by taking the average of his earnings over the 13 weeks preceding the week in which the plaintiff had his accident. The week in which the plaintiff had his accident usually has to be excluded, of course, because the plaintiff's earnings drop the moment he is injured.

Again, this is only a rule of thumb. If the plaintiff's earnings are seasonal, then a longer period has to be chosen. Similarly, if the plaintiff's income in one of the 13 weeks is clearly exceptional, because it includes substantial holiday pay, for example, or a tax rebate, then that week must be excluded from the calculation.

The net figure means what the plaintiff would have taken home. From his gross wage the plaintiff must deduct both income tax and his National Insurance contributions. He must also deduct any employee's contributions made to his employer's pension scheme: *Dews* v *National Coal Board* [1988] AC 1, [1987] 2 All ER 545. (If failure to make pension contributions during the period of incapacity will reduce the plaintiff's eventual pension entitlement, he has a separate claim for loss of pension rights.)

The next task is to decide what the plaintiff would have earned between the date of the accident and the date of the trial. If the plaintiff would have remained in the same job, and if that job would have been paying the same at the date of trial as it was at the date of the accident, the plaintiff's claim takes one of two forms. If he has not been working at all, it is the net, pre-accident, weekly figure multiplied by the number of weeks between accident and trial. If he has been working, but has not earned as much, then the correct approach is to multiply the net, pre-accident, weekly figure by the number of weeks between the accident and the trial and then deduct the money in fact earned over the same period. To calculate the loss week by week is wrong.

If the plaintiff would have changed jobs, or if the job he was doing at the time of the accident would have been paying a different rate by the time the case comes to trial, then the normal straightforward calculation has to be modified. In every case the principle is the same, however: the court tries to reconstruct what would have happened to the plaintiff had the accident not occurred.

The suggestion that the plaintiff would have changed jobs may come either from the plaintiff (who claims, for example, that he would have achieved promotion six months after the accident) or from the defendant (who says that the plaintiff's job was about to vanish in any event, though he would have been offered employment at a lower wage in a factory ten miles away). Whether the change would have in fact occurred is a matter for the party who makes the assertion to prove by evidence, but the effect on the calculation is clear: from the date on which the change would have occurred, the calculation is based not on the plaintiff's pre-accident earnings, but on what he would have been earning in his new job. Apart from that, the calculation is constructed exactly as before. If someone else is doing the job which the plaintiff says he would have filled, that person's wages over the relevant period are the best evidence.

The same principle applies where the plaintiff says that the rate for his own pre-accident job would have increased between the date of the accident and the date of the trial. Where the plaintiff was one of half a dozen doing the same job, the task is easy; the earnings of one of his workmates will be a good guide to what the plaintiff could have expected to earn over the same period, provided, of course, the evidence shows that both would have earned the same level of bonus, or overtime, or commission. Where the plaintiff was the only person employed by a particular organisation to do a particular job, and he has not been replaced while off sick, then it will be necessary to look to the earnings of someone in a similar position in another organisation for a comparison.

As long as the defendant is not the plaintiff's employer, gathering evidence should present no problem. Where he is, he will give details of the plaintiff's pre-accident earnings without difficulty, but usually no more. Thus if the plaintiff wants to prove that his earnings would have increased, and to prove that by making a comparison with the earnings of one of his former workmates, he will have to find a former workmate who is prepared to provide the information and, if necessary, give evidence in court against his employer.

The plaintiff's trade union can sometimes help in locating comparable earners. If no comparable earner is available or prepared to give evidence, information can be obtained from the Department of Employment's *New Earnings Survey*. Based on the Department's own research, the *Survey* gives each year the average gross earnings for a wide range of jobs. It can be obtained from HMSO bookshops, from good commercial bookshops or by writing to:

HMSO Publications Centre
PO Box 276
LONDON SW8 5DT

The *Survey* is published annually in six volumes. The entire publication costs £66. Each volume can be bought separately for £11.50. The volumes are arranged as follows:

- PART A: Analyses giving selected results for full-time employees in particular age groups, industries, occupations and regions;

171

summary analyses for broad categories; and a description of the whole *Survey*

- PART B: Analyses of earnings and hours for particular groups of employees
- PART C: Analyses of earnings and hours for particular industries
- PART D: Analyses of earnings and hours for particular occupations
- PART E: Analyses of earnings and hours by region, county and age group
- PART F: Distribution of hours; joint distributions of earnings and hours. Statistics for part-time female employees.

(b) Employee paid monthly

Exactly the same principles apply to a loss sustained by a salaried employee, but the calculations have to be based on monthly, rather than weekly, figures. For most employees in regular employment, the level of earnings in the three months preceding that in which the plaintiff was injured will give an accurate picture. Again, if the plaintiff's earnings are seasonal, or if he is dependent on commission which is earned erratically, a longer period must be chosen to produce a true average.

(c) The self-employed

The calculation of a loss of earnings sustained by a self-employed person can be difficult. As in the case of an employee, the first task is to discover what the plaintiff was earning at the time of his accident.

Employees' claims are generally calculated on weekly or monthly figures. In most cases this will be impossible for self-employed persons, partly because their gross earnings are variable and partly because the expenses that have to be deducted from their gross earnings fall at random times of the year: a car, for example, has to be insured only once a year, but to deduct the premium from the gross earnings made in the week in which it is paid would be completely misleading.

Where the plaintiff is well established in his business or profession, he will have — or ought to have! — accounts that have been agreed with the Inland Revenue for the purpose of assessing his income tax liability. The preparation of accounts is almost always behindhand, but it should be possible to bring them up to date before the plaintiff has to prepare his statement of special damages. This should always be the first priority in preparing a claim on behalf of a self-employed person. Unless the accident fell right at the beginning of the plaintiff's accounting year, it will also be necessary for the purposes of the claim, if not for tax purposes, to prepare an account for the period between the beginning of the plaintiff's accounting year and the date of the accident.

Once again, as in the case of an employee, the next task is to decide what the plaintiff would have earned between the date of the accident and the date of the trial. Again, where the plaintiff is well established, his last three or four years' profit should show a trend. If the profit has been stable over that period, the plaintiff is entitled to claim that it would have remained stable unless some new factor belies that assumption — since the accident a new supermarket has opened up within a few minutes' drive of the plaintiff's corner shop, for example.

In all but the simplest businesses it is vital to look beyond the bare profit figure. A static profit may, for example, conceal a rising turnover. The business is becoming less profitable: why? Have costs been rising? If so, which ones? Have prices been falling? Again, why? If the costs would have continued to rise, or the prices to fall, does the evidence suggest that the plaintiff could have continued to raise turnover to keep profits steady? In a big claim the defendant is very likely to instruct an accountant to analyse the plaintiff's figures, so it is important to be realistic from the outset about the health of the business.

The most difficult cases are those in which at the time of the accident the plaintiff had just launched a business. The difficulty is twofold. Not only does he not have any trading records from which pre-accident earnings can be calculated, but there is also no evidence to show how successful this particular plaintiff would have been in this particular business at this particular time. Judges and insurance companies tend to take a pessimistic view of the prospects of a brand-new business, and first-class evidence will be needed to establish any loss of earnings at all. This can be difficult to obtain: the best evidence, that of other people with similar qualifications engaged in the same business in the same area, is unlikely to be forthcoming, since those people will be the plaintiff's competitors. If the plaintiff can lead firm evidence about the contracts he had won, or was on the point of winning, he has the basis of a claim, but he must make proper allowance for the costs he would have incurred in carrying out those contracts.

Wherever a court is going to be asked to draw broad inferences about the profits a business would have made, the plaintiff should instruct an accountant to prepare a report. This will make projections based on whatever figures are available. The intellectual leap the inferences demand is in fact no less daunting just because accountant's evidence is available, but Judges make the leap with more confidence when it is.

4. Medical expenses

The assessment of medical expenses between the date of the accident and the date of trial should present no problem. The plaintiff's solicitor should be in a position to prepare a statement setting out everything his client has spent not only on professional fees and hospital charges but also on the minor items that are very often forgotten — prescription charges, for example, or the cost of buying proprietary painkillers. The overall loss is simply the total of the sums so spent.

The schedule prepared in this way will eventually form part of the overall statement of special damage (which is dealt with in Chapter 31). Wherever possible, claimed expenditure should be supported by a receipt.

5. Travelling expenses

The claim for travelling expenses can be substantial, but it is likely to be difficult to quantify. In a few cases a plaintiff who has travelled exclusively by public transport will have kept an accurate record of the purpose, destination and cost of each journey, but most rely on some form of estimate.

The first step is to work out how many journeys the plaintiff has made, and to where. Where the plaintiff has kept a diary, those journeys can be set out in date order in a statement. Where he has not kept a record, an estimate has to be made, based on a week or month as appropriate.

Say the plaintiff has been off work for nine months, during which he has been taking a bus to the chemist's to collect his prescription, sometimes once a week, generally twice a week, sometimes three times and occasionally four: he has no record of his journeys. An estimate based on two journeys a week will be broadly accurate, giving a loss of:

$$9 \times 4 \times 2 \times 2 = 144$$

single journeys.

The second stage depends on the means of transport the plaintiff has used. Where he has made the journeys by public transport, it should be possible to calculate the loss exactly. If the fare in our example was 90p each way, the plaintiff's total claim under this head will be:

$$£\ 144 \times 0.9 = 129.60.$$

If the claim is substantial, and the plaintiff cannot remember, the carrier can be asked for details of his fares at the appropriate time.

Where the plaintiff has made the journeys in his own car, his lawyer will have to formulate the claim on the basis of the number of miles travelled. He will then claim a sum per mile to reflect the cost of petrol, the increased depreciation and the increased maintenance attributable to travel caused by the accident, rather than to travel for normal purposes. The Automobile Association publishes useful tables setting out the cost per mile of running a car: the cost varies directly with the engine capacity and inversely with the number of miles driven per year. These figures are not strictly what is required for these purposes, since they take account of the fixed costs that the plaintiff would have incurred anyway, but the current figure for a small car doing the average annual mileage is unlikely to provoke a quarrel with the defendant's insurance company.

Where the plaintiff has begged a lift from a friend or relative, he will be able to recover reasonable sums given to that relative or friend to cover his loss. Again, the Automobile Association's figures are unlikely to be thought unreasonable.

6. Cost of professional nursing care

Assessment of the cost of professional nursing care between the date of the accident and the date of the trial should be no more difficult than the assessment of medical expenses (see above). It follows the same principles.

7. Cost of amateur nursing care

This can be assessed in one of two ways. Where a relative has taken time off work — or even given up work altogether — to look after the plaintiff, he will have suffered a loss of earnings which can be calculated in exactly the same way as the plaintiff's own. The duty to mitigate loss means that the relative must have acted reasonably. In most cases it would be unreasonable for a husband or wife to give up work altogether to look after a spouse who needs only a few hours' nursing a week; it would certainly be unreasonable for a high earner to give up work when, even after tax, it would be cheaper to employ a professional nurse.

Where the relative continues working, but gives up leisure time to look after the plaintiff, his loss can often be assessed as the cost of buying the same services in the commercial market. The relative will almost certainly have no formal nursing skills, so if his services were to be replaced commercially, they would be provided by an auxiliary nurse. The weekly loss between the date of the accident and the date of trial is therefore the product of two figures: the number of hours devoted to the plaintiff each week by his relative and the cost per hour of obtaining an auxiliary nurse through an agency. The weekly figure can then be multiplied by the number of weeks during which the relative has provided those services; if the level has changed significantly since the accident, then a separate calculation will have to be carried out for each period over which the level of services remained constant.

8. Cost of providing special accommodation

These costs fall into two categories: the cost of modifying the plaintiff's existing home and the cost of buying other, suitable accommodation. The approach required in each case is different.

Where the plaintiff has been able to modify his own home, his claim falls into two parts. The first part will be for the money he has spent on the modifications. Quantifying this part of the claim is straightforward: the expenses are simply set out in date order in a statement and the claim is for the sum of the expenses.

Modifications are expensive, but they are unlikely to increase the value of the house; indeed in most cases they will reduce it. The loss represented by this reduction is the second half of the plaintiff's claim. His advisers will have to obtain evidence from a chartered surveyor of the value of the house in its original condition and with the modifications.

The date of the valuation may be significant in times of rapidly rising or falling property values. The aim of the award of damages being to put the plaintiff in the position in which he would have been if the accident had never occurred, the relevant date ought to be immediately before trial.

Where the plaintiff has been forced to move into accommodation which is either suitable as it stands or (unlike his former home) can be adapted to his needs, his claim falls into three parts. The first part will be the reasonable cost of sale, purchase and removal. This will include solicitors' and estate agents' fees, stamp duty, Land Registry fees, removers' charges and the reasonable cost of buying new household items which could not be brought from the existing home — fitted carpets, for example, or built-in cookers.

The second part of the claim will be the cost of carrying out any modifications which prove necessary. This is calculated in exactly the same way as the cost of modifying the plaintiff's own home.

If the new home has cost more to buy than the old, the third element of the claim will be the cost of tying up the extra capital required. As explained in Chapter 19, the cost of this is reckoned to be two per cent a year: calculation of the loss from the date of the accident to the date of trial is a simple matter of multiplying two per cent of the additional capital by the number of years that have passed since purchase.

9. Cost of special equipment

Again, where this has already been incurred by the date of trial, the calculation is a matter of arithmetic.

10. Cost of modifying car

This, too, is a matter of arithmetic.

11. Cost of special diet

The claim here is for the difference between the cost of what the plaintiff would have been eating if the accident had not occurred and what he has actually been eating. In a simple case — where, for example, the plaintiff has to buy one particular, additional food — the advocate can make an estimate, supported by evidence, of the annual or monthly cost of buying that food and multiply it by the number of years or months that have passed since the accident. The evidence must deal, of course, with the number of purchases per year or month and the cost of each purchase.

Where the plaintiff has been forced to restructure his diet altogether, the problem is more difficult. In such cases the plaintiff will have to put together a typical shopping-list for a typical month before the accident: the cost of that shopping-list will then have to be multiplied by the number of months between the accident and the trial. The product will have to be deducted from the sum the plaintiff has spent on food since his accident: the balance is his claim under this head. Over a long period some allowance will have to be made for inflation.

This example neatly illustrates the importance of asking a plaintiff to keep a diary from as early a stage as possible. Where the plaintiff has not kept a diary, his expenditure on food since the accident will have to be estimated.

176

12. Increased cost of living

Calculation of the increase in the plaintiff's cost of living between the accident and the trial should be straightforward. Where the increase is caused by an entirely new expense, the plaintiff need only assemble the relevant bills. Where it is due to an increased consumption of something he was using before the accident, the plaintiff's claim is for the present cost of providing that commodity less what he would have been spending if the accident had not occurred.

If the plaintiff has kept his old bills, this calculation will present no problem. Where, for example, a plaintiff claims that he has to spend more on electricity to keep warm, his bills for the last four quarters before the accident should show his annual consumption. The important figure is the number of units used. Multiplied by the present price per unit, that figure is the present cost of buying the amount of electricity the plaintiff was using before the accident: the difference between that cost and the cost of the plaintiff's present annual consumption is the plaintiff's annual loss, which is in turn multiplied by the number of years since the accident. If the cost of electricity has changed over that period, separate calculations will have to be done for the period between each unit price change.

Where the plaintiff has not kept his old bills, some kind of estimate will be necessary. This must be based on evidence. If the plaintiff says, for example, that he now burns a one-bar electric fire all day between November and March, and says that before the accident he would normally have been out of the house from 7 am to 7 pm from Monday to Friday, he is buying an extra twelve kilowatt-hours' electricity per day, five days a week, for about 20 weeks a year: once the unit cost is known, the calculation is straightforward.

13. Lost perks

The only difficulty posed by the claim for loss of perks is that of putting a value on them. In principle it is the cash cost of replacing the lost perk. Where the plaintiff has lost a company car, for example, and is now running a car of his own, the claim is for the annual cost multiplied by the number of years since the accident. The annual cost is not confined to the running costs, but includes depreciation: for these purposes the tables published by the Automobile Association are very helpful, if the defendant can be persuaded to agree them. If not, the practitioner will have to make some attempt to work out what his client is spending on his car, making due allowance for the capital lost every time the car has to be replaced.

An employee who has perks receives part of his remuneration in kind, but pays the tax on that part of his remuneration out of income that has already been taxed. From the cash cost of replacing the lost perk must, therefore, be deducted the tax which no longer has to be paid.

Checklist

1. Refer to the heads of loss identified by using the checklist for Chapter 19.
2. Quantify the loss under each head between the date of the accident and the date of the statement of special damage.
3. Remember to recalculate the loss under each head to the date of trial in due course.
4. If the plaintiff was an employee, seek details of his pre-accident earnings: press for discovery or serve interrogatories if necessary.
5. If the plaintiff was an employee and has not returned to his pre-accident job, seek details of the earnings of the person now doing the plaintiff's job: press for discovery or serve interrogatories if necessary.
6. If the plaintiff was an employee, seek details of his promotion prospects and potential earnings: press for discovery or serve interrogatories if necessary.
7. If necessary, identify a worker with comparable earnings. Take a proof and marshal the supporting documents.
8. Was the plaintiff self-employed? If so, are his accounts complete to the end of the accounting year before that in which his accident occurred? If not, advise the plaintiff to put their preparation in hand *at once*.
9. Are accounts needed to show the plaintiff's earnings: (a) in the accounting year in which the accident occurred; or (b) in subsequent years? If so, advise the plaintiff to put their preparation in hand *at once*.
10. Is all the evidence in the form of witness statements which: (a) satisfy the requirements of the County Court Rules; and (b) exhibit any documents to which they refer?

Chapter 22

Future pecuniary loss: theory

1. Kernel of the problem

Assessment of the plaintiff's loss to the date of trial is straightforward: he receives a lump sum representing the income he has lost, or the additional expenditure he has incurred, as a result of the accident. If by the date of the trial the plaintiff has returned to work at his full pre-accident wage, or is no longer incurring additional expenditure, his pecuniary loss can be assessed very accurately. The court may be asked to make assumptions — that the plaintiff would have been promoted within a year if the accident had not occurred, for example — but if it is prepared to make those assumptions on the evidence laid before it, the calculation of the loss is a simple matter of arithmetic.

If the plaintiff is continuing to suffer loss at the date of trial, however, two separate problems arise. What loss is the plaintiff likely to suffer in the future? And how is the court to turn that loss into lump-sum compensation?

Although it presents practical difficulties caused by the need to predict the future on the basis of the evidence currently available, the first question presents no theoretical problem. Does the evidence show that it is more likely than not that this plaintiff, currently unable to work owing to his injuries, will be able to return to work of some kind at some time in the future? If so, when? What kind of work will he be able to do? How much will he earn? How much would he have been earning if the accident had not happened?

Turning that loss into lump-sum compensation, on the other hand, gives rise to problems that are as much theoretical as practical. In a few cases the plaintiff's accident will cause a future loss of capital, but in most cases, whether the plaintiff says that the accident will prevent him from earning the wages he would otherwise have earned, or says that the accident will cause him to spend money he would not otherwise have spent, his loss is a loss of income and, what is more, a loss of income in the future; in contrast, the only compensation the court can award is damages — that is an immediate capital sum. This mismatch between the nature of the loss and the nature of the compensation produces three separate problems:

- the problem of acceleration;
- the problem of inflation;
- the problem of mortality.

2. The problem of acceleration

The nature of this problem can be illustrated by an example. The plaintiff's claim is heard on the second anniversary of his accident. He has not worked since the accident, and the medical evidence shows that he will never work again. At the time of the trial he is 55 years old; in the normal course of events he would have retired at 60. Before the accident he was earning £10,000 a year after tax; the rate for the job is still the same. At the time of the trial building societies are paying nine per cent a year net of tax at the standard rate on their ordinary accounts.

Between the date of the accident and the date of the trial the plaintiff has lost two years' net salary, namely £20,000: an award of £20,000 is thus fair compensation for this loss. An award of £50,000 is not, on the other hand, fair compensation for the five years' prospective loss of earnings between the date of the trial and the date on which the plaintiff would have retired in the normal course of events; for on the assumption that the plaintiff will pay his damages into a building society and draw from them at the rate of £10,000 a year to replace his lost wages, he will have over £13,000 left at the end of the five-year period, and so receive more than a quarter too much compensation.

Precisely the same problem arises where the plaintiff has lost the right to receive a capital sum at a future date. If the evidence shows that but for the accident the same plaintiff would have received a capital sum of £50,000 at a date five years after the date of trial, an immediate award of £50,000 represents compensation of £77,000; for again, if the plaintiff leaves his damages in the building society until the date on which he would have had the capital sum in the normal course of events, he will receive (such is the power of compounding) nearly £27,000 in interest. On the other hand, if he uses the capital sum immediately, he will also be over-compensated, since he is enjoying the capital sum five years too soon.

The problem is compounded where the plaintiff is a child. If a boy of 14 is so badly injured that he will never work and, looking at his school record and hearing evidence of what the boy may have said about his plans to his parents, teachers and friends before the accident, the Judge concludes that he would have left school at 18, would not have gone on to higher education, but would have found a job within six months of leaving school, the plaintiff is not only receiving at the beginning of his working life compensation for a loss that (in part at least) he would not have suffered until the end of his working life, but he is also receiving that compensation four years before he would have started work at all.

Although these three examples refer to cases in which the plaintiff is claiming a loss of future income or capital, precisely the same considerations affect a claim for future expenditure. An award of £50,000 now is not fair compensation for expenditure of £10,000 a year over the next five years, because the plaintiff will earn compound interest on that part of the money which has not yet been spent.

3. The problem of inflation

Accelerated receipt gives the plaintiff too much compensation; inflation gives him too little. Even when interest rates are 9 per cent a year net of basic rate income tax, £50,000 now will be too little to compensate the plaintiff for the loss of five years' income at £10,000 a year if the rate of inflation is 13 per cent. If the lost income has risen smoothly at the rate of inflation, it will have reached over £18,000 a year by the end of the fifth year and the total income lost over the period of five years will be £69,000; even with compound interest at 9 per cent a year on the reducing capital the immediate award of £50,000 will have left the plaintiff with £7,600 less than he needs to make good his loss. The problem will be worse in serious cases where the interest from the damages is subject to tax at a higher rate.

This example assumes, of course, that the wage for the job the plaintiff can no longer do has risen precisely in step with inflation. It may have risen less quickly, but in general over long periods the rise in average earnings has in the recent past consistently outstripped inflation.

4. The problem of mortality

Anyone with enough morbid curiosity can find out when he can expect to die. For every individual of an given age, there is a life expectancy. In general terms it is the average number of years by which an individual answering a particular description can expect to survive his present age. The sum of age plus life expectancy always increases with age, because even a man of 105 has some life expectancy. For any given individual, the accuracy of the forecast increases with the narrowness of the description used. There is a figure for men of 37 born and resident in England and Wales: for the broad category of men of 37 born and resident in England and Wales it will be accurate. If the subject falls into the narrower category of male *manual* workers of 37 born and resident in England and Wales, however, a figure for that narrower category will be more accurate, for any given man answering that description, than the general figure for men of 37 born and resident in England and Wales. On the other hand, for a male office worker of 37 it will be less accurate than the more general figure.

Although each figure represents the truth, it represents only a statistical truth. Provided that the raw data are accurate and the statistical methods sound, life tables tell the truth about the section of the population to which they relate, but they say nothing at all about any individual member of that population: he may have an incipient melanoma, which will kill him within a year, or he may survive to receive the Queen's telegram. In one sense, the statistical truth is the only ascertainable truth: no doctor can forecast accurately when any given individual is going to die. On the other hand, an actuary's calculations are much more accurate than the crude average figure might suggest, since they take statistical account of the contingencies of life. That includes, of course, the probability that a given individual will depart from the average by living a shorter or longer time.

The consequences for compensation are far-reaching. The aim is to provide a capital sum which, by exhausting itself over the period for which the income could have been expected to last, replaces a lost income stream (or compensates for additional expenditure). A sum awarded on the basis of statistical truth may produce a gross injustice in any given case. An award based on a life expectancy of 30 years will be unjust to the defendant if the plaintiff dies from causes unrelated to the accident within five, because his heirs will inherit a capital sum which would not have existed but for the accident. On the other hand, if the plaintiff confounds the life tables and lives for 40 years, his compensation will be exhausted long before he dies.

5. The solution to the problems

The courts might have adopted a solution based on expert evidence. An actuary can deal with the problems of both acceleration and mortality by a calculation that takes account not only of the number of years that a person answering the plaintiff's description can be expected, on average, to survive, but also of the chance that the particular plaintiff in question will live for a longer or shorter period than the average. The problem of inflation could be dealt with to a limited extent by hearing expert evidence about current investment conditions and practice.

The English courts have refused to adopt this approach, largely because they have consistently misunderstood the nature of actuarial evidence. The courts have instead adopted a rough-and-ready, commonsense approach; unsatisfactory in itself, the approach is further vitiated by being based on a false premiss. The courts' approach uses two figures, called the multiplicand and the multiplier.

The first step is to assess the plaintiff's continuing annual loss. This loss is calculated at the date of trial, so any inflation between the date of the accident and the date of trial is taken automatically into account. The loss must be calculated separately for each head of damage, producing, for example, separate annual figures for loss of earnings and cost of future care. In each case the figure so produced is called the multiplicand.

Under each head the award of damages represents the capital sum produced by multiplying the multiplicand by a figure, called the multiplier, which is intended to take account of the problems of acceleration, inflation and mortality. The product of this multiplication is supposed to be that capital sum which, if eroded steadily during the period of the loss for which it is compensation, but invested in the meantime, will last for the period of the loss, but no longer.

The approach is rough-and-ready because (with very rare exceptions) the choice of multiplier is conventional and arbitrary, being governed by decisions made in similar cases in the past, rather than by evidence about the real conditions in any particular case. What is worse, the conventional multipliers tacitly assume that the plaintiff will invest his damages in a low-risk investment yielding between four and five per cent a year net. The snag, of course, is that there is no such investment, and has not been for very many years.

6. Dealing with acceleration

The rough-and-ready approach deals with the problem of acceleration by choosing multipliers which tacitly assume a discount rate of between four and five per cent a year. In other words, applied to a given multiplicand, the multiplier should produce that capital sum which, if eroded steadily during the period of the loss for which it is compensation, but invested at between four and five per cent a year net in the meantime, will produce an annual sum equal to the multiplicand for the period of the loss, but no longer.

7. Dealing with inflation

The courts deal with future inflation by ignoring it. Evidence about the likely future course of inflation is inadmissible: *Lim Poh Choo* v *Camden and Islington Area Health Authority* [1980] AC 174 at 193, [1979] 2 All ER 910 at 922. The courts expect the plaintiff himself to deal with future inflation by prudent investment (*Cookson* v *Knowles* [1979] AC 556 at 571F-572A, [1978] 2 All ER 604 at 611b–d), even though the real rate of return which they assume is entirely unrealistic.

8. Dealing with mortality

At the date of trial the medical evidence will show one of two things about the plaintiff's life expectancy. In a few cases it will have been reduced by his injuries; in the great majority of cases it will not.

If the plaintiff's life expectancy has been reduced by his injuries, the position is straightforward. In assessing compensation for a loss which will continue for the rest of the plaintiff's life, the courts will choose a multiplier which reflects the doctors' assessment.

Where the plaintiff's expectation of life is unaffected by his injuries, the courts will adopt the conventional multiplier for a person of his age, sex and occupation. These conventional multipliers tacitly assume that the plaintiff will live for the average length of time a person of the plaintiff's age, sex and occupation can be expected to survive.

9. A new problem: contingency

The problems of acceleration, inflation and mortality are ones which affect the injured plaintiff in the real future. The way in which each of these imponderables turns out over the remainder of his life will determine whether his compensation is too great or too little.

By its very nature, however, the calculation of the plaintiff's future loss is an assessment of what would have happened in a future which by definition is not the one the plaintiff will now enjoy. Like the real future of the injured plaintiff, the hypothetical future of the uninjured plaintiff is subject to imponderable factors such as inflation, mortality and contingency. These, too, must be taken into account.

10. Dealing with hypothetical inflation

The hypothetical inflation which the plaintiff would have faced if he had not been injured is the same as the real inflation which he faces now that he has been injured. The courts deal with it in the same way, that is by ignoring it.

As a consequence of this rule the calculation of the plaintiff's continuing loss must be based on a multiplicand which reflects the rate of loss at the date of the trial. This applies equally to a claim for continuing loss of earnings and to a claim for continuing expenditure caused by the accident. Thus if the plaintiff claims that he would have remained in his pre-accident work for the rest of his working life had the accident not occurred, the basis of the calculation of his future loss of earnings is the rate that that job is paying at the date of trial, even though it is likely to increase with inflation in the future.

11. Dealing with hypothetical mortality

The hypothetical life expectancy of the uninjured plaintiff may be the same as the life expectancy of the plaintiff once he has been injured, but it need not be. It can be greater or less. The difference can affect not only the calculation of losses which will continue for the rest of the plaintiff's life, but also those which (like loss of earnings) will come to an end at some date in the future (in that case, the normal retirement date for the plaintiff's pre-accident occupation).

Consider three cases. Take first the case of a bank teller who is injured in a road accident in such a way that he will not work again, though his life expectancy is not reduced. His pre-accident job did not expose him to any untoward hazards, so he can have expected to live as long as anyone else — for the average period, in other words. The accident has not changed that. It follows that mortality need only be taken into account once: in calculating compensation for those losses which will continue for the rest of his life, the court must choose a multiplier which reflects his real life expectancy at the date of trial.

Consider now a test pilot. He is also injured in a road accident in such a way that he will not work again, though his life expectancy is not reduced. His pre-accident work was very dangerous and he stood a good chance of being killed before reaching retirement: his life expectancy has probably increased, if anything, as a result of the accident. Here mortality needs to be taken into account twice.

The assessment of compensation for those losses which will continue for the rest of his life is straightforward, the court choosing a multiplier which reflects his real life expectancy at the date of trial; since he is no longer a test pilot, it is likely to be the same as that for anyone of his age and sex. The calculation of his future loss of earnings, on the other hand, must take account of the fact that he was a test pilot and ran a real risk of being killed. That is done by reducing the multiplier which on the basis of age alone would be appropriate to the period between the accident and the date on which the plaintiff could have expected to retire had the accident not occurred.

An entirely different case is that of a bank teller who is injured in a road accident in such a way that he will not work again and his life expectancy is reduced to five years. Compensation for those losses which will continue for the rest of his life must be based on a real life expectancy of five years, whereas the calculation of his future loss of earnings will be based on the risk of premature death run by a healthy bank teller. Since that is very low, it will be the multiplier appropriate to the whole of the period between the accident and the date on which the plaintiff could have expected to retire had the accident not occurred.

12. Dealing with hypothetical contingency

The hypothetical future of which the injured plaintiff has been deprived will have contained contingencies other than the risk of premature death. The assessment of his future loss must attempt to take account of these hazards of life.

A steel erector, like the test pilot, runs a serious risk of injury. So, too, does a man or woman who engages in a dangerous sport such as hang-gliding. The economy, too, contains risks. The plaintiff is being compensated only for the loss of money he would in fact have earned, so the courts must take account of the fact that an unskilled man might well have found himself out of work for long periods in any event; that a development in technology might have rendered a skill worthless; that a businessman might have been forced out of business by a change in market conditions; and so on. In each case they do so by adjusting the multiplicand, the multiplier, or both.

13. An alternative solution

There is an alternative to the use of conventional multipliers. Despite its obvious attractions, it has not yet been adopted by the courts.

The system of conventional multipliers evolved at a time when there was no investment which was both safe and proof against inflation. That changed with the introduction in 1981 of Index-Linked Government Stock. The stock is as safe as the British Government and both its maturity value and the dividends it pays in the meantime rise in step with the Retail Price Index. The yield on Index-Linked Government Stock generally lies between 2.5 and 3.5 per cent a year.

With this change in mind a Working Party set up by the various professional bodies representing actuaries, barristers, solicitors and advocates under the chairmanship of M Ogden QC produced in 1984 a set of tables which set out the appropriate actuarial multipliers for:

- pecuniary loss for life (males);
- pecuniary loss for life (females);
- loss of earnings to pension age 65 (males);
- loss of earnings to pension age 60 (females);
- loss of pension commencing age 65 (males);
- loss of pension commencing age 60 (females).

The tables allow only for mortality, so the multipliers they give must be adjusted to take account of such other contingencies as ill health, redundancy, early retirement and so on. For each category of loss, however, the table gives a multiplier appropriate both to the plaintiff's age and to the current, real, net, annual return on investments, set out in steps of half a percentage point between 1.5 and 5 per cent.

The tables are entitled *Actuarial Tables with Explanatory Notes for Use in Personal Injury and Fatal Accident Cases*, but are usually known as the Ogden Tables. A second edition of the tables was published by Her Majesty's Stationery Office in September 1994. The Appendix to this book reproduces the multipliers appropriate to the 3, 3.5, 4, 4.5 and 5 per cent rates. In November 1993 the Chancellor of the Exchequer announced that the age at which women are entitled to draw the State retirement pension is to be raised to 65 from 2010. The tables now include actuarial multipliers to reflect this change, which will be phased in over ten years.

The tables are a useful ruler against which to measure the conventional multipliers, but practitioners should bear two points in mind. Until the courts can be persuaded to adopt a realistic figure for the return on investments, the tables must be used to select multipliers appropriate to the conventional rate of 4.5 per cent, rather than the realistic rate of 2.5 to 3.5 per cent.

In theory the tables are not admissible in evidence unless agreed. In Scotland, however, the Inner House of the Court of Session decided in *Docherty as Curator Bonis to O'Brien* v *British Steel Plc* 1991 SLT 477 to take judicial notice of the Ogden Tables, an approach which has since been followed in England and Wales and approved by the Judicial Studies Board. It will be a very long time, however, before the Ogden Tables supplant the conventional method of assessing multipliers. In *Hunt* v *Severs* [1994] 2 All ER 385 at 396g to 397d the House of Lords acknowledged that nowadays 'actuarial tables tend to figure more prominently in the evidence on which courts rely' but nevertheless reversed the decision of the Court of Appeal ([1993] 4 All ER 180), which had substituted a multiplier based on actuarial tables for the conventional multiplier chosen by the trial judge. Lord Bridge said that 'some discount in respect of life's manifold contingencies is invariably made' from any multiplier taken from statistical tables: even then, an appellate court could replace a conventional multiplier only where a multiplier based on statistics gave a 'demonstrably' more accurate assessment.

Chapter 23

Future pecuniary loss: practice

1. Use of multiplicand and multiplier

In general the calculation of all the plaintiff's future loss has to fit the framework of multiplicand and multiplier. Separate calculations will be needed for each head of damage, since each head of damage will have a different multiplicand; in many cases each will have a different multiplier, too.

2. Calculation of the multiplicand

In principle, calculation of the multiplicand presents no problem. A calculation of the plaintiff's loss of earnings between the accident and the trial can be easily extended to put a figure on his continuing annual loss at the date of trial. If the plaintiff is not working, and is not likely to work in the future, he has a claim for total loss of earnings, the multiplicand being the net annual salary he would have been earning at the date of trial. If he is back at work, earning less than he was before the accident and is (inflation aside) never likely to earn more, the multiplicand will be the difference between the net annual salary he would have been earning at the date of trial and the net annual salary he is in fact earning at the date of trial. If the plaintiff is not working at the date of trial, but is capable of working, then (provided jobs within his capacity are available) the multiplicand will be the difference between what he would have been and could now be earning.

Precisely the same principles apply to a continuing expense, like the cost of medicines or the cost of additional heating. Where the loss is an entirely new expense, like the recurrent cost of medicine, the annual cost is the multiplicand. Where the loss is an increase in a pre-existing expense, like the cost of additional heating, the multiplicand will be the difference between what the plaintiff is spending per year on heating at the date of trial and what he would have been spending had the accident not occurred.

The multiplicand must always be an annual figure. A figure representing a weekly or monthly loss must be converted to an annual figure. This principle causes particular difficulties with:

- erratic loss;
- sporadic loss.

3. Erratic loss

The multiplicand is sometimes called upon to represent an erratic loss which is not easily expressed as an annual figure. An actor, for example, may be out of work for more than half his working life, even if he is successful; when not working in theatre, he may do a variety of odd jobs. In some years he may earn a lot of money; in others very little.

If a person in such a position has a claim for future loss of earnings, his continuing loss at the date of trial must be expressed as an annual figure. This can be achieved by looking either forward or backward.

If at the time of his accident the plaintiff was on the point of landing a long-term contract to play a part in a soap opera, for example, his net annual salary under that contract represents his continuing annual loss and therefore forms the basis of the multiplicand. Such cases will be rare, however, and the plaintiff's continuing annual loss will have to be calculated by looking at his pre-accident, rather than prospective, earnings. So, for example, if the actor has been in the profession for some time, it will usually be possible to produce an annual figure — and so a multiplicand — by taking his average net earnings over the last five or six years.

In a calculation of this kind it is permissible to take past inflation into account, since it is only evidence about the future course of inflation that is inadmissible. Before taking the average of the plaintiff's earnings in, say, the five years before the accident each year's earnings can be updated by a factor representing inflation, provided, of course, that there is evidence to show that actors' earnings have been increasing in line with inflation over this period.

4. Sporadic loss

A good example of sporadic loss is the cost of carrying out modifications which enable an injured person to drive his car. Although it recurs every time the plaintiff changes his car, it does not form an annual expense. The multiplicand must, however, represent an annual loss.

Before a sporadic loss of this kind can be calculated, therefore, the expense must be reduced to an annual figure. The plaintiff first needs expert evidence to show how often the expense is likely to be incurred; he then needs expert evidence to show how great the expense is likely to be each time it is incurred. Dividing the expense by the number of years between each incidence produces the multiplicand.

Thus if the evidence shows the plaintiff will have to change his car every five years and will have to spend (at today's prices) £900 each time on modifications, the multiplicand under this head will be:

$$£ \frac{900}{5} = 180$$

5. Choosing the multiplier

Future loss covers the period from the date of the trial to the date on which the loss will cease. It follows that the multiplier must be calculated as at the date of trial, not as at the date of the accident: *Pritchard* v *Cobden* [1988] Fam 22, [1987] 1 All ER 300.

Putting a figure on the multiplier is the point at which parties most often fall out in their calculation of the plaintiff's future loss. Chapter 17 described the assessment of damages for pain, suffering and loss of amenity by comparison with comparable cases. The choice of multiplier is a precisely similar process.

Appendix I to Chapter 6 of *Kemp* is a table of multipliers in personal injury cases. This is the best starting-point. The table lists cases by the plaintiff's age, youngest first: where the information is available, the table also includes his pre-accident occupation and life expectancy. The table then shows for each case the multiplier chosen in calculating the damages under each head of future loss. Where the case is reported in *Kemp*, it is cross-referenced.

The practitioner using the table tries to find a plaintiff whose circumstances are as close as possible to his client's. The multiplier used in that case is then likely to be a good guide to his own.

Table 10 in paragraph 680 of the *Report of the Pearson Royal Commission on Civil Liability and Compensation for Personal Injury* (1978 Cmnd 7054) sets out the multipliers used to calculate prospective losses for periods of between five and 40 years, in five-year steps. These figures, which were compiled from an analysis of decided cases, can be used to check the multiplier suggested by the practitioner's own research.

6. Taking account of contingency

In principle, rough-and-ready though it is, this framework should produce very simple calculations. In practice, however, it is bedevilled by the problems caused by contingency. This contingency will be of one of two kinds:

- what might be;
- what might have been.

Most of this chapter will deal with the various ways in which the courts accommodate these contingencies in practice.

7. What might be

These are the contingencies of the real world in which the injured plaintiff now finds himself. A plaintiff is injured in such a way that he has been unable to return to work; at the date of the trial he is still unfit. The medical evidence suggests, however, that there is still room for improvement and in due course the plaintiff may find work of some kind, though perhaps not perhaps commanding as high a salary as his pre-accident job. Such a set of facts confronts the court with a number of contingencies. Will the plaintiff make the progress for which the doctors hope? If so, when will he be fit for work? What kind of work will be able to do? How long will it take him to find a job once he is fit? What will it pay? How secure will it be?

8. What might have been

These are the contingencies of the world in which the plaintiff would have lived had the accident not occurred. The plaintiff will never work again, so he has a claim for total loss of earnings. But how safe was his pre-accident job anyway? Was he likely to be made redundant? Might he not have been injured in some other way even if the accident had not occurred? Problematic as the contingencies of the real world are, the assessment of these hypothetical contingencies is much more difficult.

9. Contingencies to be accommodated

There is no limit to the number of contingencies that calculations of this sort must accommodate. In the broadest possible terms, however, the contingencies which must be taken into account fall into seven categories:

- period of loss;
- prospective inflation;
- prospective taxation;
- increasing loss;
- decreasing loss;
- plaintiff's prospects unknown;
- lost years.

10. Period of loss

The most important contingency to be taken into account is the period for which the plaintiff will continue to suffer any given loss. When will it start? When will it come to an end?

The period will fall into one of two classes: losses that will last for the whole of the plaintiff's life and those that will last for a shorter period. In either case this is a contingency which affects the multiplier rather than the multiplicand.

Where the loss will continue for the whole of the plaintiff's life, the multiplier must reflect his life expectancy. If the plaintiff's life expectancy has not been reduced by his injuries, the multiplier will be based on the average life expectancy of persons answering the plaintiff's description; if his life expectancy has been reduced, the multiplier will be based on the number of years the doctors expect him to live. The commonest loss which will last for the rest of the plaintiff's life is the cost of future care — ranging from 24-hour nursing in the most serious cases to prescription charges in the least.

(a) Period of loss: life

A loss for life sounds dramatic. It may indeed be a very big claim — the cost, for example, of constant nursing care for life. Such cases are unlikely to be heard in the county court, but many losses which are small in themselves will continue for the rest of the plaintiff's life. If, for example, the plaintiff can no longer manage the heavy housework which he did before the accident, the cost of employing part-time help is a loss which will last for the rest of his life.

In theory, at least, some very long-term losses of this kind will come to an end before the plaintiff's death: it is most unlikely, for example, that a man would have been digging his garden or repairing his car in his eighties, even if he had not been injured. Unless the plaintiff is very elderly at the date of trial, however, the day when he will stop doing these tasks is so far in the future that in practical terms the cost of employing someone else to do them can be treated as a loss for life.

Because the courts have chosen to ignore actuarial evidence, a multiplier based on the average life expectancy of persons answering the plaintiff's description will be chosen not on the basis of life tables, or of the expert evidence of an actuary, but by comparison with multipliers chosen in previous cases involving similar plaintiffs.

Where the plaintiff's life expectancy has been reduced by his injuries, the multiplier must reflect the number of years the doctors expect him to live. Occasionally previous cases will suggest a suitable figure, but very often the calculation will have to proceed from first principles. If the plaintiff has a claim for the continuing cost of care for the rest of his life, but is only expected to live five years, then his compensation will be a capital sum five times his annual loss but discounted by four or five per cent a year to take account of accelerated receipt.

(b) Period of loss: less than life

A loss may last for a shorter period than the plaintiff's life for either or both of two reasons. It may come to an end before he dies; or it may not yet have begun.

The commonest example of a loss which will cease before the plaintiff dies is loss of earnings, which will in general come to an end at the date at which the plaintiff would have retired if the accident had not occurred. In such a case the multiplier reflects the period between the date of the trial and the plaintiff's normal retirement date. Again, the multiplier must be chosen by looking at earlier cases involving plaintiffs of the same kind.

Age is not the only relevant factor. Provided that a sufficiently close parallel can be found, adoption of the multiplier used in the earlier case automatically takes account of other factors, in particular the risks peculiar to the plaintiff's sex and occupation. Women live longer than men, and steel-erectors and divers are both more likely to be injured at work than barristers: if the plaintiff is a 25-year-old, male steel-erector, therefore, comparison with the multiplier adopted in an earlier case involving a 25-year-old, female barrister will be less useful than comparison with a case involving a 28-year-old, male diver. The aim is to match age, sex and occupation exactly; the trick is to match as many of the three as closely as possible.

Cases sometimes throw up a factor for which authorities do not provide a precedent. A chartered accountant may take part in dangerous pastimes like bungee-jumping: his job is free from risk, but his hobby is not. If he is injured in such a way that he has a claim for loss of earnings for the rest of his working life, the multiplier adopted in an earlier case involving a chartered accountant (or solicitor, barrister, or someone else whose job is equally free from risk) of the same age will have to be reduced to take account of the additional risk of injury or premature death the plaintiff had accepted by taking up an inherently dangerous sport.

Precedent is a good guide to the choice of multiplier to represent the period between the accident and retirement. It is less useful where, for example, the evidence shows that the plaintiff will be capable of only light work for the next three to five years, but will then be able to return to his pre-accident employment. In such cases the multiplier used to calculate the plaintiff's future loss of earnings must represent a period which is short, but uncertain. In such cases a very rough-and-ready approach is adopted: the court is likely to take a multiplier of 3.5 or even 3, reflecting both acceleration and the chance that the plaintiff may return to his pre-accident work sooner rather than later.

Where the period is very short, the court is unlikely to reduce the multiplier to take account of acceleration. If the evidence shows that the plaintiff is likely to return to work in about 18 months, the correct multiplier is 1.5.

A plaintiff very often faces losses in the future which have not begun by the date of trial. A labourer with a knee injury may, for example, be back at work at the date of trial, but be likely in the future to develop osteo-arthritis so severe that he will have to give up heavy manual work in 10 to 15 years. Similarly, a boy who needs constant nursing care may be at home at the date of trial, but likely to need institutional care within five years, when he will be too big and heavy for his parents to handle.

Once again, earlier cases will sometimes help, but it is often better to adopt a hybrid approach. The multiplicand will represent the plaintiff's annual loss at the date when it will begin: the multiplicand can be increased to take into account such contingencies as the promotion the plaintiff could have expected but for the accident between the trial and the date at which the loss will begin, but it must ignore prospective inflation. To that multiplicand is applied the multiplier appropriate to the plaintiff at the date when the loss will begin: to take account of acceleration the capital sum produced by that multiplication is then further discounted at four or five per cent a year over the period between the date on which the loss is likely to begin and the the date of trial.

(c) Period of loss: need for two multipliers

Where the plaintiff is to be compensated for two kinds of loss, one of which will last for a longer period than the other, two separate multipliers will be needed. Many cases of future loss will involve one multiplier for the loss of earnings calculation and another for calculation of future expenses. In general the first will be smaller than the second, because the plaintiff's loss of earnings will cease, at the latest, at his normal retirement age, whereas the additional expenses are with him for life.

An example may help to illustrate the nature of the calculation. A man of 28 is so badly injured that he will never return to his pre-accident work. The trial takes place two years after the accident, when the plaintiff is 30. His life expectancy is a further 44 years. In the normal course of events he would have retired at 60. He will need regular out-patient treatment for the rest of his life.

At the date of trial the plaintiff's net loss of earnings is running at £3,000 a year. His care is costing £3,000 a year. The award for loss of earnings will be £3,000x, where x, the multiplier, is the figure that produces a capital sum which, if eroded for the next 30 years, but invested in the meantime, will produce a real return of £3,000 a year. Similarly the award for cost of future care will be £3,000y, where y, the multiplier, is the figure that produces a capital sum which, if eroded for the next 44 years, but invested in the meantime, will produce a real return of £3,000 a year. y is not, of course, the same as x. When the plaintiff reaches 60, his loss of earnings will cease and so the fund produced by applying x should in theory be exhausted; the fund produced by applying y, on the other hand, will have to continue paying £3,000 for another 14 years.

Comparison of the multipliers adopted by the courts in cases of this kind will show that the difference between x and y is not as great as the difference between the periods they are supposed to represent might suggest. Practitioners should press in court for realistic differences, but while negotiating bear in mind that Judges are more likely to be swayed by authority than logic.

(d) Period of loss: need for three multipliers

The calculation of future loss will call for as many multipliers as there are separate periods of loss. Consider the case of a plaintiff of 40 who suffers a severe orthopaedic injury that reduces his mobility. Mobility is essential to his pre-accident job, but he can be retrained and once retrained will be able to find a job which pays as much as his pre-accident work. Retraining will take four years at college. Before the accident the plaintiff was an employee, working from an office; once retrained, he will be self-employed, working at home, so he will incur extra expense in heating and lighting his own home. He will need drugs for the rest of his life. If the plaintiff had remained in his pre-accident work, he would have retired at 55. His expectation of life is unaffected.

This is a case which calls for three multipliers, because each loss will run for a different period. His claim for loss of earnings covers four years. His claim for the extra cost of heating and lighting covers the eleven years from the end of his period of training, because on retirement he would have had to meet those expenses in any case. His claim for the cost of drugs covers the longest period, namely the rest of his life.

11. Prospective inflation

The multiplicand must ignore the possibility of future inflation, since evidence about the likely future course of inflation is inadmissible: *Lim Poh Choo* v *Camden and Islington Area Health Authority* [1980] AC 174 at 193, [1979] 2 All ER 910 at 922. If inflation is the only factor likely to affect a continuing loss, it follows that the loss must be treated as static: the loss the plaintiff is experiencing at the date of trial will therefore be treated as his continuing loss for the indefinite future.

It is easy to forget that this rule applies not just to losses which have begun at the date of trial and will continue into the future; it applies also to losses which have not yet begun. Thus if the medical evidence shows that a plaintiff will need institutional care in ten years' time, his advisers must call expert evidence to prove the current cost of care in the kind of institution the plaintiff will need. The likelihood of inflation over the next ten years is ignored.

12. Prospective taxation

The conventional multipliers assume a net return of between four and five per cent a year and so automatically make allowance for tax at the standard rate. The same multipliers are to be used even where the award is so big that the income it will produce is going to attract tax at a higher rate: *Hodgson* v *Trapp* [1989] AC 807, [1988] 3 All ER 870.

13. Increasing loss

A prospective increase in the plaintiff's continuing loss caused by anything other than inflation can be dealt with in one of two ways. Either the multiplicand is increased to reflect average earnings or the multiplier is split to cover different periods.

Suppose that the evidence shows that a man aged 50 would have remained in his pre-accident post for the next five years, at the end of which he could have expected promotion to a post which he would have occupied for the last ten years of his working life; the current net salary for his pre-accident job is £10,000 a year, while the job to which he could have expected promotion is currently paying £15,000 a year net. The plaintiff's average net annual loss over this period is:

$$£ \frac{(5 \times 10,000) + (10 \times 15,000)}{15} = 13,333.$$

Multiplication of this figure by the multiplier appropriate to a man of

50 in the plaintiff's occupation produces the capital sum representing his loss under this head.

The more difficult method is to split the multiplier. This requires the practitioner to choose a multiplier appropriate to the whole period of 15 years, then apply one-third of that multiplier to a loss of £10,000 a year, two-thirds to the loss of £15,000.

Both approaches have been sanctioned by the courts. Since no point of law of general importance is involved, reported decisions on this topic are rare. One example (which uses the first approach) is *Housecroft* v *Burnett* [1986] 1 All ER 332.

The cost of future care can also represent an increasing loss, particularly when the plaintiff is a child. In many cases of this kind the plaintiff's parents will continue to care for him for as long as they can, but there will come a time when the plaintiff has to be cared for in an institution. Institutional care will be much more expensive than care at home. In such cases the multiplier must be split, one applying to the multiplicand representing the period during which the plaintiff will be at home, the other to the multiplicand representing the annual cost of institutional care.

14. Decreasing loss

A prospective decrease is dealt with in exactly the same way as a prospective increase. The commonest example is that of a plaintiff who, unable to work at the date of trial, can nevertheless hope to return to work in due course. If the chance of returning to work is too slender to make a detailed calculation realistic, the courts sometimes take account of the possibility that the plaintiff will return to work at some unspecified time in the future by reducing the multiplier.

15. Plaintiff's prospects unknown

Where the plaintiff is a child or adolescent, the hypothetical future which forms the basis of his claim for future loss of earnings may be extremely difficult to assess. The contingencies of this unknown future are reflected both in the multiplicand and in the multiplier.

(a) Plaintiff's prospects unknown: adjusting the multiplicand

The evidence may show that the plaintiff will never work, or it may show that he will work in only a very limited capacity. In either case the assessment of the plaintiff's future loss will rest on the evidence of doctors and of experts in training, rehabilitation and employment. In both cases, however, the greatest difficulty lies in determining what the plaintiff would have achieved if he had not been injured.

In many cases the court will assume that the plaintiff would have earned an average wage. Depending on the evidence, this may be the national average for manual workers, for non-manual workers or for workers generally. Where the child has been at school long enough for his teachers to form some assessment of his capabilities, their evidence will be relevant; in most cases the court will hear about the plaintiff's family and the background against which he would have grown up.

Where the evidence suggests that the plaintiff's chances of obtaining well-paid work were above average, the court may well fix a multiplicand which is, say, 50 per cent above the appropriate national average. In exceptional cases, where the evidence about the child's prospects is very strong, the courts will conclude that he would have taken up a particular area of work.

Two contrasting decisions of the Court of Appeal indicate the way in which the courts tackle this problem. The first is an example of the normal approach, the second of the exceptional.

In *Croke* v *Wiseman* [1982] 1 WLR 71 at 83C, [1981] 3 All ER 852 at 862c:

'The judge [at first instance] assessed the future loss of earnings at £5,000 per annum. He arrived at this figure by taking the national average wage for a young man. In my view, he was justified in doing so. This child came from an excellent home, the father is an enterprising man starting his own business and the mother is a qualified teacher; they have shown the quality of their characters by the care they have given their child and their courage by the fact that they have continued with their family even after this disaster befell them. The defendants cannot complain that they are unfairly treated if against this background the judge assumes that the child will grow up to lead a useful working life and be capable of at least earning the national average wage.'

Contrast *Cassel* v *Riverside Health Authority* [1992] PIQR Q1. The plaintiff in that case was eight years old. Rose J heard evidence about the plaintiff's family and background and found a pattern of effort and success; he came to the conclusion that the the child would have had good prospects of entering a profession, in particular the legal profession, if he had wished. He also held that he would probably have started work at 23 and retired at 65. Accepting evidence that a man who was destined for partnership in a medium-sized firm of City solicitors or accountants could expect to be earning £16,000 a year at age 24 and £100,000 at age 65, he fixed a multiplicand of £35,000.

On appeal the defendants conceded that the plaintiff would have had above-average employment prospects, but contended that this could be reflected in a multiplicand of one and a half times the national average for non-manual workers (less than £15,500). The Court of Appeal upheld Rose J.

(b) Plaintiff's prospects unknown: adjusting the multiplier

A plaintiff can make a claim for future loss of earnings only if the evidence shows that he would in fact have chosen to work. He is being compensated for loss of actual earnings, not loss of earning capacity: *per* Diplock LJ in *Browning* v *War Office* [1963] 1 QB 750 at 766, [1962] 3 All ER 1089 at 1096A. Whether an adult plaintiff would have tried to find work can usually be gauged from his pre-accident record; in the case of a child this is an imponderable. Whether even a willing plaintiff would in fact have found work is, of course, a separate problem; again a child does not have the working history from which the plaintiff's success in finding work can be assessed.

To these difficulties is added the problem of double acceleration. When replaced by lump-sum compensation, a child's lost earnings are accelerated not only by the period of his working life, but also by the period between the date of the trial and the date on which he would normally have expected to start work. In practice the courts tend to roll all these imponderables into one and make a substantial discount from the multiplier which would be appropriate if it were based solely on the plaintiff's expectation of life. *Croke* v *Wiseman* [1982] 1 WLR 71, [1981] 3 All ER 852 is again a good example. *Per* Griffiths LJ at page 83E and 862e:

> 'Assuming the child was able to start work at 18 and lived to the age of 40, his working life would be 22 years. According to the actuarial tables put in at the trial, the appropriate multiplier to apply for such a period was 8.876. But that is a mathematical figure based upon the certainty that earnings would have continued over that period. It makes no allowance for the large discount that must be given for the immediate receipt of the capital sum at least 11 years before earnings would commence; nor does it allow a discount for the possibility that the child might never have become an earner. Taking these factors into account, I think there should be a substantial further discount on the multiplier, which I would reduce to five years.'

In *Kemp* at paragraph 6−049 practitioners will find a useful note of multipliers adopted in cases involving children.

16. Lost years

Where a plaintiff's life expectancy has been reduced by his injuries, 'lost years' is a term used to describe the period between the age at which he is likely to die and the age at which he would have been likely to die if his life had not been so shortened. In *Pickett* v *British Rail Engineering* [1980] AC 136 the House of Lords held that a plaintiff whose life has been shortened can recover damages for the loss of pecuniary benefits he would have received during the lost years. The commonest example of such benefits is the wages the plaintiff would have earned between the age at which he is likely to die and the age at which he would have expected to retire but for the accident.

Although a plaintiff who is still alive has a claim for money he would have earned in the lost years, his estate, once he dies, does not. That is the effect of s 4(2) of the Administration of Justice Act 1982, which abolished the rule laid down by the House of Lords in *Gammell* v *Wilson* [1982] AC 27, [1981] 1 All ER 578 that a claim made by the deceased's estate under the Law Reform (Miscellaneous Provisions) Act 1934 in respect of an injury sustained by the deceased before his death includes a claim for the money he would have earned in the lost years. The rationale behind the change is that the deceased's dependants already have a claim for loss of their dependency in the lost years under the Fatal Accidents Act 1976: to allow the estate also to recover is to require the defendant to pay twice in respect of the same loss.

The lost years claim made by the deceased's estate was no different in principle from the lost years claim that can still be made by a living plaintiff. The principles laid down in the cases leading up to *Gammell* v *Wilson* are accordingly still relevant in deciding how to calculate the loss.

(a) Circumstances giving rise to a lost years claim

A claim for a pecuniary benefit which would have been enjoyed during the lost years arises only where the reduction in the plaintiff's life expectancy is enough to have a significant effect on the multiplier. A man of 36 can expect to live about as long as he has already lived. A reduction of five years in his life expectancy will have no effect on the multiplier used to calculate his future loss of earnings; a reduction of 20 years, on the other hand, will.

(b) Nature of lost years claim

The commonest claim is in respect of the wages the plaintiff would have earned in the years he has lost. He must be able to produce evidence on which his lost earnings can be estimated. If no such evidence is available, the court cannot award a conventional sum based on the assumption that the plaintiff would have earned something: *Gammell* v *Wilson* [1982] AC 27, [1981] 1 All ER 578.

Lost years claims are not restricted to loss of earnings. In *Adsett* v *West* [1983] QB 826, [1983] 2 All ER 985 the court allowed a claim in respect of the income from assets in his father's estate that the plaintiff would probably have inherited at some time during the lost years.

(c) Claim by a child

In *Gammell* v *Wilson* [1982] AC 27, [1981] 1 All ER 578 the House of Lords said that a young child is unlikely to be able to make a claim for loss of earnings during the lost years. This is not a statement of law, but an observation of fact. The claim relates to a time so far into the future that there is unlikely to be any evidence on which to base an assessment of the child's earnings; any award would therefore be pure speculation. If such evidence is available, however, a claim can be made; the older the child, the more likely it is that such evidence will be available.

(d) Deduction of living expenses: principles

A claim for pecuniary loss in the lost years must always be reduced by the amount of the plaintiff's living expenses in the lost years. The reason is, of course, that having died the plaintiff will not incur those expenses.

There are two kinds of case in which prospective living expenses have to be assessed and then deducted from a claim for damages. The first is a claim by a plaintiff, who is still alive, in respect of pecuniary loss in the lost years; the second is a claim under the Fatal Accidents Act 1976 by the dependants of someone who has already died. The principles used in the two types of case are so closely related that they can be understood only as a whole.

A claim under the Fatal Accidents Act 1976 is for compensation for loss of dependency — for loss, in other words, of the financial support the dependants would have received from the deceased if he had not been killed. In theory a claim for loss of support from the deceased's income requires the court to calculate how much the deceased would have contributed to the cost of the dependants' accommodation, food, clothing, household goods, heating and so on. In practice the courts adopt a rule of thumb based on conventional percentages, unless there is compelling evidence to show that the rule of thumb does not reflect the true position.

The rule of thumb requires the court to assume that the deceased would have spent on his dependants the whole of his income less the proportion needed for his own living expenses, hobbies and entertainment. In the absence of evidence to the contrary, that proportion is purely conventional. In the case of a married, but childless, wage-earner it is one-third.

In effect the courts assume that one-third of the wage is spent on the wage-earner alone, one-third on his dependent wife and one-third on expenditure that benefits them both equally — mortgage payments for example. The reason for deducting only the one-third that the wage-earner spends on himself, rather than the third the wage-earner spends on himself plus one half of the one-third that he spends on joint expenditure, is that the widow was dependent for the whole of such benefits on the wage-earner: deprived of that wage-earner's support, she cannot live in half a house or drive half a car.

Though formulated in terms of wage-earning husband and dependent wife, these rules apply equally, of course, to a widower who was dependent on his wife. Where the couple have children, the conventional deduction falls from one-third to one-quarter.

Can the same approach be used to determine the living expenses that have to be deducted from a claim for loss of pecuniary benefits in the lost years? In *Harris* v *Empress Motors* [1983] 3 All ER 561 the Court

Future pecuniary loss: practice

of Appeal said no. A claim for loss of pecuniary benefits in the lost years looks at the situation not from the dependants' point of view, but from the deceased's. As a benefit, the house financed by the payment of a mortgage is indivisible; as an expense, however, the instalments due under a mortgage can be regarded as being paid one half for the wage-earner's benefit, one half for his dependent wife's.

In that case at page 575c the court laid down three basic rules:

'1. The ingredients that go to make up 'living expenses' are the same whether the victim be young or old, single or married, with or without dependants.
2. The sum to be deducted as living expenses is the proportion of the victim's net earnings that he spends to maintain himself at the standard of life appropriate to his case.
3. Any sums expended to maintain or benefit others do not form part of the victim's living expenses and are not to be deducted from the net earnings.'

(e) Deduction of living expenses: practice

In the broadest terms victims in this context fall into one of three categories:

*   single victim;
*   married victim without children;
*   married victim with children.

In *White* v *London Transport Executive* [1982] QB 489, [1982] 1 All ER 410 the court came to the conclusion that a single man living at home would have one-third of his income available after meeting his living expenses; on moving into a flat of his own he would find that proportion dropping to one-quarter. Where the plaintiff is a young man, the court should not assume that he would have remained single: *Harris* v *Empress Motors* [1983] 3 All ER 561 at 577b. On the other hand, the court is likely to assume that an older man would have remained single if he was already a confirmed bachelor at the date of the accident.

Where the plaintiff is married without children, the court is likely to regard his living expenses in the lost years as being the one-third that the wage-earner would have spent on himself plus one half of the one-third that he would have spent on expenditure for the joint benefit of himself and his dependent wife — in other words one half of his net earnings:

$$\frac{1}{3} + \left(\frac{1}{2} \times \frac{1}{3}\right) = \frac{1}{2}$$

Just as the courts will not assume that a young bachelor would have remained single, they will not assume that a young couple would have remained childless. Where the plaintiff has (or would have been likely to have) children, the proportion of his income that the plaintiff can spend

200

exclusively on himself falls to one-quarter (as in a claim under the Fatal Accidents Act 1976); the proportion of his income going into joint expenditure remains at about one-third, but the proportion of that joint expenditure which benefits the plaintiff falls to $1/(x + 2)$, where x is the number of children.

With two children, therefore, the proportion which the plaintiff would have spent on himself will be:

$$\frac{1}{4} + \left(\frac{1}{4} \times \frac{1}{3}\right) = \frac{1}{3}$$

and with four:

$$\frac{1}{4} + \left(\frac{1}{6} \times \frac{1}{3}\right) = \frac{11}{36}$$

17. Future medical expenses

An injured person often faces the prospect of further treatment at some time in the future. This gives rise to two distinct claims.

The first claim is for the estimated cost of the treatment itself. However distant the date at which treatment will be needed, the cost is the current cost, since inflation between the date of the trial and the date of the treatment will be covered by investing the money in the meantime.

If the treatment is such that the plaintiff will have to take time off work, he also has a claim for loss of earnings. The doctor who gives evidence about the need for the further treatment must estimate the length of time the plaintiff is likely to be away from work.

18. Damages for disability on the open labour market

Per Lloyd LJ in *Foster* v *Tyne and Wear County Council* [1986] 1 All ER 567 at 570h, the assessment of damages for disability on the open labour market is 'essentially an imprecise and speculative exercise'. At 570a the same Judge said that one of the few principles to emerge from the authorities in this area is that there is no rule of thumb; in each case the court has to assess the plaintiff's handicap, as an existing disability, by reference to what may happen in the future.

In assessing damages the court must ask two questions. Is there a real (as opposed to speculative) risk that the plaintiff will lose his job? If so, what are his chances of finding another? If the answers to these questions are 'Yes' and 'Worse than average' respectively, the plaintiff has a claim for damages under this head.

Although the plaintiff must run an appreciable risk of unemployment, the risk need not be greater than that run by other persons of his age, qualifications and experience. It can even arise from the possibility that he may want to change his job for personal reasons. What must be greater than the average, however, is the difficulty that he will face in finding another job if he is thrown on to the labour market.

Where the claim is small, a county court Judge will generally assume that anyone with a disability will be at the back of the queue for whatever jobs are available, particularly in times of high unemployment. Where the plaintiff intends to mount a substantial claim, however, his advisers should commission a report from an employment consultant. Relying on statistics showing the number of jobs available in any given area for persons of his age, qualifications and experience, coupled with statistics showing the number of qualified applicants for each job, an employment consultant can estimate how much longer the plaintiff will take to obtain a job than an uninjured person of the same age, qualifications and experience.

In theory the award of damages under this head is not the plaintiff's current net weekly earnings multiplied by the number of additional weeks it will take him to land a job in competition with uninjured persons of the same age, qualifications and experience. The Court of Appeal has said that a calculation based on multiplicand and multiplier cannot provide a complete answer, but county court Judges feel more comfortable if they can explain their award as being so many weeks' or months' loss of earnings.

If the plaintiff has by the date of trial returned to his pre-accident work, or to work paying as much as his pre-accident work, his claim for disability on the open labour market will stand alone. If he has taken up work paying less than his pre-accident work, on the other hand, it will be coupled with a claim for future partial loss of earnings; in such a case, of course, the potential loss which underpins his claim for damages for disability on the open labour market will be loss of the earnings of his post-accident, rather than his pre-accident, job.

A plaintiff who makes a claim for total future loss of earnings has no claim for disability on the open labour market; for it is necessarily his case that he will not be thrown onto the labour market. On the other hand, the mere fact that the plaintiff is not in work at the date of trial does not bar the claim: *Cook* v *Consolidated Fisheries* [1977] ICR 635 at 640B. So an unemployed plaintiff who contends that he will be able to return to work at some time in the future can make a parallel claim for a disability on the open labour market which will arise only when he starts looking for work.

Most awards represent less than two years' loss of earnings. This does not reflect any rule, however; in *Foster* v *Tyne and Wear County Council* [1986] 1 All ER 567 the Court of Appeal upheld an award equivalent to nearly five years' salary.

Checklist

1. Identify all losses that are continuing at the date of trial.
2. If there is a claim for loss of earnings, consider whether the claim depends on proving the wages of a comparable earner. Is such an earner available and willing to give evidence?
3. If not, consider using the *New Earnings Survey*.

4. Reduce each continuing loss to an annual figure.
5. Separate the continuing losses into two categories: (1) those that will last for the rest of the plaintiff's life; and (2) those that will last for a shorter period (usually until the date on which he would have retired in any event).
6. Choose a suitable multiplier for those losses that will last for the rest of the plaintiff's life. Consult *Kemp* and the *Actuarial Tables with Explanatory Notes for Use in Personal Injury and Fatal Accident Cases*.
7. Choose a suitable multiplier for those losses that will last for a shorter period than life. Consult *Kemp* and (where the loss is until retirement) the *Actuarial Tables*.
8. Remember that the *Actuarial Tables* are not admissible unless proved. Seek the defendant's agreement to their use.
9. What contingencies need to be accommodated? How will they affect the multiplier? What evidence is needed?
10. Is all the evidence in the form of witness statements which: (1) satisfy the requirements of the County Court Rules; and (2) exhibit any documents to which they refer?

Chapter 24

Recouping State benefits

1. Starting date for new rules

An injured plaintiff may receive State benefits for the two or three years between the accident and the trial. How are those benefits to be treated if he succeeds in recovering damages?

The Social Security Act 1989 introduced entirely new rules where compensation is paid after 3 September 1990 in respect of:

- an accident or injury occurring on or after 1 January 1989; or
- a disease, if the victim's first claim for a relevant benefit in consequence of the disease is made on or after 1 January 1989.

Payment of compensation for:

- an accident or injury suffered before 1 January 1989; or
- a disease in respect of which benefit is claimed before 1 January 1989

is governed by the provisions of the Law Reform (Personal Injuries) Act 1948.

2. Legislation

The relevant rules are now contained in:

- Part IV of the Social Security Administration Act 1992, which replaces the Social Security Act 1989;
- the Social Security (Recoupment) Regulations 1990, SI 1990/322, as amended.

The Social Security (Recoupment) Regulations 1990 were made under the Social Security Act 1989. Despite the repeal of that Act the Regulations will continue in force by virtue of the Social Security (Consequential Provisions) Act 1992 until new regulations are made under the Social Security Administration Act 1992.

The statutory provisions are extremely detailed. What follows is an outline of the most important rules.

3. 'Compensation payment'

The rules apply to compensation payments. A compensation payment is defined by s 81(1) of the Social Security Administration Act 1992 as:

'... any payment falling to be made (whether voluntarily, or in pursuance of a court order or an agreement, or otherwise) —

(a) to or in respect of the victim in consequence of the accident, injury or disease in question, and

(b) either —

  (i) by or on behalf of a person who is, or is alleged to be liable to any extent in respect of the accident, injury or disease, or

  (ii) in pursuance of a compensation scheme for motor accidents but does not include benefit or an exempt payment or so much of a payment as is referable to costs incurred by any person.'

The scheme is not restricted to awards of damages made in court: it applies also to any agreement under which one party pays to another compensation in 'money or money's worth' (s 81(1)) in respect of an accident, injury or disease.

4. Exempt payments

Certain compensation payments are exempt from the scheme. These are listed in s 81(3) of the Act and reg 4 of the Regulations. The most important are:

- any small payment, as defined by the Social Security (Recoupment) Regulations 1990: that is, any compensation payment, or aggregate of two or more compensation payments, made to the same victim in respect of the same accident, injury or disease, which does not exceed £2,500 (s 81(3)(a));
- any payment made under the Vaccine Damage Payments Act 1979 (s 6(4) of which provides its own scheme for deduction) (s 81(3)(e));
- any payment made in the exercise of a discretion out of property held subject to a trust in a case where no more than 50 per cent by value of the capital contributed to the trust was directly or indirectly provided by persons who are, or are alleged to be, liable in respect of —

  (a) the accident, injury or disease suffered by the victim in question; or

  (b) the same or any connected accident, injury or disease suffered by another (s 81(3)(g)):

  in practice, disaster relief funds more than half of which have come from public donations;
- any compensation payment made by British Coal in accordance with the NCB Pneumoconiosis Compensation Scheme set up by an agreement made on 13 September 1974 between the Government and the mining unions (reg 4(b));

- any payment made to a victim in respect of sensorineural hearing loss where the loss is less than 50 db in one or both ears (reg 4(c));
- any contractual amount paid to an employee by an employer of his in respect of a day's incapacity for work (reg 4(d)).

5. The essence of the scheme

The essence of the scheme is contained in s 82(1) of the Act, which provides:

'A person (the "compensator") making a compensation payment, whether on behalf of himself or another, in consequence of an accident, injury or disease suffered by any other person (the "victim") shall not do so until the Secretary of State has furnished him with a certificate of total benefit and shall then —

(a) deduct from the payment an amount, determined in accordance with the certificate of total benefit, equal to the gross amount of any relevant benefits paid or likely to be paid to or for the victim during the relevant period in respect of that accident, injury or disease;

(b) pay to the Secretary of State an amount equal to that which is required to be so deducted; and

(c) furnish the person to whom the compensation payment is or, apart from this section, would have been made (the "intended recipient") with a certificate of deduction.'

In outline therefore:

- the defendant cannot pay compensation until he has a certificate showing the whole of the benefit paid to the plaintiff in respect of the injury or disease for which the plaintiff is claiming damages;
- when he pays the damages, the defendant must deduct and repay to the state the whole of the benefit paid to the plaintiff in respect of the injury or disease for which the plaintiff is claiming damages.

State benefits are deducted from the whole of the plaintiff's damages, whatever the head under which they have been awarded or agreed. It follows that a successful plaintiff may recover nothing at all, particularly where his damages have been reduced to take account of his contributory negligence.

Section 82(1) contains a number of terms that have a precise meaning:

- 'relevant benefit';
- 'relevant period';
- 'total benefit';
- 'certificate of total benefit';

6. 'Relevant benefit'

Fifteen benefits are defined by reg 2 of the Regulations as 'relevant' for the purposes of s 82 of the Act:

- attendance allowance;
- disablement benefit (including disablement pensions) payable in accordance with ss 57–63 of the Social Security Act 1989;
- family credit;
- income support under Part II of the Social Security Act 1986, including personal expenses addition, special transitional additions and transitional addition as defined in the Income Support (Transitional) Regulations 1987;
- invalidity pension and allowance. These benefits, known collectively as invalidity benefit, will be replaced by a new benefit, called incapacity benefit, when the Social Security (Incapacity for Work) Act 1994 is brought into force by statutory instrument;
- mobility allowance;
- benefits payable under schemes made under the Industrial Injuries and Diseases (Old Cases) Act 1975;
- reduced earnings allowance;
- retirement allowance;
- severe disablement allowance;
- sickness benefit. This benefit will also be replaced by incapacity benefit when the Social Security (Incapacity for Work) Act 1994 is brought into force;
- such proportion of statutory sick pay as the employer is entitled to recover from the state by virtue of regulations made under s 158(1) of the Social Security Contributions and Benefits Act 1992 — namely 80 per cent. This applies only to statutory sick pay paid up to 5 April 1994, since on 6 April the relevant part of s 158(1) ceased to have effect by virtue of s 1 of the Statutory Sick Pay Act 1994;
- unemployment benefit;
- disability living allowance;
- disability working allowance.

If income support (and that includes personal expenses addition, special transitional additions and transitional addition as defined in the Income Support (Transitional) Regulations 1987) is paid on the same instrument as invalidity pension and allowance, severe disablement allowance, sickness benefit or unemployment benefit, that, too, must be taken into account for the purposes of s 82 of the Act: reg 2(2) of the Regulations.

7. 'Relevant period'

Under s 81(1) of the Act the 'relevant period' begins:

- in the case of a disease, on the date on which the victim first claims a relevant benefit in consequence of the disease; or

- in the case of an accident or injury, on the day on which the accident or injury occurred.

In either case the period ends:

- on the day on which a compensation payment is made in full and final settlement; or
- (if later) after five years.

8. 'Total benefit'

This is defined by s 81(1) of the Act as 'the gross amount referred to in section 82(1)(a)'. That is 'the gross amount of any relevant benefits paid or likely to be paid to or for the victim during the relevant period'.

9. 'Certificate of total benefit'

The person responsible for paying compensation cannot do so until he has obtained a certificate of total benefit: s 82(1). The responsibility for obtaining the certificate rests with the compensator: s 84(1). Certificates are issued by:

Compensation Recovery Unit
Department of Social Security
Reyrolle Building
Hebburn
Tyne & Wear
NE31 1XB
Telephone: 091-225 8030 and 091-225 8542

The contents of the certificate are laid down by s 84(2):

'(a) the amount which has been, or is likely to be, paid on or before a specified day by way of any relevant benefit which is capable of forming part of the total benefit;

(b) where applicable —

   (i) the rate of any relevant benefit which is, has been, or is likely to be paid after the date so specified and which would be capable of forming part of the total benefit; and

   (ii) the intervals at which any such benefit is paid and the period for which it is likely to be paid;

(c) the amounts (if any) which, by virtue of provisions, are to be treated as increasing the total benefit; and

(d) the aggregate amount of any [payments made to the Secretary of State under the recoupment provisions] made on or before a specified date (reduced by so much of that amount as has been paid by the Secretary of State to the intended recipient before that date in consequence of [Part IV of the Act]).'

The specified date will not be earlier than the date on which the compensator applied for the certificate (s 95(1)(b)) and is usually a date immediately before issue of the certificate. The certificate remains in force until a date given in the certificate (s 84(5)); this is generally eight weeks from the issue of the certificate. Section 84(4) gives the Secretary of State power to estimate 'in such manner as he thinks fit, any of the amounts, rates or periods' in the certificate.

If the certificate expires, the case cannot be settled, nor a judgment satisfied, until a fresh certificate has been received. A compensator cannot apply for a fresh certificate while an existing certificate is in force: s 84(5).

10. Appeals against certificate

Section 97 of the Act gives the Secretary of State power to review any certificate of total benefit if he is satisfied that it was issued 'in ignorance of, or was based on a mistake as to, some material fact or that a mistake (whether in computation or otherwise) has occurred in its preparation'. The Secretary of State can confirm the certificate or issue a new one, but he cannot increase the total benefit.

Section 98 provides for an appeal against the certificate of total benefit by the compensator, the victim or the intended recipient. An appeal which raises medical questions (as defined) is determined by a medical appeal tribunal; an appeal about amount, rate or period will be heard by a social security appeal tribunal. There is a further appeal in either case on a point of law to a Social Security Commissioner.

Unlike a review under s 97, an appeal under s 98 can go either way. Section 99 requires the Secretary of State to repay any excess and recover any shortfall.

11. Time for issuing certificate

Under s 95(1)(a) the Secretary of State is under an obligation to issue a certificate of total benefit within four weeks of the date on which the application for a certificate is received. Provided the compensator has made a correct application, and has received a written acknowledgement of its receipt, his duty to deduct and repay to the state is unenforceable if the Secretary of State does not issue a certificate of total benefit within four weeks.

12. Duty to deduct

Section 82(1) of the Act creates the obligation to deduct the amount specified in the certificate of total benefit and to pay it to the Secretary of State. Section 83 provides that the obligation to make payment arises immediately before the compensation payment is made, and must be met within 14 days of its arising.

13. Multiple compensation payments

Section 86 deals with cases in which the compensator makes more than one payment — where, for example, he makes one or more interim payments. In those cases the certificate of total benefit obtained with a view to making the second payment will show the total benefit paid to the victim to the date of the second payment, but will reduce the amount to be deducted from the second payment by the amount already deducted from the first. The compensator must rely on the certificate of total benefit; if it does not show the reduction, the compensator must ignore the reduction, deduct the full total benefit and leave the Secretary of State to repay the excess to the victim. If the duty to deduct from the first payment became unenforceable because the Secretary of State was late in furnishing the certificate of total benefit, it is revived by the second payment, which must be reduced by the whole of the total benefit paid to the date of the second payment.

The same rules apply where the second or subsequent compensation payment is made by a different compensator from the first. Section 87, however, allows any two or more compensators paying compensation to the same victim for the same accident, injury or disease to give notice to the Secretary of State that they are collaborating: each of them will then be entitled to add to the sum shown on his certificate of total benefit as already paid to the Secretary of State any sum deducted and paid by one of his collaborators.

14. Payment into court

The defendant can make a payment into court:

- before applying for a certificate of total benefit; or
- after applying for a certificate of total benefit.

If he makes a payment into court before applying, he must:

- allow in his calculations for the sum he will have to pay to the Secretary of State;
- apply for a certificate of total benefit on or before the date on which he makes the payment into court; and
- as soon as he is notified that the sum in court has been paid out, pay to the Secretary of State the sum shown in the certificate of total benefit.

The safer course is to apply for a certificate of total benefit first. In those cases the defendant:

- withholds from the sum paid into court the sum shown on the certificate of total benefit;
- notifies the Court of the amount withheld from the sum paid in, which is treated as increased by the amount withheld; and

- as soon as he is notified that the sum in court has been paid out, pays to the Secretary of State the sum shown in the certificate of total benefit.

These rules are contained in s 93 of the Act.

County Court Form N 243, the notice of payment into court, requires the defendant to state whether he has made a deduction in accordance with the recoupment provisions. The prescribed wording is:

'The defendant has withheld from this payment into court the sum of £ in accordance with Section 12(2)(a)(i) of the Social Security Administration Act 1992.'

In general a defendant cannot make an offer of the kind approved in *Calderbank* v *Calderbank* [1976] Fam 93, [1975] 3 All ER 333 in any case in which a payment into court can be made. To protect a defendant who wishes to make an offer from the risk of paying money into court before he has received a certificate of total benefit, however, O 11 r 10 CCR allows the defendant to make an offer a copy of which is filed at court in a sealed envelope; when the question of costs falls to be decided, the court shall:

'in exercising its discretion as to costs, take into account any offer which has been brought to its attention.'

Such an offer can be made only once the defendant has applied for a certificate of total benefit. An offer made in this way ceases to be effective seven days after the defendant receives a certificate of total benefit.

15. Contributory negligence

The statutory scheme operates with full force even though the plaintiff's damages may have been reduced to take account of his own negligence.

16. Structured settlements

Section 88 of the Act makes special provisions for structured settlements (see Chapter 26). If the relevant period as defined by s 81(1) has not already come to an end under the provisions of that subsection, it is deemed to do so on the date on which settlement is reached. That is the date on which the parties enter into the agreement for the structured settlement, unless it is one which requires the approval of the court, in which case it is the date on which approval is given.

On that date the compensator becomes liable to make to the Secretary of State a single payment of the amount referred to in s 82(1)(a) — namely 'the gross amount of any relevant benefits paid or likely to be paid to or for the victim during the relevant period'. A review under s 97 or an appeal under s 98 may later show that the amount so paid was wrong. If it was too much, the excess is refunded to the compensator; if too little, the shortfall is made up by the intended recipient.

The payments made under the annuity for which the structured settlement provides are exempt payments. The insurance company which is liable to pay the annuity is never the compensator for the purposes of the recoupment provisions.

If any further compensation becomes payable to the victim outside the structured settlement, the relevant period is defined by s 81, not s 88.

17. DSS v Legal Aid Board

The Legal Aid Board wins: section 90 provides that if the compensation is, after deduction of the relevant benefits, insufficient to satisfy the Legal Aid charge, the Secretary of State shall make a payment to make good the deficiency.

The plaintiff loses: any payment the Secretary of State makes in accordance with this provision is treated as increasing the total benefit.

18. Foreign compensator

Where compensation is to be paid by a foreign compensator, the duty to notify the Department of Social Security of the claim, to apply for the certificate of total benefit and to pay to the Secretary of State an amount equivalent to the total benefit falls not on the compensator, but on the victim. Forms explaining the mechanics of recoupment in these circumstances can be obtained from the Compensation Recovery Unit.

Checklist

1. Is this an exempt payment? See paragraph 4 above.
2. Note especially the exemptions for:
    (a) claims not exceeding £2,500;
    (b) *sensorineural* (but not other) deafness cases under 50 db.
3. Does this claim exceed £2,500? If not, the recoupment provisions will not apply, but deduction under the Law Reform (Personal Injuries) Act 1948 will: see Chapter 25, paragraph 2.
4. Has the plaintiff received any of the benefits listed in paragraph 6 above? If so, ask to see the documents and try to work out how much of each he has received.
5. Check the certificate of total benefit. Should the plaintiff be advised to ask for a review or to appeal?
6. Is the source of compensation a foreign compensator? If so, remember that *the duty to notify the Department of Social Security of the claim, the duty to apply for the certificate of total benefit and the duty to pay to the Secretary of State an amount equivalent to the total benefit all fall on the plaintiff.* Apply to the Department immediately for the necessary forms.

Chapter 25

Other benefits

1. The general rule

The plaintiff recovers compensation for money he has lost, or expenditure he has incurred, as a result of the accident. As a general rule, if he has received a financial benefit as a result of the accident, his damages must be reduced to the extent of that benefit: *Hodgson* v *Trapp* [1989] AC 807, [1988] 3 All ER 870.

The plaintiff may, for example, receive payments under a job-release scheme; if so, they will be deductible: *Crawley* v *Mercer* The Times 9 March 1984. Similarly a plaintiff may be unable to take paid work — because, for example, he needs to be admitted frequently to hospital — but be able to make good use of the time by taking a course of study; if he does so, and receives a student grant, his claim for loss of earnings will be reduced by the amount of the grant. Since he has received the grant only because he has taken a course of study, and since he would not have been able to take the course of study but for the accident (because he would have been working), the grant is a benefit received as a result of the accident.

Benefits of this kind fall into six broad categories:

- relevant benefits (as defined by the Social Security Administration Act 1992) in cases not exceeding £2,500;
- contractual sick pay;
- redundancy payment where the redundancy has been caused by the accident;
- saving in living expenses: maintenance in a public institution;
- saving in living expenses: maintenance in a private institution;
- saving in work expenses.

2. Relevant benefits in cases not exceeding £2,500

Where the amount of the compensation payment made to the victim does not exceed £2,500 (and so the recoupment provisions of the Social Security Administration Act 1992 do not apply), s 2(1) of the Law Reform (Personal Injuries) Act 1948 provides that one half of certain benefits paid to the plaintiff as a result of the injury in the five years following the date on which the cause of action arose shall be deducted from his damages. The rule applies to all damages, not just damages for loss of earnings.

The benefits to which this rule applies, called the 'relevant benefits', are those listed in reg 2 of the Social Security (Recoupment) Regulations 1990, SI 1990/322, as amended:

- attendance allowance;
- disablement benefit (including disablement pensions) payable in accordance with ss 57–63 of the Social Security Act 1989;
- family credit;
- income support under Part II of the Social Security Act 1986, including personal expenses addition, special transitional additions and transitional addition as defined in the Income Support (Transitional) Regulations 1987;
- invalidity pension and allowance. These benefits, known collectively as invalidity benefit, will be replaced by a new benefit, called incapacity benefit, when the Social Security (Incapacity for Work) Act 1994 is brought into force by statutory instrument;
- mobility allowance;
- benefits payable under schemes made under the Industrial Injuries and Diseases (Old Cases) Act 1975;
- reduced earnings allowance;
- retirement allowance;
- severe disablement allowance;
- sickness benefit. This benefit will also be replaced by incapacity benefit when the Social Security (Incapacity for Work) Act 1994 is brought into force;
- such proportion of statutory sick pay as the employer is entitled to recover from the state by virtue of regulations made under s 158(1) of the Social Security Contributions and Benefits Act 1992 — namely 80 per cent. This applies only to statutory sick pay paid up to 5 April 1994, since on 6 April the relevant part of s 158(1) ceased to have effect by virtue of s 1 of the Statutory Sick Pay Act 1994;
- unemployment benefit;
- disability living allowance;
- disability working allowance.

If income support (and that includes personal expenses addition, special transitional additions and transitional addition as defined in the Income Support (Transitional) Regulations 1987) is paid on the same instrument as invalidity pension and allowance, severe disablement allowance, sickness benefit, or unemployment benefit, that, too, is a relevant benefit for these purposes: reg 2(2) of the Social Security (Recoupment) Regulations 1990, SI 1990/322.

Two or more payments made to the same victim in respect of the same injury are called connected payments. Connected payments are aggregated for the purpose of deciding whether the compensation payment exceeds £2,500: s 85(1) of the Social Security Administration Act 1992.

3. Contractual sick pay

If the plaintiff's employer has paid sick pay under a contractual obligation (and the sick pay is not refundable), the plaintiff's claim for loss of earnings must be reduced by the amount he has received. This rule applies even when the plaintiff's employers make the payments from the proceeds of an insurance policy they have taken out to cover such an eventuality: *Hussain* v *New Taplow Paper Mills Ltd* [1988] AC 514, [1988] 1 All ER 541.

4. Redundancy payment where the redundancy has been caused by the accident

If the plaintiff is made redundant as a result of his accident, any redundancy payment he receives must be deducted from his claim for loss of earnings: *Wilson* v *National Coal Board* 1981 SLT 67. The plaintiff's claim for loss of earnings is based on the assumption that but for the accident he would have continued in work; since his redundancy payment is therefore something he would not have received but for the accident, it must be deducted from his claim for the loss caused by the accident.

The converse is true, of course. If the plaintiff's redundancy has nothing to do with the accident, his redundancy payment is not to be deducted from his claim for loss of earnings; equally, however, his loss of earnings cannot be assessed on the assumption that he would have continued working if the accident had not occurred.

5. Saving in living expenses

(a) Maintenance in a public institution

Under s 5 of the Administration of Justice Act 1982 the plaintiff is obliged to deduct from his claim for loss of income — but not for anything else:

'...any saving to the injured person which is attributable to his maintenance wholly or partly at public expense in a hospital, nursing home or other institution.'

Thus if a plaintiff with severe injuries is kept in a National Health Service hospital for a year following his injuries, he must give credit against his claim for, say, loss of earnings for the money he has saved in that year on his own living expenses.

(b) Maintenance in a private institution

Where the plaintiff claims the cost of being looked after in a private institution, he must give credit for the domestic element in the cost of that care. This reflects what he would have spent had he remained at home.

The extent of the deduction will depend on whether the plaintiff is single or married. If he is single, he will have saved the entire cost of maintaining his own home, and will be obliged to give credit for that part of the cost of his care which represents the cost of providing the accommodation, feeding him, providing warmth, light, clean linen, and so on. On the other hand, if he is married, he is still obliged to provide a home for his wife and so will probably have saved only the cost of his food and laundry.

The same principle applies where the plaintiff is being looked after at home. He cannot claim for those expenses he would have incurred even if he had not been injured.

The defendant cannot claim to deduct from the cost of care the money the plaintiff spent on his living accommodation before the accident: *Shearman* v *Folland* [1950] 2 KB 43, [1950] 1 All ER 976. The reason is that the court is not entitled to take into account the style in which the plaintiff chose to live, or the way in which he chose to spend his money: in that case the plaintiff had been living in a hotel before the accident.

6. Saving in work expenses

If the plaintiff incurs expenses in earning his living, then any saving in those expenses that he makes as a result of being unable to work must be deducted from his claim for loss of earnings: *Lim Poh Choo* v *Camden and Islington Area Health Authority* [1980] AC 174, [1979] 2 All ER 910. Where the plaintiff is self-employed, the calculation of his claim for loss of earnings will probably make this deduction automatically, since he will have paid tax before the accident only on what was left of his receipts after deduction of allowable expenses.

Is the cost of commuting an expense for which a plaintiff who can no longer work should give credit? In theory the answer is probably yes, but in practice no, unless the cost of travelling is exceptional: *Dews* v *National Coal Board* [1988] AC 1, [1987] 2 All ER 545. It can always be argued (as it was by the defendants in that case) that the cost of commuting is an expense of the plaintiff's way of life rather than of his job.

7. The exceptions

To this general rule there are seven main exceptions:

- contractual sick pay paid under an obligation to repay;
- relevant benefits in cases exceeding £2,500;
- repayable benefits;
- proceeds of insurance policies;
- pensions;
- charitable assistance;
- gratuitous provision of accommodation.

8. Contractual sick pay paid under an obligation to repay

The plaintiff's employers will often continue to pay his wages while he is unfit to work through injury on condition that if the plaintiff subsequently makes a claim against a third party for damages in respect of his injuries, he will include a claim for loss of earnings and pay anything he recovers under that head to his employers. In some cases this condition will have been written into the plaintiff's contract of employment, so creating a binding obligation; in others it will be an understanding only, creating merely a moral obligation. Whether or not the obligation to repay is legally binding, sums paid in these circumstances are not to be deducted from the plaintiff's claim for loss of earnings: *Dennis* v *London Passenger Transport Board* [1948] 1 All ER 779. If the plaintiff is obliged to make a claim, effectively on his employer's behalf, for wages paid during his absence through injury, his claim is limited to the net amount he has received, even though his employer will have deducted and paid on his behalf income tax and National Insurance contributions.

9. Relevant benefits in cases exceeding £2,500

Where the amount of the compensation payment made to the victim exceeds £2,500 (and so the recoupment provisions of the Social Security Administration Act 1992 do apply), any State benefit which is among those listed in reg 2 of the Social Security (Recoupment) Regulations 1990, SI 1990/322, as amended, is to be disregarded in the assessment of damages: s 81(5) of the Social Security Administration Act 1992. These, the so-called 'relevant benefits', are listed at paragraph 2. above (pages 213–214).

10. Repayable benefits

The same rule applies to any benefit which the plaintiff receives from a third party as a result of the accident but is under an obligation to repay in the event of recovery. It was applied in *Berriello* v *Felixstowe Dock & Railway Co* [1989] 1 WLR 695 to an Italian disability benefit which the plaintiff was, by Italian law, obliged to repay if he recovered damages in respect of the loss for which the benefit had been paid.

11. Proceeds of insurance policies

If the plaintiff has an insurance policy which makes payment in the event of injury, the proceeds are not deducted from the plaintiff's damages: *Bradburn* v *Great Western Railway Co* (1874) LR 10 Ex 1. The plaintiff has paid good money for a contract providing protection in the event of injury: it would be unjust to give the benefit of that contract to the tortfeasor.

12. Pensions

If the plaintiff has a pension which becomes payable as a result of his injuries (for example, because he has to retire early), the pension payments are not deducted from any claim for loss of earnings: *Parry* v *Cleaver* [1970] AC 1, [1969] 1 All ER 555. The plaintiff has paid for his pension directly or indirectly: directly to the extent that he has paid contributions, indirectly to the extent that he has accepted a lower wage in return for the employers' contributions to a pension scheme. In either case it would be unjust to give the benefit of that pension to the tortfeasor.

This exception applies even if the defendant is the plaintiff's employer and so paying the pension: *Smoker* v *London Fire and Civil Defence Authority* [1991] 2 AC 502, [1991] 2 All ER 449. It applies also to the state retirement pension: *Hewson* v *Downs* [1970] 1 QB 73, [1969] 3 All ER 19.

This exception applies only to claims for loss of earnings. If therefore the plaintiff receives a disability pension as a result of his injuries, but suffers a reduction in his retirement pension, he must deduct from any claim he makes for loss of his retirement pension what he expects to receive by way of disability pension over the same period.

13. Charitable assistance

A plaintiff may receive money from charity, either through a public appeal or through a particular organisation that exists to help people with his particular disability. In neither case are his damages reduced: *Hussain* v *New Taplow Paper Mills Ltd* [1988] AC 514, [1988] 1 All ER 541.

This rule applies also to payments made *ex gratia* by the plaintiff's employer. In *Cunningham* v *Harrison* [1973] QB 942, [1973] 3 All ER 463 Lord Denning MR applied it to a pension paid *ex gratia* by the plaintiff's employer. Similarly, in *McCamley* v *Cammell Laird Ltd* [1990] 1 WLR 963, [1990] 1 All ER 854 the defendants, who were the plaintiff's employers, had effected an insurance policy which provided for payment to the defendants should any of their employees suffer injury, whether or not the defendants (or indeed anyone) might be to blame. The plaintiff, who had known nothing of the policy and had paid nothing, directly or indirectly, towards the premiums, was injured as a result of the defendants' negligence. The defendants paid the proceeds of the insurance policy to his solicitors: the Court of Appeal held that the payment had been made *ex gratia* and was not to be deducted from the plaintiff's damages. The whole point of effecting the policy had been to allow the defendants to make a payment as an act of benevolence in the event of injury, and the payment had not been made on account of any sum which the defendants were legally obliged to pay.

14. Gratuitous provision of accommodation

The plaintiff may have a job which provides free board and lodging. If so, and if as a result of the accident he goes away to be looked after by a relative, or stays with a friend, he has a claim for the value of the free board and lodging he has lost, even though he has been housed and fed free of charge by someone else. He is not obliged to deduct the value of the free board and lodging he has received from the relative or friend: *Liffen* v *Watson* [1940] KB 556.

Checklist

1. Does this claim exceed £2,500? If not, the recoupment provisions will not apply, but deduction under the Law Reform (Personal Injuries) Act 1948 will: see paragraph 2. above (pages 213–214).
2. Has the plaintiff benefited in any of the ways listed in paragraph 1. above (page 213) as a result of the accident?
3. If so, quantify the benefit.
4. Remember that the plaintiff may have to prove the value to him of the benefit he has received: assemble the relevant evidence.
5. Is all the evidence in the form of witness statements which: (1) satisfy the requirements of the County Court Rules; and (2) exhibit any documents to which they refer?

Chapter 26

Structured settlements

1. Introduction

Structured settlements will not be found in the county court, since at present at least they are suitable only for the most serious cases. Because they amount to an entirely new way of compensating plaintiffs for their injuries, however, and because, if their history in the United States of America and Canada is a good guide, they are likely to develop rapidly, they represent a change of which all practitioners should be aware. A lawyer who fails to consider a structured settlement in an appropriate case is probably negligent. What follows is the briefest outline of the way in which they work.

The Law Commission is currently considering structured settlements. Practitioners should therefore be alert to the possibility of a major change in the law.

2. Defining the problem

Traditional damages which represent compensation for a continuing loss or expense are supposed to be that capital sum which, if eroded steadily during the period of the loss for which it is compensation, but invested in the meantime, will last for the period of the loss, but no longer. The only certainty of such a calculation is that it is bound to result in injustice for someone. If the plaintiff lives longer than expected, his compensation will be exhausted before he dies. If inflation rises to the point where he can no longer obtain a real return on his investments after tax, he will be forced to live on pure capital, which will thus be eroded more quickly than it should. On the other hand, if the plaintiff walks under a bus as he leaves court, the beneficiaries of his estate will be enriched by the inheritance of a capital sum to which they have no moral right at all.

3. A possible solution

The only solution to this problem is to compensate the plaintiff by the purchase of an investment which generates cash for so long (but only for so long) as he is alive. The only investment that answers this description is a life annuity. An annuity is a right sold in return for a capital sum to receive income for a specified period in the future. Any period can be specified; a life annuity is an annuity for the rest of the annuitant's life.

4. Nature of structured settlements

A structured settlement uses an annuity to convert part of the capital sum the defendant is paying as compensation into an income stream which will last for the rest of the plaintiff's life, but no longer. In essence the defendant:

- pays part of the plaintiff's damages in the form of a conventional lump sum;
- undertakes a contractual obligation to pay the plaintiff damages by instalment for the rest of his life;
- funds that obligation by purchasing from a life office a life annuity on the plaintiff's life.

5. Power to create structured settlements

Structured settlements can be created only by agreement between the parties. The tax advantages of structured settlements arise out of an agreement reached in 1987 between the Inland Revenue and the Association of British Insurers: it is therefore essential that any proposed settlement falls within the terms of that agreement.

The courts have no power to award or impose a structured settlement. The courts have, however, enthusiastically endorsed structured settlements in cases (such as those involving a minor or mental patient) where a compromise between the parties has required judicial approval.

6. Structure of structured settlements

Structured settlements are very technical. No one should contemplate the use of a structured settlement without taking the best advice available.

In essence, however, a structured settlement divides the plaintiff's loss into two parts. The plaintiff receives in cash the sum he will need to set up his life after his accident — to convert his house, adapt his car and so on. He also receives in cash a fund to cover unexpected contingencies in the future. Once those requirements have been met, the general insurer, who represents the defendant, purchases from a life office a life annuity to fund a contractual obligation to pay damages by instalments for life.

The greatest advantage from the plaintiff's point of view is the elimination of the risk that his damages will be exhausted before he dies. Furthermore, provided the settlement meets the requirements laid down by the Inland Revenue, the instalments of damages are not taxable in the plaintiff's hands, since they are regarded as instalments of capital. In general, the greater security and freedom from tax on the investments that would otherwise be required to provide his income prompt the plaintiff to settle for less: by the same token, even when the administrative costs of setting up a structured settlement have been taken into account, the saving to the general insurer makes the disposal of a claim in this way an attractive proposition.

Chapter 27

Loss of pension rights

1. The problem

An injured plaintiff may never work again, or may be unable to earn as much as he did before the accident. In the first case he will be able to make no pension contributions; in the second he will almost certainly be able to make only reduced contributions. In either case the value of his pension rights when he reaches retirement will be less than it would have been had the accident not occurred. If the pension scheme to which he has been contributing provides only an annuity, he will lose income; if it also provides a capital sum on retirement, that, too, is likely to be reduced. It makes no difference, of course, whether the pension contributions are paid by the plaintiff or by his employer.

Unless the plaintiff has already retired by the date of trial, any claim for loss of pension rights will be a claim for prospective loss. The problem is to put a present value on a loss, whether of income or capital, which will not accrue until far into the future.

2. The traditional solution

The most recent and authoritative decision on the traditional approach is that of the Court of Appeal in *Auty* v *National Coal Board* [1985] 1 WLR 784, [1985] 1 All ER 930. Mr Auty was a coalminer, prevented by his injury from working at the coalface: as a result he would suffer a loss of earnings until age 50, when he had intended to retire in any case. He and his wife were both 34 years old.

In outline the National Coal Board's pension scheme provided Mr Auty at age 65 with an annual income on retirement and a lump sum equal to three years' pension. If he were to die after the normal retirement age, his widow would receive a pension equal to two-thirds of his. If he were to die within five years of retirement, Mrs Auty would receive the balance of five years' pension in a lump sum. If he were to die in service, she would receive a lump sum plus two-thirds of the pension which would have been payable to Mr Auty if he had retired through incapacity on the date of his death. The parties had agreed that Mr Auty's injury, and consequent inability to maintain the high wages he had been earning before the accident, would reduce by £633 a year the pension he could expect to receive at age 65.

The Judge at first instance took Mr Auty's expectation of life at age 65 to be 6.68 years. Being a woman, Mrs Auty could expect to live a further 5.58 years after her husband's death. The standard rate of tax being (as it was in 1985) 30 per cent, a gross loss of £633 a year represented an annual loss of:

$$£ 633 \times 0.7 = 443.10$$

Since Mrs Auty's pension after her husband's death would be two-thirds of his, the total number of years at £433 the Autys had lost was:

$$£ 6.68 + \left(\frac{2 \times 5.58}{3}\right) = 10.4$$

The judge chose a multiplier of 7. Applying the multiplier of 7 to the net annual loss of £433 and adding a lump sum of three times the gross pension payment, the Judge calculated a total loss at age 65 of:

$$£ (7 \times 443) + (3 \times 633) = 5000$$

The choice of a multiplier of 7 to represent a loss which was likely to extend over 10.4 years makes an appropriate allowance both for the accelerated receipt at age 65 of a pension which would have been paid over the period between age 65 and the likely date of death and for the chance of premature mortality. It does not, of course, make any allowance for the additional acceleration over the period between age 65 and age 34: for the fact, in other words, that Mr Auty was being compensated by an award of damages at age 34 for a loss which he would not suffer until age 65.

To deal with that additional acceleration, the Judge discounted the award of £5,000 a year by 5 per cent a year, arriving at a figure of £1,100. From that he deducted a further £300 (or roughly 27 per cent) to cover such contingencies such as voluntary early retirement, redundancy, dismissal, supervening ill health, disablement, or death before age 65 — death being the major discount. That produced a figure of £800, to which the Judge added £200 to compensate for the reduction in the benefit that would be paid to Mrs Auty if Mr Auty were to die in service; the overall award under this head was therefore £1,000. The Court of Appeal approved this line of reasoning.

3. Using tables

The Multiplier Tables in the Appendix to this book can be used to simplify calculations of this kind. The third column, headed 'Loss of pension commencing age 65' for males and 'Loss of pension commencing age 60' for females, contains multipliers which make an appropriate allowance not only for the accelerated receipt at age 65 (or 60) of a pension which would have been paid over the period between age 65 (or 60) and the likely date of death and for the chance of premature mortality, but also for the additional acceleration over the period between age 65 (or 60) and the plaintiff's current age.

Thus if a boy of 16 is injured in such a way that he will lose an annual pension of £1,000 at age 65, the actuarially correct award to compensate for this loss, given an annual rate of return of 4.5 per cent in the meantime, is £1,000 x 0.7 = £700. A glance at the first column in the same table shows that the actuarially correct multiplier at the same annual rate of return for a man of 65 (the age at which the loss will commence) is 8.8. By receiving at 16 what he would not normally have received until 65 the boy can look forward to 65 − 16 = 49 years' compound interest before he needs to draw on the damages to compensate him for the loss he has suffered. Secondly, he runs a risk, which can only be expressed statistically, of dying before he reaches age 65. The difference between the figure of 8.8 in the first column and the figure of 0.7 in the third column takes account of both these factors.

If a boy receives £700, a girl of the same age should receive £1,600 to compensate her for the same loss. The difference reflects both her earlier retirement and her longer life expectancy.

If the plaintiff is female, and in 1994 was younger than 44, these tables cannot be used. From 2010 the earliest age at which a woman can draw her State pension is to be progressively increased until it reaches 65 in 2020.

However useful, these tables are not admissible in evidence. A Judge may be persuaded to take judicial notice of them, but it is much safer to seek the agreement of the other side to admit them in evidence.

4. An alternative solution

An alternative solution to this problem is gaining ground as the basis for negotiated settlements. If the accident had not occurred, the plaintiff would have retired at age 60 with a pension of £x a year; as it is, he will retire at age 60 with a reduced pension of £y. His loss is therefore £ (x − y) a year from age 60 for life.

The simplest way of quantifying that loss is to obtain from a number of insurance companies quotations for the present cost of providing this particular plaintiff with a pension of £ (x − y) a year from age 60 for life. A similar approach can be adopted towards calculating compensation for any reduction in the lump sum the plaintiff can expect to receive on retirement.

Where the plaintiff is still working, and is able to buy pension provision of his own, the lowest quotation for a pension which gives the plaintiff what he has lost is the measure of his damage under this head. If he will have to pay commission to an agent for arranging the pension provisions, that commission forms part of his loss and should be added to the claim. Where the plaintiff is not in a position to buy pension provision of his own, his loss will be slightly less than the lowest quotation, since that includes an element of profit for the insurance company. As he does not intend to buy a pension with his damages, he does not need compensation to cover the element of profit that an insurance company would demand when selling him a pension.

Checklist

1. Discover what the plaintiff's pension would have been at his normal retirement date if the accident had not occurred.
2. Calculate what the plaintiff's pension is likely to be in the light of the accident at the same date.
3. Where appropriate, obtain quotations for the cost of funding the difference.
4. Remember that the plaintiff will have to prove both the premises on which the quotation is based: the pension he would have received if the accident had not occurred, and the pension he will in fact receive at the same age. Marshal the relevant evidence.
5. Is all the evidence in the form of witness statements which:
   (a) satisfy the requirements of the County Court Rules; and
   (b) exhibit any documents to which they refer?

Chapter 28

Children

1. Introduction

A minor is a person who has not yet reached 18 years of age: s 1 Family Law Reform Act 1969. In principle a minor's damages are assessed in exactly the same way as an adult's, but this chapter deals with three points that are peculiar to cases involving children. The way in which the courts deal with a claim for future loss of earnings made by a very young child has already been considered in Chapter 22.

2. Infant approval summons

The most important point a practitioner should remember when acting for a minor is that he cannot agree the damages or settle the case without the court's approval. Order 10 r 10(1) CCR provides:

'Where in any proceedings money is claimed by or on behalf of a person under disability, no settlement, compromise or payment and no acceptance of money paid into court, whenever entered into or made, shall so far as it relates to that person's claim be valid without the approval of the court.'

Despite the substitution of the word 'minor' for 'infant' in 1969, the application by which the court's approval is sought is still generally known as an infant approval summons.

3. Dealing with minors' damages

Another vital point to remember is that the damages will not be the minor's to deal with as he wishes until he reaches 18 years of age. Order 10 r 11(1) and (2) CCR provide:

'(1) Where in any proceedings —
    (a) money is recovered by or on behalf of, or adjudged or ordered or agreed to be paid to, or for the benefit of, a [minor], or
    (b) money paid into court is accepted by or on behalf of a [minor], then, unless the court otherwise directs, the money shall not be paid to the [minor] or to his next friend, guardian ad litem or his solicitor but shall be paid into or remain in court.

(2) The money and any interest thereon shall be invested, applied or otherwise dealt with as the court may from time to time direct.'

Once the plaintiff reaches 18, the money must be paid out to him unconditionally.

4. Increase between trial and receipt

Because a minor's damages may remain in court for many years, the sum received on majority may be very much greater than the sum originally awarded. The Court of Appeal held in *Gold* v *Essex County Council* [1942] 2 KB 293 that the award must make no allowance for this prospect. The reason is that the plaintiff may need the money at any time between the trial and his majority.

Chapter 29

The duty to mitigate

1. Nature of the duty

Anyone who claims compensation for a loss is under a duty to take all reasonable steps to keep his loss to a minimum. A failure to take such steps is generally called a failure to mitigate. The duty to mitigate is not heavy: *Banco de Portugal* v *Waterlow* [1932] AC 452 at 506.

2. Burden of proof

The burden of proving a failure to mitigate lies on the defendant: *Steele* v *Robert George & Co (1937) Ltd* [1942] AC 497, a decision of the House of Lords. Whether a not a plaintiff has acted, or is acting, reasonably is a question of fact in each case.

3. Categories of failure to mitigate

There is no limit to the type of failure that may be alleged, but the allegations generally encountered fall into six broad categories:

- failure to seek medical treatment;
- failure to return to work;
- refusal to take uncongenial employment;
- unwarranted retraining at defendant's expense;
- failure to mitigate expense;
- failure to claim State benefit.

4. Failure to seek medical treatment

A plaintiff who has been injured may be suffering greater pain or disability than he need simply because he refuses treatment. If his refusal is unreasonable, he will be able to recover damages only for the degree of pain or disability he would have been suffering if he had undergone the appropriate treatment.

Whether the plaintiff's refusal is reasonable depends very much on the facts of the individual case. The question is whether the plaintiff has reached a reasonable decision in the light of the medical advice he has been given. In deciding this question the court will not try to resolve a difference of medical opinion over the desirability of a particular course of treatment: *Richardson* v *Redpath, Brown & Co Ltd* [1944] AC 62 at 68. On the other hand, the mere fact that the advice comes from the defendant's doctor is irrelevant: *McAuley* v *London Transport Executive* [1957] 2 Lloyd's Rep 500.

Much will depend on the nature of the disability and the nature of the treatment. A refusal is likely to be held unreasonable if, for example, a serious disability could be largely removed by a simple, safe surgical procedure. On the other hand, if that same surgical procedure carries an appreciable risk, or is particularly unpleasant, the court is unlikely to hold the plaintiff's refusal to submit to treatment unreasonable, even though the statistics show that the procedure is far more likely than not to be successful.

If the plaintiff unreasonably refuses treatment, his damages will be assessed as though he had undergone the treatment and obtained the degree of benefit to be expected from it: *Morgan* v *T Wallis Ltd* [1974] 1 Lloyd's Rep 165.

5. Failure to return to work

The complaint most commonly made by defendants is that the plaintiff has failed to return to work. If the plaintiff has suffered a devastating injury, or has suffered only a moderate injury but is so close to the normal retirement age that he is unlikely to find work of any kind, then a court will accept that he will never work again. It cannot be stressed too strongly, however, that in all but the most exceptional cases it is almost impossible to establish a total future loss of earnings. Unless he has the clearest medical evidence to the effect that the plaintiff is permanently unfit for work of any kind, the best advice a solicitor can give the client for whom he is preparing a personal injury claim is to find a job — any job!

It does not matter what kind of a job it is, or what it pays. Nor does it matter that the plaintiff intends to abandon it the moment his case is over. The measure of his damage is the difference between what he would have been earning had the accident not occurred and what he is in fact earning at the time of trial. Judges find it much easier to award a substantial sum based on that calculation than to award even modest sums based on the premise that the plaintiff will never work again.

The plaintiff should try to find work for which his qualifications and experience fit him, of course, but if he cannot, the more menial the job, the better: for the more menial the job, the greater will be the Judge's regard for his determination to return to work.

Even if he tries hard to find work, the plaintiff may fail. A failure to find work despite strenuous efforts is good evidence in support of a claim that the plaintiff will never work again; the plaintiff should therefore be advised to keep a diary of his attempts to find work and to keep any letters of rejection he receives.

6. Refusal to take uncongenial employment

Where the plaintiff is unemployed, the courts are likely to have scant sympathy with evidence that the only jobs available are uncongenial. Once the plaintiff has made the effort to return to work, however, the plaintiff will not generally be expected to take work he finds unpleasant simply to boost his earnings by a few pounds a week. In one unreported case, for example, the Court of Appeal held that a married man of 59 was not acting unreasonably in refusing a job which would have involved night work, which he had never done and for which he had a strong dislike, when the increase in his income would have been all of 15 per cent.

If the defendant's insurers complain that the plaintiff is acting unreasonably in refusing an unpleasant job which would pay more, they should be reminded that damages can be awarded for loss of congenial employment.

7. Unwarranted retraining at defendant's expense

A plaintiff who is unable to return to his pre-accident work sometimes seeks to train for other work and to recover from the defendant both the earnings he will lose and the cost of the training he proposes to undertake. Whether this is a reasonable way of reducing the plaintiff's claim for loss of earnings is, once again, a question of fact in each case.

If the plaintiff can take without retraining a job in which he will earn as much, or almost as much, as he was earning before the accident, then he will not be able to claim the cost of retraining. He cannot, in other words, ask the defendant to fund a change to a more congenial occupation: if he dislikes the only work for which he is fitted, his claim (if any) will be for loss of congenial employment.

If the plaintiff is going to make a claim of this kind, he must have good prospects of completing the course of training on which he is proposing to embark. Equally, of course, the qualification he is seeking must give him a good chance of a job which pays more than any job he could find without retraining.

Rowden v *Clarke Chapman & Co Ltd* [1967] 3 All ER 608 is a good example of a case in which the plaintiff was held to have acted reasonably in following this route. Mr Rowden was a steel-erector who was injured in such a way that he could not return to his pre-accident work. On his return to work he was assigned for a short period to light duties at his pre-accident wage; having been made redundant, he obtained a job first as a storeman (at a lower wage), then as a shop steward (at his original wage). He then embarked on a six-month course for retraining as a welder. The evidence showed that even slightly disabled welders could earn high wages if highly skilled.

The defendants accepted that Mr Rowden's decision to retrain as a welder was reasonable. In his judgment Mocatta J endorsed the decision as reasonable. If Mr Rowden had chosen to remain a steel-erector, he would have been unable to do the really heavy and dangerous work, and so might have been unable to earn the full rate of pay for very long. Equally, Mr Rowden could not expect to remain a shop steward indefinitely.

8. Failure to mitigate expense

The plaintiff is under a duty to keep to a minimum any expense which is caused by the accident. Thus if a plaintiff is injured in such a way that he cannot live alone in the house in which he was living at the time of the accident, but would be able to live alone if the house were modified, he cannot claim the cost of employing someone to look after him, since he could mitigate his loss by carrying out the modification.

9. Failure to claim State benefit

The provisions of the Social Security Administration Act 1992 now require the defendant to deduct from the plaintiff's damages and repay to the Secretary of State a sum equal to the total of the State benefits the plaintiff has received in the first five years after the accident. In the great majority of cases, therefore, a failure to claim benefit cannot as a matter of fact amount to a failure to mitigate. Even where the recoupment provisions do not apply, a failure to claim State benefits does not as a matter of law amount to a failure to mitigate: *Eley* v *Bedford* [1972] 1 QB 155, [1971] 3 All ER 285.

10. Reasonable expenses of mitigating

The plaintiff can recover the reasonable expenses of mitigating his loss. One example is the cost of an operation to reduce disability; another is the loss Mr Rowden (see above) suffered while obtaining a qualification which would in the long term reduce his claim for loss of earnings.

Checklist

1. Consider the plaintiff's prospects of returning to work.
2. Advise the plaintiff to try to get a job of any kind.
3. Advise the plaintiff to keep a diary of his attempts to find work.
4. Advise the plaintiff to keep any letters of rejection he may receive.
5. Is this a case for an employment consultant?
6. Should the plaintiff consider retraining?

Chapter 30

Interest

1. Power to award

In the county court the power to award interest is conferred by s 69 of the County Courts Act 1984. In the form in which they apply to actions for personal injuries where the damages exceed £200, the relevant subsections provide:

'(1) Subject to county court rules, in proceedings (whenever instituted) before a county court for the recovery of a debt or damages there shall be included in any sum for which judgment is given unless the court is satisfied that there are special reasons to the contrary simple interest, at such rate as the court thinks fit or may be prescribed, on all or any part of the debt or damages in respect of which judgment is given, or payment is made before judgment, for all or any part of the period between the date when the cause of action arose and —

(a) in the case of any sum paid before judgment, the date of payment; and

(b) in the case of any sum for which judgment is given, the date of judgment.

(5) Interest under this section may be calculated at different rates in respect of different periods.'

By subsection (6), personal injuries are defined as 'including any disease and any impairment of a person's physical or mental condition'.

2. Heads of damage

For the purposes of calculating interest the plaintiff's damages fall under four main heads:

- General damages for pain, suffering and loss of amenity;
- Special damages, in the strict sense of pecuniary loss to the date of trial;
- General damages for future loss;
- Damages for disability on the open labour market.

3. General damages for pain, suffering and loss of amenity

In normal circumstances interest on general damages for pain, suffering and loss of amenity runs:

- from the date on which the summons was served;
- to the date of judgment;
- at two per cent a year.

This guideline was laid down by the House of Lords in *Wright* v *British Railways Board* [1983] 2 AC 773, [1983] 2 All ER 698.

In the same case the House of Lords suggested that there might be cases — where liability cannot seriously be contested, for example, and the plaintiff's long-term medical outlook is already clear at the date of the letter before action — in which interest should run from that date. Such cases are extremely rare.

4. Special damages, in the strict sense of pecuniary loss to the date of trial

In theory the plaintiff is entitled to interest:

- on each item of special damage;
- from the date on which the loss accrued;
- to the date of judgment;
- at the Special Rate of interest (formerly the Short Term Investment Rate).

In most cases, however, the financial losses which the plaintiff suffers between the accident and trial fall evenly throughout that period. In practice therefore the courts adopt a rough-and-ready approach to the calculation, awarding interest:

- on the total of special damages;
- from the date of the accident;
- to the date of judgment;
- at one half of the Special Rate of interest (formerly the Short Term Investment Rate).

This guideline was laid down by the Court of Appeal in *Jefford* v *Gee* [1970] 2 QB 130, [1970] 1 All ER 1202. It is to be adopted in the great majority of cases, but should not be followed where the facts of the case make it manifestly unfair to either the plaintiff or the defendant. Where the plaintiff sustains heavy loss in the weeks immediately after the accident, for example, but thereafter suffers virtually no loss in the two years or so before the case comes to trial, the court should go back to first principles and award interest at the full rate from the date on which the loss accrued: *Ichard* v *Frangoulis* [1977] 1 WLR 556, [1977] 2 All ER 461.

If the plaintiff intends to ask the court to depart from the normal rough-and-ready approach, he must say so in his pleading and set out the facts which justify such a departure. The defendant must be in a position to assess the strength of the plaintiff's argument and so make a proper payment into court.

In *Dexter* v *Courtaulds Ltd* [1984] 1 WLR 372, [1984] 1 All ER 70 Lawton LJ gave two examples of the special circumstances that would justify a departure from the principle laid down in *Jefford* v *Gee*. In the first example a high earner suffered a substantial loss of income in the three or four weeks immediately after the accident, but no loss once he had returned to work. In the second the plaintiff had paid out of his own pocket for expensive medical treatment which enabled him to return to work and so mitigate his claim for loss of earnings. In both examples several years had passed between the plaintiff's return to work and the trial.

In most cases the plaintiff's claim will represent a specific financial loss to the plaintiff. A claim for the cost of amateur nursing care by one of the plaintiff's relatives often represents only a notional expenditure, however, since the relative has given up leisure rather than gainful employment. The Court of Appeal has held that damages awarded under this head should nevertheless be regarded as special damages for the purpose of calculating interest: *Roberts* v *Johnstone* [1989] QB 878, [1988] 3 WLR 1247.

5. General damages for future loss

Damages which are awarded to compensate the plaintiff for any loss which he will incur in the future do not attract an award of interest.

6. Damages for disability on the open labour market

Damages for disability on the open labour market awarded under the rule in *Smith* v *Manchester Corporation* (1974) 17 KIR 1 do not attract interest: *Clarke* v *Rotax Aircraft Equipment Ltd* [1975] 1 WLR 1570, [1975] 3 All ER 794. Although the award represents compensation for a present disability, the loss to which that disability gives rise will fall on the plaintiff in the future.

7. Third party proceedings

If the defendant joins as third party a party whom the plaintiff then adds as second defendant, an award of interest against the second defendant should run from service of the third party notice: *Slater* v *Hughes* [1971] 1 WLR 1438, [1971] 3 All ER 1306.

8. Special Interest rate

The Special Interest rate varies from time to time. The notes to s 69 of the County Courts Act set out in *The County Court Practice* in the section headed 'Personal Injury and Death' give the rate from 1 October 1965 to the last change before the current edition went to press; more recent changes can be found in *Current Law*. The rate over the last ten years has been:

From 1 April 1983	12.50 %
From 1 April 1984	12.00 %
From 1 August 1986	11.50 %
From 1 January 1987	12.25 %
From 1 April 1987	11.75 %
From 1 November 1987	11.25 %
From 1 December 1987	11.00 %
From 1 May 1988	9.50 %
From 1 August 1988	11.00 %
From 1 November 1988	12.25 %
From 1 January 1989	13.00 %
From 1 November 1989	14.25 %
From 1 April 1991	12.00 %
From 1 October 1991	10.25 %
From 1 February 1993	8.00 %

From time to time the Law Society's *Gazette* publishes a ready-reckoner prepared by Mr RM Nelson-Jones, a partner in Field Fisher Waterhouse, which shows the cumulative figure for interest from each month over the last few years to the date of publication. The ready-reckoner takes account of any fluctuation in the rate of interest over the period it covers.

9. Date of judgment

The date of judgment for the purposes of an interest calculation is the date on which a judgment quantifies the sum to be paid by the defendant to the plaintiff. If therefore the plaintiff obtains an interlocutory judgment for damages to be assessed, interest will continue to run under s 69 of the County Courts Act 1984 until the assessment of damages. This was decided by the House of Lords in *Thomas* v *Bunn* [1991] 1 AC 362, [1991] 1 All ER 193.

10. Interest must be pleaded

Order 6 r 1A CCR requires a claim for interest to be expressly pleaded. If such a claim is not pleaded, interest cannot be recovered unless the pleading is amended: *Ward* v *Chief Constable of Avon and Somerset* (1985) 129 Sol Jo 606. If the plaintiff intends to rely on circumstances which justify a departure from the guideline laid down in *Jefford* v *Gee* [1970] 2 QB 130, [1970] 1 All ER 1202, he must set out those circumstances in his pleading: *Dexter* v *Courtaulds Ltd* [1984] 1 WLR 372, [1984] 1 All ER 70.

11. Effect of delay

If the plaintiff is unreasonably dilatory in bringing or prosecuting his action, the court may shorten the period for which it awards interest: *Birkett* v *Hayes* [1982] 1 WLR 816 at 825E−F, [1982] 2 All ER 710 at 717d−e.

Checklist

1. Calculate interest on general damages at two per cent a year from service of the summons until date of judgment (or earlier settlement).
2. Is this a case which justifies departure from the normal rule laid down in *Jefford* v *Gee*?
3. If so, calculate separately the interest due on each item of special damage at the full rate from the date on which it occurred until date of judgment (or earlier settlement).
4. If not, calculate the interest due on the special damages as a whole at half the appropriate rate from the date of the accident until date of judgment (or earlier settlement).

Chapter 31

The statement of special damages

1. Obligation to file statement

Order 6 r 1(6) CCR requires the plaintiff in an action for personal injuries to file with his Particulars of Claim a 'statement of the special damages claimed'. This is defined by r 1(7) as:

'a statement giving full particulars of the special damages claimed for expenses and losses already incurred and an estimate of any future expenses and losses (including loss of earnings and of pension rights).'

As pointed out in Chapter 16, compensation for future expenses and losses is not strictly special damages, but the term is used loosely to mean the damages awarded for everything except pain, suffering and loss of amenity. Although the rules refer to a statement, practitioners usually speak of a schedule of special damage.

2. Aim of statement

The aim of the statement of special damages is fivefold:

- to enable the defendant to see at a glance what the plaintiff is claiming and to decide item by item whether he is prepared to meet the claim subject to liability;
- to prompt early agreement of those items that can be agreed subject to liability;
- if an item cannot be agreed, to enable the defendant to identify the particular point at issue. If a claim for future loss of earnings cannot be agreed, for example, the statement should be laid out in such a way that the defendant can identify the particular element he is challenging: the figure claimed for the plaintiff's continuing gross loss of earnings, the calculation which converts that gross figure into a net loss, the age at which the plaintiff says he would have retired if the accident had not occurred, the choice of multiplier, and so on;
- if part of a claim really cannot be agreed, to isolate those items on which the Judge will have to hear evidence and argument;
- to focus the attention of Judge, advocates and witnesses on the point(s) in issue.

3. Form of statement

The form of the statement is not prescribed. The choice of layout will depend on the complexity of the case. In the simplest case, the statement need be no more than a list, totalled at the foot of the page. In the most complex cases the statement will be a document running to perhaps a dozen pages and prepared by an accountant.

However complex the statement, it should always make clear at a glance what the plaintiff is claiming. If it runs to more than a page, therefore, it should begin with a single-page summary setting out the plaintiff's claim under each head.

It goes without saying that the statement must be typewritten. If the plaintiff has kept his own handwritten diary of expenses, it cannot simply be photocopied and added to a typewritten summary.

Every item on the statement should be numbered. If the parties cannot agree, the statement will be used in court; if the items are not numbered, a witness who is asked to refer to an item on the schedule is bound to stumble in giving his evidence and so annoy the Judge unnecessarily.

The statement of special damage should carry the title of the action. Papers often go astray.

The statement should also be dated. Statements are often updated as the action progresses, so it is important to see which is the most recent.

4. Content of statement

It is often difficult to know how much to put into the statement and how much to leave out. If the client has been attending hospital as an outpatient for two or three years, for example, and perhaps attending a physiotherapist at the same time, and has kept a detailed record of the journeys, listing them day by day, should every single journey appear in the statement of special damage?

In general the answer is yes: the more detail the statement contains, the better. The more detail the statement contains, however, the more frequently its contents need to be summarised. In such a case the statement would contain not merely a single-page summary of the whole claim, but also a separate summary dealing with the claim for travelling expenses: that summary might, for instance, give two figures for each calendar year since the accident, the first being the total sum spent on travelling to hospital, the second the total sum spent on travelling to the physiotherapist.

Similar questions arise over the extent to which calculations should be set out in the statement. Again, the answer is the more, the better: the more transparent the claim, the more likely it is to be agreed subject to liability. Again, too, the more detailed the calculations, the greater the need for summaries. If the plaintiff's pre-accident earnings varied because they were seasonal, for example, the statement might set out his gross loss of earnings since the accident month by month over a period of, say, three years, then set out for each tax year the calculation which converts those gross earnings into a net loss; in such a case the section of the statement which deals with the plaintiff's loss of earnings should have its own summary giving a single figure for the net loss for each tax year. The total of those annual figures will then be carried forward to the overall summary.

The claim for loss of earnings is often based on the plaintiff's average net earnings in the 13 weeks before the accident. Where the defendant is the plaintiff's employer, there is no need to set out the figures from which that average has been calculated, since he will have been the source of the information in the first place; where the defendant is not the plaintiff's employer, on the other hand, he will want to check the data.

5. Matching the evidence

The statement should take whatever form will make the plaintiff's claim readily intelligible. The overriding requirement, however, which is often forgotten, is that the schedule should match the evidence to be called at trial.

The form of the evidence should dictate the form of the statement. Thus if the documents on which the plaintiff will rely to establish his loss of earnings are based on calendar years rather than tax years, then the statement of special damage should be based on calendar years, too. In the same way an accountant might divide his calculation of the plaintiff's net loss into, say, three separate periods, the beginning of each period corresponding to an increase in the rate for the job the plaintiff can no longer do: in such a case the statement should adopt the same periods.

A statement that does not reflect the evidence to be called is useless. Where, for example, the statement uses calendar years, but the supporting documentary evidence is based on tax years, it may be impossible to verify the figures in the statement by looking at the documentary evidence.

A failure to match the statement to the evidence can cause more subtle problems. The statement is intended as a tool to isolate, and to enable the Judge to deal with, the points that remain contentious at trial. Consider the case of the plaintiff who has not worked since the accident. His employers review their employees' salaries on 1 June each year. The plaintiff contends that between 1 June 1992 and 31 May 1993 he would have been earning £12 an hour; the defendant says he would have earned only £10. If the statement calculates the plaintiff's loss of earnings in periods running from 1 June to 31 May, it is a simple matter to insert in the statement whichever figure the Judge finds to have been the more likely hourly rate for the period 1 June 1992 to 31 May 1993 and then do the necessary calculations to arrive at a net loss over that period. If the statement is arranged by calendar years, on the other hand, or by tax years, the advocates will have to recalculate two periods rather than one if the Judge finds against the plaintiff.

The statement of special damages

6. Layout of statement: simple cases

In the simplest case the statement of special damage need be no more than a list. Consider the case of a motor-cyclist who is knocked off his machine, but suffers nothing worse than a few grazes and a week or so of severe headaches. The statement might look like this:

IN THE ISLEWORTH COUNTY COURT **Case No 9300101**

BETWEEN: ANTHONY RECKLESS Plaintiff
and
PETER INNOCENT Defendant

PLAINTIFF'S STATEMENT OF SPECIAL DAMAGE

	£
(1) Cost of replacing helmet	75.00
(2) Cost of replacing glasses	120.00
(3) 1 day's net loss of earnings @ £55	55.00
(4) Cost of travelling to optician's:	
2 journeys @ 90p return	1.80
(5) Medicines: 2 packets Headeeze @ £1.16	2.32
3 tubes Stingeeze @ 64p	1.92
	256.04

Interest on £256.04
03.09.92 – 31.01.93, 119 days @ 11.25% pa 9.39
01.02.93 – 24.03.93, 52 days @ 8.00% pa 2.92
12.31

Interest will continue to accrue at the rate of 5.6p a day.

The Plaintiff will contend for interest at the full rate from 3rd September 1992 on the grounds that all the above losses had accrued by that date.

DATED 24th March 1993

7. Setting out loss of earnings: short periods

In all but the simplest cases the claim for loss of earnings should be set out in full. The source of the data on which the calculation is based should appear at the foot. Similarly, if the calculation is based on assumptions, these, too, should come after the calculation, so keeping the calculation itself as uncluttered as possible.

If the plaintiff was injured on 1 June 1992, and was off work as a result of his injuries for six weeks, the section of the statement which deals with his loss of earnings (Section B in this example) might look like this:

240

B. LOSS OF EARNINGS   £

The plaintiff was off work as a result of the accident until
13th July 1992, a period of 6 weeks.

His net pre-accident earnings were £206.35 a week

6 weeks @ £206.35 =   1238.10

The figure of £206.35 a week is the average of the plaintiff's gross
earnings, less income tax and employee's National Insurance
contributions, in the 13 weeks ending 30th May 1992.

Now consider a slightly more complicated case. The same plaintiff is in
a job which requires seasonally high levels of overtime in May and June,
but no substantial overtime during the rest of the year. Here the average
of the plaintiff's earnings in the 13 weeks prior to the accident will not
be a good guide to the plaintiff's post-accident loss, for two reasons.
First, his earnings in the last four weeks will have been substantially
higher than his earnings in the previous nine. Secondly, the weekly
earnings he has lost in June will be higher than his average earnings over
the previous 13 weeks, because only four of those included overtime.

In such a case it will be necessary to deal with the plaintiff's basic wages
and overtime separately. Add one more complication: the plaintiff's
take-home pay in the week beginning 19 April 1992 was not typical,
because he had to work three extra shifts to cover for a sick colleague.
In those circumstances the section of the statement dealing with loss of
earnings might look like this:

B. LOSS OF EARNINGS   £

The plaintiff was off work as a result of the accident until
13th July 1992, a period of 6 weeks.

(1) His net pre-accident basic wage was £206.35 a week

    6 weeks @ £206.35 =   1238.10

(2) His net pre-accident earnings from overtime were
    £72.60

    4 weeks 2 days @ £72.60 =   311.14

TOTAL LOSS OF EARNINGS   1549.24

241

NOTE:

  (a) The figure of £206.35 a week is the average of the plaintiff's gross basic pay, less income tax and employer's National Insurance contributions, in the 14 weeks ending 30th May 1992 excluding the week beginning 19th April 1992.

  (b) The week beginning 19th April 1992 has been excluded from this calculation. The plaintiff's earnings in that week were unusually high because he was covering for a sick colleague.

  (c) The plaintiff's job requires him to work overtime in May and June, but not at other times of the year. In May the plaintiff worked an average of 12 hours' overtime a week.

  (d) The calculation assumes that the plaintiff would have been required to work as many hours' overtime in June as May.

  (e) The plaintiff's net pay for overtime is £6.05 an hour.

8. Setting out loss of earnings: longer periods

Where the plaintiff's loss of earnings covers only a few weeks or months, it can safely be calculated as a multiple of his weekly net pre-accident earnings — or, of course, his monthly net pre-accident earnings, if he was paid monthly. Where the loss covers more than one tax year, however, the lost earnings are likely to suffer tax at differing rates: in such cases, it is necessary to set out the gross figures and show the calculations by which they are converted into a net loss.

Take, for example, the case of an employee, a single woman, earning £42,500 a year when she is seriously injured in a road accident on her way back from a party on New Year's Day 1991. Her employers continue to pay her in full for six months, but when it becomes clear that she is not going to return to work in the immediate future, dismiss her on 30 June 1991. She is out of work for a further 18 months, but lands a job paying as much as her pre-accident work from 1 January 1993. She contends that the gross salary from her pre-accident job would have increased by 3 per cent on 1 January 1992.

The plaintiff's loss between 1 July 1991 and 5 April 1992 falls into Tax Year 1991–92; between 6 April 1992 and 1 January 1993 it falls into Tax Year 1992–93. In 1991–92 income tax was levied at 25 per cent on the first £23,700 and at 40 per cent on the remainder; the single person's personal allowance was £3,295. National Insurance contributions for employees who have not contracted out of the state earnings related pensions scheme was two per cent on the first £2,704 a year plus nine per cent on earnings between £2,704 and £20,280. In 1992–93 income tax was levied at 20 per cent on the first £2,000, at 25 per cent on the next

£21,700 and at 40 per cent on the remainder; the single person's personal allowance was £3,445. National Insurance contributions for employees who have not contracted out of the state earnings related pensions scheme was two per cent on the first £2,808 a year plus nine per cent on earnings between £2,808 and £21,060.

In such a case the section of the statement dealing with the plaintiff's claim for loss of earnings (Section B once again) might look like this:

B. LOSS OF EARNINGS   £

1. Expected gross earnings Tax Year 1991 – 92
    (a) 06.04.91 – 31.12.91
        270 days @ £42500 a year =   31438.36
    (b) 01.01.92 – 05.04.92
        96 days @ £43775 a year =   11513.42
        Total   42951.78

2. Expected gross earnings Tax Year 1992 – 93 to 31st
    December 1992

        06.04.92 – 31.12.92
        270 days @ £43775 a year =   32831.51

3. Expected net earnings Tax Year 1991 – 92

        Gross earnings   42951.78
           LESS personal allowance   3295.00
        Taxable pay   39656.78

        Income tax:
        @ 25% on first £23700   5925.00
        @ 40% on remainder £39656.78 – 23700 =
        15956.78   6382.71
        Total income tax   12307.71

        Employee's National Insurance contributions:
        @ 2% on first £2704   54.08
        @ 9% between £2704 and £20280   1581.84
        Total NI contributions   1635.92

        Net pay:
        Gross pay   42951.78
        LESS income tax   12307.71
           NI contributions   1635.92
                                                                29008.15

4. Expected net earnings Tax Year 1992 – 93 to 31st
    December 1992

Gross earnings	32831.51
LESS personal allowance	3445.00
Taxable pay	29386.51
Income tax:	
@ 20% on first £2000	400.00
@ 25% on next £21700	5425.00
@ 40% on remainder £29386.51 − 23700 = 5686.51	2274.60
Total income tax	8099.60
Employee's National Insurance contributions:	
@ 2% on first £2808	56.16
@ 9% between £2808 and £21060	1642.68
Total NI contributions	1698.84
Net pay:	
Gross pay	32831.51
LESS income tax	8099.60
NI contributions	1698.84
	23033.07

5. Net loss of earnings:

(a)	Net loss Tax Year 1991 – 92	29008.15
(b)	Net loss Tax Year 1992 – 93 to 31.12.92	23033.07
(c)	LESS net earnings paid to 30.06.91	7184.50
	TOTAL NET LOSS OF EARNINGS	44856.72

NOTES:

(a) At the time of the accident the plaintiff was earning £42500 a year.

(b) Owing to her inability to return to work the plaintiff's employers
dismissed her on 30th June 1991.

(c) The plaintiff's employers paid her salary in full from the date of the
accident to 30th June 1991. The figure of £7184.50 at 5(c) is the net
sum so paid in Tax Year 1991 – 92.

(d) The plaintiff's earnings would have increased by 3% to £43775 from
1st January 1992: see 1(b) above

(e) The plaintiff returned to work on 1st January 1993 and ceased to
suffer a loss of earnings on that date: see 2. and 4. above.

9. Setting out loss of earnings: continuing loss

Where the plaintiff claims a continuing loss of earnings, the statement should break the calculation of that part of the claim into two sections. The first sets out the continuing annual loss at the date of trial; the second shows the multiplier for which the plaintiff is contending and gives the capital sum it produces.

The plaintiff in our previous example went back to work on 1 January 1993, earning as much as if the accident had not occurred. Suppose instead that her new job pays £40,000 a year rather than the £43,775 she would have been earning if the accident had not occurred: she will suffer a continuing loss of earnings. Suppose, too, that her age, job and normal retirement age suggest a multiplier of 6. In such a case the statement of special damage will contain an additional section — here called Section C — as follows:

C. FUTURE LOSS OF EARNINGS £

1. Continuing loss per annum:

Gross continuing loss £43775 − 40000 =	3775
LESS tax @ 40%	1510
Net continuing loss	2265
2. The plaintiff will contend for a multiplier of 6	6
TOTAL CLAIM FOR FUTURE LOSS OF EARNINGS	13590

NOTE:

(a) The plaintiff is currently earning £40,000 a year gross.

(b) If the accident had not occurred, the plaintiff would have been earning £43,775 a year gross.

10. Cross-reference to documents

In more complex cases it may be helpful to key the statement to the documentary evidence that supports it. If so, the statement should have an additional column on the right: each figure in that column refers to the appropriate page in the bundle of documents.

11. Setting out other losses

In general other losses should be set out in much the same way as the plaintiff's claim for loss of earnings. If any of the plaintiff's losses is continuing at the date of the statement, two statements will be needed, one dealing with loss to date, the other using an appropriate multiplier to deal with future loss.

12. An example

Mr D Brown is a scaffolder. At the time of his accident he was working for Unsteady Scaffolds Ltd. On 16 June 1990 he fell and injured his back at work. At the time of the accident Mr Brown was earning a basic wage of £280 a week gross for a standard week of 32 hours plus overtime at the rate of £11.16 an hour gross thereafter. Unsteady Scaffolds continued to pay Brown's basic wage for the 26 weeks following the accident, a total of £5,100.42. From the beginning of Tax Year 1991–92 Brown was able to return to work, but never regained his pre-accident level of earnings. He was dismissed on the grounds of incapacity by Unsteady Scaffolds on 30 April 1993.

On 1 September 1991 the rate of pay for Brown's job was increased to £287.50 gross per week basic and £11.96 gross per hour overtime. On 1 September 1992 it was increased again to £291 gross per week basic and £12.31 gross per hour overtime. It has not been increased since. In the last complete Tax Year before the accident, namely 1989–90, Brown had worked a total of 452 hours' overtime.

At the date of the accident the plaintiff had earned £5,222.02 net in Tax Year 1990–91. After the accident he received a tax rebate of £236.22.

Brown earned £9,764.33 net in Tax Year 1991–92 and £10,234.48 net in Tax Year 1992–93. In Tax Year 1993–94 Brown earned only £55.01, because he was dismissed by Unsteady Scaffolds Ltd on 30 April 1993. To the date of the statement of special damage, 14th September 1994, Brown has earned nothing in Tax Year 1994–95.

Brown will need painkillers for the rest of his life. As a result of the accident he has lost on average one and a half days' work every week. Since he has therefore been spending an additional one and a half days a week at home, he has been forced to spend more on heating and on providing the lunch he used to receive free at work. He has incurred expense in travelling to and from hospital; he also lost a number of items of property in the accident itself.

Brown was born on 1 October 1940. Had the accident not occurred, he would have continued working to age 55.

In such a case the schedule of special damage might look like this. The schedule incidentally illustrates the point that a case should not be in the High Court just because the likely damages exceed £50,000, if the only reason for their exceeding £50,000 is a large claim for loss of earnings.

IN THE CHELMSFORD COUNTY COURT   **Case No CH 94106**

BETWEEN:

DAVID BROWN

and   Plaintiff

UNSTEADY SCAFFOLDS LIMITED

Defendants

PLAINTIFF'S SCHEDULE OF SPECIAL DAMAGE

SUMMARY

	£
A. Loss of earnings to date	34256.03
B. Cost of medicines to date	142.54
C. Cost of extra heating and food to date	356.36
D. Miscellaneous expenses to date	95.43
E. Future loss	15242.41
F. Interest on special damages	7657.66
	57750.43

SECTION A

Loss of earnings to date

	£
(1) Net loss in Tax Year 1990−1	3425.27
(2) Net loss in Tax Year 1991−2	4483.59
(3) Net loss in Tax Year 1992−3	4492.22
(4) Net loss in Tax Year 1993−4	14794.53
(5) Net loss in Tax Year 1994−5	7060.42
	34256.03

Notes

1. The Plaintiff has never returned to his pre-accident earnings.

2. At the time of the accident the Plaintiff was earning:

   (1) a basic wage of £280 a week gross for standard week of 32 hours; plus

   (2) overtime at the rate of £11.16 an hour gross thereafter.

3. In the last complete Tax Year before the accident, namely 1989−90, the Plaintiff had worked a total of 452 hours' overtime.

4. On 1st September 1991 the rate of pay for the Plaintiff's job was increased to £287.50 gross per week basic and £11.96 gross per hour overtime.

5. On 1st September 1992 the rate of pay for the Plaintiff's job was increased to £291 gross per week basic and £12.31 gross per hour overtime.

6. In Tax Year 1990−91 the Plaintiff should have earned gross:

   £ (52 × 280) + (452 × 11.16)
   = £ 19604.32

7. In Tax Year 1991−92 the Plaintiff should have earned gross:

    (a) from 6th April 1991 to 31st August 1991, a period of 21 weeks:

    £ (21 × 280) + $\dfrac{21 \times 452 \times 11.16}{52}$

    = £ 7917.13

    (b) from 1st September 1991 to 5th April 1992, a period of 31 weeks:

    £ (31 × 287.50) + $\dfrac{31 \times 452 \times 11.96}{52}$

    = £ 12135.26

    (c) a total for the year of:

    £ 7917.13 + 12135.26
    = £ 20052.39

8. In Tax Year 1992−93 the Plaintiff should have earned gross:

    (a) from 6th April 1992 to 1st September 1992, a period of 21 weeks:

    £ (21 × 287.50) + $\dfrac{21 \times 452 \times 11.96}{52}$

    = £ 8220.66

    (b) from 1st September 1992 to 5th April 1993, a period of 31 weeks:

    £ (31 × 291) + $\dfrac{31 \times 452 \times 12.31}{52}$

    = £ 12338.07

    (c) a total for the year of:

    £ 8220.66 + 12338.07
    = £ 20558.73

9. In Tax Year 1993−94 the Plaintiff should have earned gross:

    £ (52 × 291) + (452 × 12.31)
    = £ 20696.12

10. In Tax Year 1994−95 the Plaintiff should have earned gross from 6th April 1994 to the date hereof (14th September 1994), a period of 23 weeks:

    £ (23 × 291) + $\dfrac{23 \times 452 \times 12.31}{52}$

    = £ 9145.05

The statement of special damages

11. The Plaintiff is entitled to the following tax allowances:

    −   Tax Year 1990−91   £ 3005
    −   Tax Year 1991−92   £ 3295
    −   Tax Year 1992−93   £ 3445
    −   Tax Year 1993−94   £ 3445
    −   Tax Year 1994−95   £ 3445

12. The Plaintiff is not contracted out of the State Earnings Related Pension Scheme.

13. In Tax Year 1990−91 income tax was payable at 25 per cent on the first £20700.

    Thus the Plaintiff's tax liability would have been:

    $$£ (19604.32 - 3005) \times 0.25$$
    $$= £ 4149.83$$

14. In Tax Year 1990−91 National Insurance contributions were payable at:

    (a)   two per cent on the first £46 a week; plus

    (b)   nine per cent on the balance up to £350 a week.

    £19604.32 a year is equivalent to £377.01 a week

    Thus the Plaintiff's liability for National Insurance contributions would have been:

    $$£ (46 \times 0.02) + [(350 - 46) \times 0.09]$$
    $$= £ 28.28 \text{ a week,}$$

    equivalent to £1470.56 a year.

15. In Tax Year 1991−92 income tax was payable at 25 per cent on the first £23700.

    Thus the Plaintiff's tax liability would have been:

    $$£ (20052.39 - 3295) \times 0.25$$
    $$= £ 4189.35$$

16. In Tax Year 1991−92 National Insurance contributions were payable at:

    (a)   two per cent on the first £52 a week; plus

    (b)   nine per cent on the balance up to £390 a week.

    £20052.39 a year is equivalent to £385.62 a week

    Thus the Plaintiff's liability for National Insurance contributions would have been:

    $$£ (52 \times 0.02) + [(385.62 - 52) \times 0.09]$$
    $$= £ 31.06 \text{ a week,}$$

    equivalent to £1615.12 a year.

17. In Tax Year 1992–93 income tax was payable at:

    (a)   20 per cent on the first £2000; plus

    (b)   25 per cent on the next £23700 – 2000 = £21700.

    Thus the Plaintiff's tax liability would have been:

    £ (2000 × 0.2) + [(20558.73 – 3445 – 2000) × 0.25]
    =   £4 178.43

18. In Tax Year 1992–93 National Insurance contributions were payable at:

    (a)   two per cent on the first £54 a week; plus

    (b)   nine per cent on the balance up to £405 a week.

    £20558.73 a year is equivalent to £395.36 a week.

    Thus the Plaintiff's liability for National Insurance contributions would have been:

    £ (54 × 0.02) + [(395.36 – 54) × 0.09]
    =   £ 31.80 a week,

    equivalent to £1653.60 a year.

19. In Tax Year 1993–94 income tax was payable at:

    (a)   20 per cent on the first £2500; plus

    (b)   25 per cent on the next £23700 – 2500 = £21200.

    Thus the Plaintiff's tax liability would have been:

    £ (2500 × 0.2) + [(20696.12 – 3445 – 2500) × 0.25]
    =   £4187.78

20. In Tax Year 1993–94 National Insurance contributions were payable at:

    (a)   two per cent on the first £56 a week; plus

    (b)   nine per cent on the balance up to £420 a week.

    £ 20696.12 a year is equivalent to £398 a week.

    Thus the Plaintiff's liability for National Insurance contributions would have been:

    £ (56 × 0.02) + [(398 – 56) × 0.09]
    =   £31.90 a week,

    equivalent to £1658.80 a year.

21. In Tax Year 1994−95 income tax is payable at:

    (a) 20 per cent on the first £3000; plus

    (b) 25 per cent on the next £23700 − 3000 = 20700.

    Thus the Plaintiff's tax liability would be:

    £ (3000 × 0.2) + [(9145.05 − 3445 − 3000) × 0.25]
    = £1275.01

22. In Tax Year 1994−95 National Insurance contributions are payable at:

    (a) two per cent on the first £57 a week; plus

    (b) ten per cent on the balance up to £430 a week.

    £9145.05 over a period of 23 weeks is equivalent to £397.61 a week.

    Thus the Plaintiff's liability for National Insurance contributions would be

    £ (57 × 0.02) + [(397.61 − 57) × 0.1]
    = £ 35.20 a week,

    equivalent to £809.60 over a period of 23 weeks.

23. At the date of the accident the Plaintiff had earned £5222.02 net in Tax Year 1990−91.

24. The Defendants continued to pay the Plaintiff's basic wage for 26 weeks following the accident, a total of £5100.42.

25. The Plaintiff received a tax rebate of £236.22 in Tax Year 1990−91.

26. The Plaintiff earned £9764.33 net in Tax Year 1991−92.

27. The Plaintiff earned £10234.48 net in Tax Year 1992−93.

28. The Plaintiff earned £55.01 net in Tax Year 1993−94. He was dismissed by the Defendants on 30th April 1993.

29. The Plaintiff has not worked since 30th April 1993.

30. The Plaintiff's net loss in Tax Year 1990−91 is therefore:

		£
Prospective gross earnings		19604.32
LESS income tax		4149.83
	NI contributions	1470.56
	net earnings to 30th June 1990	5222.02
	paid after 30th June 1990	5100.42
	tax rebate	236.22
		3425.27

31. The Plaintiff's net loss in Tax Year 1991–92 is therefore:

	£
	£
Prospective gross earnings	20052.39
LESS income tax	4189.35
NI contributions	1615.12
net earnings	9764.33
	4483.59

32. The Plaintiff's net loss in Tax Year 1992–93 is therefore:

	£
Prospective gross earnings	20558.73
LESS income tax	4178.43
NI contributions	1653.60
net earnings	10234.48
	4492.22

33. The Plaintiff's net loss in Tax Year 1993–94 to date is therefore:

	£
Prospective gross earnings	20696.12
LESS income tax	4187.78
NI contributions	1658.80
net earnings	55.01
	14794.53

34. The Plaintiff's net loss in Tax Year 1994–95 to date is therefore:

	£
Prospective gross earnings	9145.05
LESS income tax	1275.01
NI contributions	809.60
	7060.44

SECTION B

<u>Cost of medicines to date</u>

	£
Cost	142.54

<u>Notes</u>

1. The Plaintiff has bought on average 1 packet of Kill-Kwik pain relievers every fortnight since 16th June 1990.

2. In June 1990 a packet cost 66p. A packet now costs £1.92. The Plaintiff will contend for an average cost of:

    $$£ \frac{0.66 + 1.92}{2}$$
    $$= \quad £1.29$$

3. The period between 16th June 1990 and 14th September 1994 is one of 221 weeks.

4. The total cost of medicines to date is therefore:

    $$£ \frac{1.29 \times 221}{2}$$
    $$= \quad £142.54$$

SECTION C

Cost of additional heating and food to date

	£
(1) Cost of additional electricity	62.36
(2) Cost of additional food	294.00
	356.36

Notes

1. Since the accident the Plaintiff has lost an average of 1.5 days' work a week.

2. As a result the Plaintiff has spent an extra 1.5 days a week at home.

3. Between October and April in each year (7 months) the Plaintiff has been forced to burn a 1kW electric fire for, say, an average of 5.5 hours extra per working day.

4. The average cost of 1kW of electricity over this period has been 6.23p.

5. The Plaintiff has therefore spent a total of:

$$£ \frac{0.0623 \times 5.5 \times 1.5 \times 52 \times 4 \times 7}{12}$$

$$= £ 62.36$$

on additional electricity since the accident.

6. While the Plaintiff is at work, his lunch is paid for by the Defendants. While he has been at home, the Plaintiff has been forced to prepare his own lunch at an average cost of, say, £1.

7. The Plaintiff used to take 3 weeks' holiday a year before the accident.

8. The Plaintiff has therefore spent a total of:

$$£ 1 \times 1.5 \times 49 \times 4$$

$$= £294$$

on additional food since the accident.

255

SECTION D

Miscellaneous expenses

		£
		£
(1)	Watch smashed in fall	89.99
(2)	Travelling to hospital and for x-rays: 3 trips by car, 5.5 miles each way @ 16.5p/mile	5.44
		95.43

SECTION E

Future loss

	£
(1) Future loss of earnings	14700.86
(2) Future cost of extra heating	18.77
(3) Future cost of extra food	73.50
(4) Future cost of medicines	449.28
	15242.41

Notes

1. If the Plaintiff had continued to work for the Defendants full-time, he would now be earning:

   £ (52 × 291) + (452 × 12.31)
   = £ 20696.12 a year gross.

2. At present rates of tax, the Plaintiff's tax liability on that sum would be:

   £ (3000 × 0.2) + [(20696.12 − 3445 − 3000) × 0.25]
   = £ 4162.78

3. £20696.12 a year is equivalent to £398 a week. At present rates the Plaintiff would be liable for National Insurance contributions of:

   £ (57 × 0.02) + [(398 − 57) × 0.1]
   = £ 35.24

   a week, or £1832.48 a year.

4. Thus the Plaintiff is suffering a continuing net annual loss of earnings of

   £20696.12 − 4162.78 − 1832.48
   = £14700.86

The statement of special damages

5. Had the accident not occurred, the Plaintiff would have continued working to age 55.

6. The Plaintiff will therefore contend for a multiplier for loss of earnings of 1:

Annual loss	14700.86
Multiplier	1
Future loss of earnings	14700.86

7. The present cost of electricity is 7.5p/kW. The Plaintiff is accordingly suffering a continuing annual loss of:

$$£ \frac{0.075 \times 5.5 \times 1.5 \times 52 \times 7}{12}$$

= £18.77

8. The Plaintiff will contend for a multiplier to date of retirement of 1:

Annual loss	18.77
Multiplier	1
Future cost of extra electricity	18.77

9. The present cost of lunch is £1. The Plaintiff is accordingly suffering a continuing annual loss of:

£1 × 1.5 × 49
= £73.50

10. The Plaintiff will contend for a multiplier to date of retirement of 1:

Annual loss	73.50
Multiplier	1
Future cost of extra food	73.50

11. The annual cost of buying Kill-Kwik is:
£26 × 1.92
= £49.92

12. The Plaintiff will need painkillers for the rest of his life.

13. The Plaintiff contends for a multiplier for life of 9.

14. The total future cost of painkillers is therefore:

Annual loss	49.92
Multiplier	9
Future cost of painkillers	449.28

SECTION F

Interest

(1) The total of special damages to date is:

A. Loss of earnings to date	34256.03
B. Cost of medicines to date	142.54
C. Cost of extra heating and food to date	356.36
D. Miscellaneous expenses to date	95.43
	34850.36

(2) The interest on special damages is therefore:

On £34850.36

− 16.06.90 − 31.03.91, 288 days @ 7.125% pa	1959.26
− 01.04.91 − 30.09.91, 183 days @ 6.000% pa	1048.38
− 01.10.91 − 31.01.93, 489 days @ 5.125% pa	2392.86
− 01.02.93 − 14.09.94, 591 days @ 4.000% pa	2257.16
	7657.66

Interest will continue to accrue at the rate of £3.82 a day.

DATED this 14th day of September 1994

APPENDIX:

TABLES

Income Tax and National Insurance rates from 1986

(a) Income tax rates and reliefs

Tax years end 5 April.

	Personal relief Married	Single	Tax rate
1986–1987	£3,655	£2,335	29% to £17,200 40% £17,201–£20,200 45% £20,201–£25,400 50% £25,401–£33,300 55% £33,301–£41,200 60% over £41,200
1987–1988	£3,795	£2,425	27% to £17,900 40% £17,901–£20,400 45% £20,401–£25,400 50% £25,401–£33,300 55% £33,301–£41,200 60% over £41,200
1988–1989	£4,095	£2,605	25% to £19,300 40% over £19,300

	Personal allowance	Married couple's allowance	
1990–1991	£3,005	£1,720	25% to £20,700 40% over £20,700
1991–1992	£3,295	£1,720	25% to £23,700 40% over £23,700
1992–1993	£3,445	£1,720	20% to £2,000 25% £2,001–£23,700 40% over £23,700
1993–1994	£3,445	£1,720	20% to £2,500 25% £2,501–£23,700 40% over £23,700

1994–1995	£3,445	£1,720	20% to £3,00
			25% £3,001–£23,700
			40% over £23,700

(b) Employee's National Insurance contributions

1986–1987 Lower earnings limit – £38.00 per week
£38.00–£59.99 – 5%
£60.00–£94.99 – 7%
£95.00–£285.00 – 9%

1987–1988 Lower earnings limit – £39.00 per week
£39.00–£64.99 – 5%
£65.00–£99.00 – 7%
£100.00–£295.00 – 9%

1988–1989 Lower earnings limit – £41.00 per week
£41.00–£69.99 – 5%
£70.00–£104.99 – 7%
£105.00–£305.00 – 9%

1989–1990 Lower earnings limit – £43.00 per week
£43.00–£74.99 – 5% until 5.10.89, 9% thereafter
£75.00–£114.99 – 7% until 5.10.89, 9% thereafter
£115.00–£325.00 – 9%

1990–1991 Lower earnings limit – £46.00 per week
first £46.00 – 2%
£46.00–£350.00 – 9%

1991–1992 Lower earnings limit – £52.00 per week
first £52.00 – 2%
£52.00–£390.00 – 9%

1992–1993 Lower earnings limit – £54.00 per week
first £54.00 – 2%
£54.00–£405.00 – 9%

1993–1994 Lower earnings limit – £56.00 per week
first £56.00 – 2%
£56.00–£420.00 – 9%

1994–1995 Lower earnings limit – £57.00 per week
first £57.00 – 2%
£57.00–£430.00 – 10%

NB. These details are correct for non-contracted out employees.

Appendix: Tables

Department of Social Security Benefits

Weekly amounts in £ of the main social security benefits

(a) Benefits taxable under Schedule E

	9.4.90 to 7.4.91	8.4.91 to 5.4.92	6.4.92 to 11.4.93	12.4.93 to 10.4.94	from 11.4.94
Unemployment benefit					
(Below state pension age)					
Single person	37.35	41.40	43.10	44.65	45.45
Adult dependant addition	23.05	25.55	26.60	27.55	28.05
Retirement pensions					
(Basic rates on					
contributions)					
Single person	46.90	52.00	54.15	56.10	57.60
Married couple:					
Both contributors (each)	46.90	52.00	54.15	56.10	57.60
Wife non-contributor	28.20	31.25	32.55	33.70	34.50
Over 80 age addition	0.25	0.25	0.25	0.25	0.25
(Non-contributory)					
Single person					
Married couple:	28.20	31.25	32.55	33.70	34.50
Category C	45.05	49.95	52.00	53.85	55.15
Category D over 80	56.40	62.50	65.10	67.40	69.00
Over 80 age addition	0.25	0.25	0.25	0.25	0.25
Widow's pension	46.90	52.00	54.15	56.10	57.60
Widowed mother's					
allowance	46.90	52.00	54.15	56.10	57.60
Invalid care allowance					
Individual	28.20	31.25	32.55	33.70	34.50
Adult dependant addition	16.85	18.70	19.45	20.15	20.65
Invalidity allowance					
(When paid with retirement					
pension)					
Higher rate	10.00	11.10	11.55	11.95	12.15
Middle rate	6.20	6.90	7.20	7.50	7.60
Lower rate	3.10	3.45	3.60	3.75	3.80

(b) Non-taxable benefits

	9.4.90 to 7.4.91	8.4.91 to 5.4.92	6.4.92 to 11.4.93	12.4.93 to 10.4.94	from 11.4.94
Income support (Taxable to those required to register as unemployed)					
Single householder aged 25 or over	36.70	39.65	42.45	44.00	45.70
Couple (married or unmarried) where at least one is aged 18 or over	57.60	62.25	66.60	69.00	71.70
Sickness benefit					
Standard individual	35.70	39.60	41.20	42.70	43.45
Adult dependant addition	22.10	24.50	25.50	26.40	26.90
Invalidity benefit					
Individual	46.90	52.00	54.15	56.10	57.60
Adult dependant addition	28.20	31.25	32.55	33.70	34.50
Child dependant addition	9.65	10.70	9.75–10.85	9.80–10.95	9.80–11.00
Child benefit For only, elder or eldest child					
For which payable	7.25	9.65	9.65	10.00	10.20
For each other child	7.25	7.50	7.80	8.10	8.25
One parent benefit	5.60	5.60	5.85	6.05	6.15
Industrial disablement benefit					
100%	76.60	84.90	88.40	91.60	93.20
Constant attendance allowance (max)	30.70	34.00	35.40	73.40	74.80
Exceptionally severe disablement allowance	30.70	34.00	35.40	36.70	37.40
Unemployability supplement	46.90	52.00	54.15	56.10	57.60
Reduced earnings allowance (max)	30.64	33.96	35.36	36.64	37.28

Retail Prices Index

	1984	1985	1986	1987	1988	1989	1990	1991	1992	1993	1994
January	86.84	91.20	96.25	100.00	103.30	111.00	119.50	130.20	135.60	137.90	141.30
February	87.20	91.94	96.60	100.40	103.70	111.80	120.20	130.90	136.30	138.80	142.10
March	87.48	92.80	96.73	100.60	104.10	112.30	121.40	131.40	136.70	139.30	142.50
April	88.64	94.78	97.67	101.80	105.80	114.30	125.10	133.10	138.80	140.60	144.20
May	88.97	95.21	97.85	101.90	106.20	115.00	126.20	133.50	139.30	141.10	144.70
June	89.20	95.41	97.79	101.90	106.60	115.40	126.70	134.10	139.30	141.00	144.70
July	89.10	95.23	97.52	101.80	106.70	115.50	126.80	133.80	138.80	140.70	144.70
August	89.94	95.49	97.82	102.10	107.90	115.80	128.10	134.10	138.90	141.30	144.00
September	90.11	95.44	98.30	102.40	108.40	116.60	129.30	134.60	139.40	141.90	144.70
October	90.67	95.59	98.45	102.90	109.50	117.50	130.30	135.10	139.90	141.80	
November	90.95	95.92	99.29	103.40	110.00	118.50	130.00	135.60	139.70	141.60	
December	90.87	96.05	99.62	103.30	110.30	118.80	129.90	135.70	139.20	141.90	

Figures supplied by Central Statistical Office.

Average Earnings Index

	1988	1989	1990	1991	1992	1993	1994
January	79.70	87.10	95.00	103.80	111.10	116.10	120.30
February	79.80	87.40	95.20	104.10	111.90	116.70	122.00
March	82.10	89.60	98.00	106.50	115.80	119.60	124.90
April	81.70	89.60	98.00	106.40	113.00	117.50	121.60
May	82.20	89.80	99.00	107.00	113.90	118.00	
June	83.40	91.10	100.70	107.90	114.50	118.50	
July	84.60	92.10	101.30	109.00	115.10	119.50	
August	83.80	91.10	101.00	109.20	114.60	118.20	
September	84.30	92.50	101.30	109.30	114.70	118.00	
October	85.00	93.30	101.70	109.30	116.00	118.40	
November	86.60	94.60	103.40	111.40	116.40	120.00	
December	89.30	95.80	105.50	112.30	117.90	121.60	

Figures supplied by the Department of Employment
Whole economy (unadjusted)

Multiplier Tables

MALES

Pecuniary loss for life						Loss of earnings to pension age 65						Loss of pension commencing age 65					
Age	3%	3½%	4%	4½%	5%	Age	3%	3½%	4%	4½%	5%	Age	3%	3½%	4%	4½%	5%
16	26.9	24.3	22.2	20.4	18.8	16	25.0	23.0	21.2	19.6	18.2	16	1.8	1.4	1.1	0.8	0.6
17	26.7	24.2	22.1	20.3	18.7	17	24.8	22.8	21.0	19.4	18.1	17	1.9	1.4	1.1	0.8	0.6
18	26.5	24.0	22.0	20.2	18.6	18	24.5	22.6	20.8	19.3	18.0	18	1.9	1.5	1.1	0.9	0.7
19	26.3	23.9	21.9	20.1	18.6	19	24.3	22.4	20.7	19.2	17.9	19	2.0	1.5	1.2	0.9	0.7
20	26.1	23.7	21.7	20.0	18.5	20	24.0	22.1	20.5	19.0	17.7	20	2.1	1.6	1.2	1.0	0.8
21	25.9	23.6	21.6	19.9	18.4	21	23.7	21.9	20.3	18.9	17.6	21	2.1	1.7	1.3	1.0	0.8
22	25.7	23.4	21.5	19.8	18.3	22	23.5	21.7	20.1	18.7	17.5	22	2.2	1.7	1.3	1.1	0.8
23	25.4	23.2	21.3	19.7	18.2	23	23.2	21.5	19.9	18.6	17.4	23	2.3	1.8	1.4	1.1	0.9
24	25.2	23.0	21.2	19.6	18.1	24	22.9	21.2	19.7	18.4	17.2	24	2.3	1.8	1.5	1.2	0.9
25	25.0	22.9	21.0	19.4	18.0	25	22.6	20.9	19.5	18.2	17.1	25	2.4	1.9	1.5	1.2	1.0
26	24.7	22.7	20.9	19.3	17.9	26	22.2	20.7	19.3	18.0	16.9	26	2.5	2.0	1.6	1.3	1.0
27	24.5	22.4	20.7	19.2	17.8	27	21.9	20.4	19.1	17.8	16.7	27	2.5	2.0	1.6	1.3	1.1
28	24.2	22.2	20.5	19.0	17.7	28	21.6	20.1	18.8	17.6	16.6	28	2.6	2.1	1.7	1.4	1.1
29	23.9	22.0	20.3	18.9	17.6	29	21.2	19.8	18.6	17.4	16.4	29	2.7	2.2	1.8	1.4	1.2
30	23.7	21.8	20.2	18.7	17.4	30	20.9	19.5	18.3	17.2	16.2	30	2.8	2.3	1.9	1.5	1.2
31	23.4	21.6	20.0	18.5	17.3	31	20.5	19.2	18.0	17.0	16.0	31	2.9	2.4	1.9	1.6	1.3
32	23.1	21.3	19.8	18.4	17.2	32	20.1	18.9	17.7	16.7	15.8	32	3.0	2.4	2.0	1.7	1.4
33	22.8	21.1	19.5	18.2	17.0	33	19.7	18.5	17.5	16.5	15.6	33	3.1	2.5	2.1	1.7	1.4
34	22.5	20.8	19.3	18.0	16.9	34	19.3	18.2	17.1	16.2	15.3	34	3.2	2.6	2.2	1.8	1.5
35	22.2	20.5	19.1	17.8	16.7	35	18.9	17.8	16.8	15.9	15.1	35	3.3	2.7	2.3	1.9	1.6
36	21.8	20.3	18.9	17.6	16.5	36	18.5	17.4	16.5	15.6	14.8	36	3.4	2.8	2.4	2.0	1.7
37	21.5	20.0	18.6	17.4	16.3	37	18.0	17.1	16.2	15.3	14.6	37	3.5	2.9	2.5	2.1	1.8
38	21.2	19.7	18.4	17.2	16.2	38	17.6	16.7	15.8	15.0	14.3	38	3.6	3.0	2.6	2.2	1.8
39	20.8	19.4	18.1	17.0	16.0	39	17.1	16.3	15.4	14.7	14.0	39	3.7	3.1	2.7	2.3	1.9

Age					
40	20.4	19.1	17.8	16.7	15.8
41	20.1	18.8	17.6	16.5	15.6
42	19.7	18.4	17.3	16.3	15.3
43	19.3	18.1	17.0	16.0	15.1
44	18.9	17.8	16.7	15.8	14.9
45	18.6	17.4	16.4	15.5	14.6
46	18.2	17.1	16.1	15.2	14.4
47	17.8	16.7	15.8	14.9	14.2
48	17.4	16.4	15.5	14.6	13.9
49	16.9	16.0	15.1	14.4	13.6
50	16.5	15.6	14.8	14.1	13.4
51	16.1	15.3	14.5	13.8	13.1
52	15.7	14.9	14.1	13.4	12.8
53	15.3	14.5	13.8	13.1	12.5
54	14.8	14.1	13.4	12.8	12.3
55	14.4	13.7	13.1	12.5	12.0
56	14.0	13.3	12.7	12.2	11.7
57	13.6	13.0	12.4	11.9	11.4
58	13.2	12.6	12.0	11.5	11.1
59	12.7	12.2	11.7	11.2	10.8
60	12.3	11.8	11.3	10.9	10.5
61	11.9	11.4	11.0	10.6	10.2
62	11.5	11.0	10.6	10.2	9.9
63	11.1	10.7	10.3	9.9	9.5
64	10.7	10.3	9.9	9.6	9.2
65	10.3	9.9	9.6	9.2	8.9
66	9.9	9.5	9.2	8.9	8.6
67	9.5	9.1	8.9	8.6	8.3
68	9.1	8.8	8.5	8.3	8.0
69	8.7	8.4	8.2	7.9	7.7
70	8.3	8.1	7.8	7.6	7.4

Age					
40	16.7	15.8	15.1	14.4	13.7
41	16.2	15.4	14.7	14.0	13.4
42	15.7	15.0	14.3	13.7	13.1
43	15.2	14.5	13.9	13.3	12.7
44	14.6	14.0	13.4	12.9	12.4
45	14.1	13.5	13.0	12.5	12.0
46	13.6	13.0	12.5	12.1	11.6
47	13.0	12.5	12.1	11.6	11.2
48	12.4	12.0	11.6	11.2	10.8
49	11.9	11.5	11.1	10.7	10.4
50	11.3	10.9	10.6	10.2	9.9
51	10.6	10.3	10.0	9.7	9.5
52	10.0	9.7	9.5	9.2	9.0
53	9.4	9.1	8.9	8.7	8.5
54	8.7	8.5	8.3	8.1	7.9
55	8.1	7.9	7.7	7.6	7.4
56	7.4	7.2	7.1	7.0	6.8
57	6.7	6.6	6.4	6.3	6.2
58	5.9	5.9	5.8	5.7	5.6
59	5.2	5.1	5.1	5.0	4.9
60	4.4	4.4	4.3	4.3	4.2
61	3.6	3.6	3.5	3.5	3.5
62	2.8	2.8	2.7	2.7	2.7
63	1.9	1.9	1.9	1.9	1.9
64	1.0	1.0	1.0	1.0	1.0

Age					
40	3.8	3.2	2.8	2.4	2.0
41	3.9	3.4	2.9	2.5	2.1
42	4.0	3.5	3.0	2.6	2.3
43	4.2	3.6	3.1	2.7	2.4
44	4.3	3.8	3.3	2.9	2.5
45	4.5	3.9	3.4	3.0	2.6
46	4.6	4.0	3.6	3.1	2.8
47	4.8	4.2	3.7	3.3	2.9
48	4.9	4.4	3.9	3.5	3.1
49	5.1	4.5	4.1	3.6	3.3
50	5.3	4.7	4.2	3.8	3.4
51	5.5	4.9	4.4	4.0	3.6
52	5.7	5.1	4.7	4.2	3.8
53	5.9	5.4	4.9	4.5	4.1
54	6.1	5.6	5.1	4.7	4.3
55	6.4	5.8	5.4	5.0	4.6
56	6.6	6.1	5.7	5.2	4.8
57	6.9	6.4	6.0	5.5	5.2
58	7.2	6.7	6.3	5.9	5.5
59	7.5	7.1	6.6	6.2	5.8
60	7.9	7.4	7.0	6.6	6.2
61	8.3	7.8	7.4	7.0	6.7
62	8.7	8.3	7.9	7.5	7.2
63	9.2	8.8	8.4	8.0	7.7
64	9.7	9.3	8.9	8.6	8.3
65	10.3	9.9	9.6	9.2	8.9

The figures used in these tables are based upon those produced by the Government Actuary's Department.

Multiplier Tables

FEMALES

Pecuniary loss for life

Age	3%	3½%	4%	4½%	5%
16	28.0	25.2	22.9	20.9	19.2
17	27.8	25.1	22.8	20.8	19.2
18	27.6	24.9	22.7	20.8	19.1
19	27.4	24.8	22.6	20.7	19.0
20	27.3	24.7	22.5	20.6	19.0
21	27.1	24.5	22.4	20.5	18.9
22	26.9	24.4	22.2	20.4	18.8
23	26.7	24.2	22.1	20.3	18.8
24	26.5	24.1	22.0	20.2	18.7
25	26.3	23.9	21.9	20.1	18.6
26	26.0	23.7	21.7	20.0	18.5
27	25.8	23.5	21.6	19.9	18.4
28	25.6	23.4	21.4	19.8	18.3
29	25.4	23.2	21.3	19.6	18.2
30	25.1	23.0	21.1	19.5	18.1
31	24.9	22.8	21.0	19.4	18.0
32	24.6	22.6	20.8	19.2	17.9
33	24.4	22.4	20.6	19.1	17.8
34	24.1	22.1	20.4	18.9	17.6
35	23.8	21.9	20.2	18.8	17.5
36	23.5	21.7	20.1	18.6	17.4
37	23.2	21.4	19.9	18.5	17.2
38	22.9	21.2	19.6	18.3	17.1
39	22.6	20.9	19.4	18.1	16.9

Loss of earnings to pension age 60

Age	3%	3½%	4%	4½%	5%
16	24.3	22.4	20.7	19.2	17.9
17	24.0	22.1	20.5	19.1	17.8
18	23.7	21.9	20.3	18.9	17.7
19	23.4	21.7	20.1	18.8	17.5
20	23.1	21.4	19.9	18.6	17.4
21	22.8	21.2	19.7	18.4	17.2
22	22.5	20.9	19.5	18.2	17.1
23	22.1	20.6	19.2	18.0	16.9
24	21.8	20.3	19.0	17.8	16.7
25	21.4	20.0	18.7	17.6	16.6
26	21.1	19.7	18.5	17.4	16.4
27	20.7	19.4	18.2	17.1	16.2
28	20.3	19.1	17.9	16.9	16.0
29	19.9	18.7	17.6	16.6	15.7
30	19.5	18.4	17.3	16.4	15.5
31	19.1	18.0	17.0	16.1	15.3
32	18.7	17.6	16.7	15.8	15.0
33	18.2	17.2	16.3	15.5	14.7
34	17.8	16.8	16.0	15.2	14.5
35	17.3	16.4	15.6	14.9	14.2
36	16.8	16.0	15.2	14.5	13.9
37	16.3	15.5	14.8	14.2	13.5
38	15.8	15.1	14.4	13.8	13.2
39	15.3	14.6	14.0	13.4	12.9

Loss of pension commencing age 60

Age	3%	3½%	4%	4½%	5%
16	3.7	2.8	2.2	1.7	1.3
17	3.8	2.9	2.3	1.8	1.4
18	3.9	3.0	2.4	1.8	1.4
19	4.0	3.1	2.5	1.9	1.5
20	4.2	3.3	2.6	2.0	1.6
21	4.3	3.4	2.7	2.1	1.7
22	4.4	3.5	2.8	2.2	1.8
23	4.5	3.6	2.9	2.3	1.8
24	4.7	3.7	3.0	2.4	1.9
25	4.8	3.9	3.1	2.5	2.0
26	5.0	4.0	3.2	2.6	2.1
27	5.1	4.2	3.4	2.7	2.2
28	5.3	4.3	3.5	2.9	2.4
29	5.4	4.5	3.7	3.0	2.5
30	5.6	4.6	3.8	3.1	2.6
31	5.8	4.8	4.0	3.3	2.7
32	6.0	4.9	4.1	3.4	2.9
33	6.1	5.1	4.3	3.6	3.0
34	6.3	5.3	4.5	3.8	3.2
35	6.5	5.5	4.6	3.9	3.3
36	6.7	5.7	4.8	4.1	3.5
37	6.9	5.9	5.0	4.3	3.7
38	7.1	6.1	5.2	4.5	3.9
39	7.4	6.3	5.4	4.7	4.1

Age					
40	22.3	20.7	19.2	17.9	16.8
41	22.0	20.4	19.0	17.7	16.6
42	21.7	20.1	18.8	17.5	16.4
43	21.4	19.9	18.5	17.3	16.3
44	21.0	19.6	18.3	17.1	16.1
45	20.7	19.3	18.0	16.9	15.9
46	20.3	19.0	17.8	16.7	15.7
47	20.0	18.7	17.5	16.4	15.5
48	19.6	18.4	17.2	16.2	15.3
49	19.2	18.0	16.9	16.0	15.1
50	18.9	17.7	16.7	15.7	14.8
51	18.5	17.4	16.4	15.4	14.6
52	18.1	17.0	16.1	15.2	14.4
53	17.7	16.7	15.8	14.9	14.1
54	17.3	16.4	15.5	14.6	13.9
55	16.9	16.0	15.1	14.4	13.7
56	16.5	15.6	14.8	14.1	13.4
57	16.1	15.3	14.5	13.8	13.1
58	15.7	14.9	14.2	13.5	12.9
59	15.3	14.5	13.8	13.2	12.6
60	14.9	14.2	13.5	12.9	12.3
61	14.5	13.8	13.2	12.6	12.0
62	14.1	13.4	12.8	12.2	11.7
63	13.6	13.0	12.4	11.9	11.4
64	13.2	12.6	12.1	11.6	11.1
65	12.8	12.2	11.7	11.3	10.8
66	12.3	11.8	11.4	10.9	10.5
67	11.9	11.4	11.0	10.6	10.2
68	11.4	11.0	10.6	10.2	9.9
69	11.0	10.6	10.2	9.9	9.5
70	10.6	10.2	9.8	9.5	9.2

Age					
40	14.7	14.1	13.5	13.0	12.5
41	14.2	13.6	13.1	12.6	12.1
42	13.6	13.1	12.6	12.1	11.7
43	13.0	12.6	12.1	11.7	11.3
44	12.4	12.0	11.6	11.2	10.8
45	11.8	11.4	11.1	10.7	10.4
46	11.2	10.8	10.5	10.2	9.9
47	10.5	10.2	9.9	9.7	9.4
48	9.9	9.6	9.3	9.1	8.9
49	9.2	8.9	8.7	8.5	8.3
50	8.5	8.3	8.1	7.9	7.7
51	7.7	7.6	7.4	7.3	7.1
52	7.0	6.8	6.7	6.6	6.5
53	6.2	6.1	6.0	5.9	5.8
54	5.4	5.3	5.2	5.2	5.1
55	4.6	4.5	4.5	4.4	4.4
56	3.7	3.7	3.6	3.6	3.6
57	2.8	2.8	2.8	2.8	2.8
58	1.9	1.9	1.9	1.9	1.9
59	1.0	1.0	1.0	1.0	1.0

Age					
40	7.6	6.6	5.7	4.9	4.3
41	7.8	6.8	5.9	5.1	4.5
42	8.1	7.0	6.1	5.4	4.7
43	8.3	7.3	6.4	5.6	5.0
44	8.6	7.6	6.7	5.9	5.2
45	8.9	7.8	7.0	6.2	5.5
46	9.2	8.1	7.2	6.5	5.8
47	9.5	8.4	7.6	6.8	6.1
48	9.8	8.8	7.9	6.8	6.4
49	10.1	9.1	8.2	7.4	6.7
50	10.4	9.4	8.6	7.8	7.1
51	10.8	9.8	9.0	8.2	7.5
52	11.1	10.2	9.4	8.6	7.9
53	11.5	10.6	9.8	9.0	8.3
54	11.9	11.0	10.2	9.5	8.8
55	12.4	11.5	10.7	10.0	9.3
56	12.8	12.0	11.2	10.5	9.8
57	13.3	12.5	11.7	11.0	10.4
58	13.8	13.0	12.3	11.6	11.0
59	14.3	13.6	12.9	12.2	11.6
60	14.9	14.2	13.5	12.9	12.3

The figures used in these tables are based upon those produced by the Government Actuary's Department.

Index

Index